STRUGGLING FOR SELF RELIANCE

Four case studies of Australian
Regional Force Projection in the
late 1980s and the 1990s

STRUGGLING FOR SELF RELIANCE

Four case studies of Australian Regional Force Projection in the late 1980s and the 1990s

BOB BREEN

THE AUSTRALIAN NATIONAL UNIVERSITY

E PRESS

Published by ANU E Press
The Australian National University
Canberra ACT 0200, Australia
Email: anuepress@anu.edu.au
This title is also available online at: http://epress.anu.edu.au/sfsr_citation.html

National Library of Australia
Cataloguing-in-Publication entry

Author:	Breen, Bob.
Title:	Struggling for self reliance : four case studies of Australian regional force projection in the late 1980s and the 1990s / Bob Breen.
ISBN:	9781921536083 (pbk.) 9781921536090 (online)
Series:	Canberra papers on strategy and defence ; 171
Notes:	Bibliography.
Subjects:	Australia--Armed Forces. National security--Australia. Australia--Defenses--Case studies.
Dewey Number:	355.033294

All rights reserved. No part of this publication may be reproduced, stored in a retrieval system or transmitted in any form or by any means, electronic, mechanical, photocopying or otherwise, without the prior permission of the publisher.

The *Canberra Papers on Strategy and Defence* series is a collection of publications arising principally from research undertaken at the SDSC. Canberra Papers have been peer reviewed since 2006. All Canberra Papers are available for sale: visit the SDSC website at <http://rspas.anu.edu.au/sdsc/canberra_papers.php> for abstracts and prices. Electronic copies (in pdf format) of most SDSC Working Papers published since 2002 may be downloaded for free from the SDSC website at <http://rspas.anu.edu.au/sdsc/working_papers.php>. The entire Working Papers series is also available on a 'print on demand' basis.

Strategic and Defence Studies Centre Publications Program Advisory Review Panel: Emeritus Professor Paul Dibb; Professor Desmond Ball; Professor David Horner; Professor Hugh White; Professor William Tow; Professor Anthony Milner; Professor Virginia Hooker; Dr Coral Bell; Dr Pauline Kerr

Strategic and Defence Studies Centre Publications Program Editorial Board: Professor Hugh White; Dr Brendan Taylor; Dr Christian Enemark; Miss Meredith Thatcher (series editor)

Cover design by ANU E Press

This edition © 2008 ANU E Press

Contents

Abstract		vii
About the Author		ix
Acronyms and Abbreviations		xi
Preface		xv
1.	Relevance, Theory and Practice of Force Projection for Australia's Defence	1
2.	Australian Force Projection 1885–1985	11
3.	Lead Up to Operation *Morris Dance*	23
4.	Responses to Crisis	31
5.	Lessons and Observations	45
6.	Lead-Up to Operation *Lagoon*	53
7.	Conduct and Aftermath of Operation *Lagoon*	71
8.	Search for Joint Command and Control	85
9.	Lead Up to Operation *Bel Isi*	93
10.	Challenges during the first 12 months	109
11.	Projection to East Timor	127
12.	Reflections and Observations	155
13.	Conclusion	165
Glossary		177
Bibliography		185
Index		213

Abstract

This monograph contains historical and comparative analyses of four Australian regional force projections in the 1980s and 1990s: (1) a contingency evacuation deployment to the waters off Fiji; (2) an armed peacekeeping operation into Bougainville; (3) an unarmed peace support intervention into Bougainville; and (4) a multinational stabilisation operation into East Timor. It uses the following framework of 10 functions of force projection to describe and analyse these interventions:

No.	Function	Elements
1.	Generic Preparation	Military capability that is made up of force structure, readiness, mobilisation and sustainability
2.	Command	Command, control, communications and computer systems
3.	Specific Preparation	Concentration of force elements in mounting or home bases, reconnaissance, reinforcement, training, administration and issue of equipment and stocks
4.	Deployment	Concentration of personnel and *matériel*, loading, movement of force elements to area of operations and, best effect arrival and pre-positioning
5.	Protection	Intelligence, surveillance, contingency rehearsal and rapid response
6.	Employment	Conduct of operations that may include maintaining deterrent presence, manoeuvre and application of firepower
7.	Sustainment	Planning and carrying out the movement of supplies and maintenance of forces through a supply chain
8.	Rotation	Reinforcement, relief, resting, retraining, re-equipping and redeployment of force elements
9.	Redeployment	Protected movement to specified locations, normally home bases
10.	Reconstitution	Return to required level of military capability

After explaining the relevance and importance of these functions, the monograph sets the scene with a short history of Australia's proficiency in force projection from 1885 until 1985. Australia depended on allies for this period. When they were not in a position to help, Australia struggled. These deficiencies increased risk at tactical tipping points in New Guinea in 1942 and in Vietnam in 1966. These were short periods when the outcomes of tactical contests had strategic consequences for Australia. Both times, Australian troops prevailed against the odds. Bravery and good luck saved Australia from political and strategic embarrassment.

After 1972, Australia's strategic emphasis moved towards more self-reliant defence and conducting joint (maritime, land and air) operations. The Australian armed forces did not learn from the tipping points of 1942 and 1966. In 1987, risks emerged during an evacuation contingency deployment to the waters off Fiji. Operations in Bougainville in 1994 and 1997–98 exposed persistent problems with preparation and deployment as well as force command, protection and sustainment. The short notice intervention into East Timor in 1999 confirmed that there was still significant room for improvement. These four projections achieved successful outcomes. However, *ad hoc* and inefficient processes demonstrated that Australia was still struggling for self reliance. For all of these interventions, Australian Defence Force (ADF) higher levels of command put the tactical level under unnecessary additional pressure that increased risk.

Despite concerted efforts to establish more effective command and control arrangements for joint operations, these case studies expose weaknesses in command and control as well as logistics. Examined collectively, they make a case for consolidating ADF command and control arrangements and matching responsibilities of joint commanders with the authority and enablers to achieve their missions. They also make a case for a permanent joint commander of ADF operations, supported by a joint integrated headquarters, and having operational control over assigned high readiness force elements from the three Services in order to rehearse the functions of force projection.

About the Author

Bob Breen's experience in first-hand research on international and regional peace support missions began in Somalia in 1993 as an historian and operations analyst and continued in Rwanda, the Middle East, Mozambique, Bougainville and East Timor periodically until 2002 when he began a PhD program at The Australian National University, graduating in 2006. He resumed work as an analyst in late 2007, when he conducted research for the Australian Defence Force Chief of Joint Operations in Iraq and Afghanistan. After publishing a book and two monographs in the early 1990s on Australian military experiences in the Vietnam War and the Korean War, his subsequent publications have related to Australia's military participation in peace missions in Somalia, Bougainville and East Timor. As an army reserve colonel during the period 1997–2002, he was also responsible for designing, developing and participating in the delivery of preparatory training programs for Australian government officials, civilian peace monitors, Australian Defence Force contingents, Australian United Nations Military Observers and politicians about to serve on or visit peacekeeping operations or UN electoral missions. Currently, he is writing the official history of Australian peacekeeping in the South Pacific during the period 1980–2005 and preparing manuscripts for publication on Australia's military force projection, battalion group operations in East Timor in 2000 and an historical analysis of the experiences of Australian junior combat leaders and small teams on contemporary peace enforcement operations.

Bob Breen is a research fellow at the Strategic and Defence Studies Centre at The Australian National University in Canberra. The research for this book was conducted before he took up this position as an author of an official history. His views in this book are his own and do not represent the views of the Department of Defence.

Acronyms and Abbreviations

1 ATF	1st Australian Task Force
1 RAR	1st Battalion, the Royal Australian Regiment
2 RAR	2nd Battalion, the Royal Australian Regiment
3 RAR	3rd Battalion, the Royal Australian Regiment
ABRI	*Angkatan Bersenjata Republik Indonesia* or Indonesian Armed Forces
ACOPS	Assistant Chief of the Defence Force–Operations
ADF	Australian Defence Force
ADFA	Australian Defence Force Academy
ADFCC	Australian Defence Force Command Centre
ADFIC	Australian Defence Force Intelligence Centre
ADHQ	Australian Defence Headquarters
AIF	Australian Imperial Force
ALG	Air Lift Group
AN and MEF	Australian Naval and Military Expeditionary Force
ANZAC	Australian and New Zealand Army Corps
ANZUS	Australia New Zealand and United States
AO	Area of Operations
APC	Armoured Personnel Carrier
APS	Australian Public Service
ASLAV	Australian Light Armoured Vehicle
AST	Australian Theatre
ASTJIC	Australian Theatre Joint Intelligence Centre
AWM	Australian War Memorial
BASB	Brigade Administrative Support Battalion
BCAT	Bougainville Crisis Action Team
BRA	Bougainville Revolutionary Army
CDF	Chief of the Defence Force
CDFS	Chief of the Defence Force Staff
CGS	Chief of the General Staff
CINC	Commander in Chief (US)
CINCPAC	Commander in Chief Pacific (US)
CIS	Computer Information Systems
CJLOG	Commander Joint Logistics

CJOPS	Chief of Joint Operations
CNS	Chief of Navy Staff
CO	Commanding Officer
COMAST	Commander Australian Theatre
COMD DJFHQ	Commander Deployable Joint Force Headquarters
COMNORCOM	Commander Northern Command
COMSPTAS	Commander Support Command Australia
COSC	Chiefs of Staff Committee
DFAT	Department of Foreign Affairs and Trade
DIO	Defence Intelligence Organisation
DJFHQ	Deployable Joint Force Headquarters
DJOPS	Director Joint Operations
DNSDC	Defence National Supply and Distribution Centre
EW	Electronic Warfare
FLSG	Force Logistic Support Group
FSB	Force Support Battalion
HF	High Frequency
HMAS	Her Majesty's Australian Ship
HMNZS	Her Majesty's New Zealand Ship
HMS	Her Majesty's Ship
HQ	Headquarters
JIO	Joint Intelligence Organisation
JLU	Joint Logistic Unit
JMOVGP	Joint Movement Group
JOC	Joint Operations Command
JTFHQ	Joint Task Force Headquarters
LCAUST	Land Commander—Australia
LCM8	Landing Craft Medium Type 8
LOGCOMD	Logistic Command
LSF	Logistic Support Force
MC	Movement Control

NAA	National Australian Archives
NCA	National Command Authority (US)
NCO	Non Commissioned Officer
NOCCC	Navy Office Contingency Co-ordination Centre
NORCOM	Northern Command
NSCC	National Security Committee of Cabinet
NZDF	New Zealand Defence Force
OC	Officer Commanding
ONA	Office of National Assessments
PACOM	Pacific Command (US)
PNG	Papua New Guinea
PNGDF	Papua New Guinea Defence Force
RAA	Royal Australian Artillery
RAAF	Royal Australian Air Force
RAN	Royal Australian Navy
RANR	Royal Australian Navy Reserve
RAR	Royal Australian Regiment
RFMF	Republic of Fiji Military Forces
RHC	Reinforcement Holding Company
RN	Royal Navy
RNZAF	Royal New Zealand Air Force
RNZN	Royal New Zealand Navy
ROE	Rules of Engagement
SAS	Special Air Service
SASR	Special Air Service Regiment
SATCOM	Satellite Communications
SCA	Support Command—Australia
SEATO	South East Asia Treaty Organisation
sitrep	*situation report*
SO1	Staff Officer Grade 1
SO2	Staff Officer Grade 2
SO3	Staff Officer Grade 3
SOFA	Status of Forces Agreement
SPPKF	South Pacific Peace Keeping Force
Spt	*support*

TMG	Truce Monitoring Group
TNI	*Tentara Nasional Indonesia* (or the Indonesian Army)
UK	United Kingdom
UN	United Nations
UNAMET	United Nations Assistance Mission–East Timor
US	United States
VCDF	Vice Chief of the Defence Force

Preface

In 1987 two events set the scene for Australian military activity in the 1990s and revived an historical paradox. In March, Defence Minister Kim Beazley released a White Paper, *The Defence of Australia 1987,* that explained a strategy of defence-in-depth of territorial sovereignty. The centrepiece was self reliance. Two months later a hastily assembled Australian military force sailed into international waters off Fiji—a contingency for evacuating Australians if there was widespread violence after a military coup. This activity, called Operation *Morris Dance*, was not about defence-in-depth. It represented enduring national obligations to Australian citizens in danger overseas.

The 1987 White Paper and *Morris Dance* symbolically revived the paradox of Australian Governments emphasising defence of sovereignty while demonstrating a predilection to project Australian military force well beyond the sea and air approaches to the homeland. The deployment of another expeditionary force from Australia's shores in May 1987 reaffirmed an historical penchant that began in 1885 for Australian governments to dispatch military forces offshore at short notice in support of discretionary strategic and humanitarian interests.

In the 1990s the paradox became more conspicuous. The Australian Defence Force (ADF) contributed forces to multi-national peace support operations in the Gulf, Cambodia, Somalia, Western Sahara, Rwanda, Papua New Guinea (PNG) (Bougainville) and Indonesia (East Timor) and humanitarian operations in northern Iraq, PNG, Irian Jaya and several South Pacific nations. Like *Morris Dance*, none of these operations defended Australia from attack but all of them were useful rehearsals of military force projection. Though most were small-scale, largely uncontested and did not involve complex manoeuvre or application of firepower, forces were assembled, prepared, employed and sustained beyond the Australian mainland in the company of allied military forces—the same mechanics for defending Australia.

Force projection is a centuries-old integrated offensive military system. It is not just an *ad hoc* flex of military muscle in times of emergency or political urgency. It is more than the act of dispatching forces. It should be the self reliant capacity to strike from mainland ports, bases and airfields that underwrites Australia's nationhood. The ADF should be maintained in a balanced and responsive posture to conduct an efficient projection cycle of preparation, command, deployment, protection, employment, sustainment, redeployment and reconstitution. If the ADF consistently gets this cycle wrong, then there is something wrong with Australia's defence.

Therefore, given that the same functions of force projection apply to all offshore operations, Australian regional peace support operations in the 1990s were valid measures of the ADF's preparedness and capability to defend Australia—the main game. This monograph audits four regional force projections within the framework of force projection and offers observations and conclusions.

Bob Breen
Canberra
August 2008

Chapter 1

Relevance, Theory and Practice of Force Projection for Australia's Defence

Relevance

As a land girt by sea, Australia has a number of military choices. It can use geographical advantage and fight enemy forces from continental beaches, and in national airspace and both on and under territorial waters. Alternatively, it can project military force to engage enemies further from the Australian homeland: closer to or in it enemies' homelands—preferably in the company of powerful allies. There is also a choice about responding to regional and international events that require military intervention: stay at home, leaving allies (and the United Nations) to face military and humanitarian emergencies alone, or participate in those operations deemed by the government of the day to be in the national interest. Australian military history testifies to the choices that Australians traditionally make. The Australian people and their governments invariably choose regional and international force projection over 'fortress defence' and isolationism.

Australia also has a geographical dilemma and more military choices. The continent is vast and divided into southern and eastern heartlands, where most Australians live, and a remote western and northern crescent hinterland. This hinterland can be likened to a curved archipelago located forward of the heartlands. It is comprised of an island of people and infrastructure in the southwest, near Perth, and isolated pockets of people and economically important resources and infrastructure extending north to another island of people and infrastructure near Darwin and then east across northern Australia to the Torres Strait Islands. How should Australia defend this national archipelago? Will there be sufficient warning time and political will to permit mobilisation and deployment of sufficient military force from the south and east coasts to the west and north? What proportion of Australia's armed forces should be located in the west and north? Australian military and political responses during the Second World War show that Australians will defend their national archipelago. Western and northern basing and conduct of major exercises in northern Australia in the latter two decades of the twentieth century confirm their choice. The strategic preference is to do so through a combination of pre-positioning forces and projecting military force from the heartlands to the hinterland.

Theory

The functions of military force projection are as old as the formation of nation-states. In rudimentary form, they predate them. From the earliest times when humans gathered in collective defence of their territory, or for conquest, they have executed all or some functions with varying degrees of capacity, proficiency and sophistication. Some clarification and definition is necessary before specifying the purpose and method of this monograph. The following table summarises the 10 enabling functions and describes their supporting elements:

No.	Function	Elements
1.	Generic Preparation	Military capability that is made up of force structure, readiness, mobilisation and sustainability
2.	Command	Command, control, communications and computer systems
3.	Specific Preparation	Concentration of force elements in mounting or home bases, reconnaissance, reinforcement, training, administration and issue of equipment and stocks
4.	Deployment	Concentration of personnel and *matériel*, loading, movement of force elements to area of operations and, best effect arrival and pre-positioning
5.	Protection	Intelligence, surveillance, contingency rehearsal and rapid response
6.	Employment	Conduct of operations that may include maintaining deterrent presence, manoeuvre and application of firepower
7.	Sustainment	Planning and carrying out the movement of supplies and maintenance of forces through a supply chain
8.	Rotation	Reinforcement, relief, resting, retraining, re-equipping and redeployment of force elements
9.	Redeployment	Protected movement to specified locations, normally home bases
10.	Reconstitution	Return to required level of military capability

Force projection begins with functions that culminate in deployment.[1] Most nation-states maintain pre-positioned extant military capability (generic force preparation) under some form of command and control (force command).[2] Periodically, they mobilise extant and latent military capabilities and then prepare maritime, land and, in modern times, air force and Special Forces elements (specific force preparation) to take specified military action.[3] They then move forces to advantageous locations and circumstances, preferably after thorough reconnaissance, to begin operations (force deployment).[4] Typically, nations prefer to deploy force elements beyond their borders so that their populations remain safe and their homelands are not laid waste.

After deployment, commanders employ force elements (force employment) under designated command arrangements that are extensions of command in the homeland, while ensuring their protection (force protection) and sustainment (force sustainment).[5] During longer operations and campaigns, commanders reinforce, relieve, rest, retrain, re-equip and redeploy force elements (force rotation).

Final functions return forces to generic preparedness. After operations and campaigns end, force elements redeploy (force redeployment) back inside borders or to locations beyond borders. They reconstitute themselves (force reconstitution), either with more capability or less, depending on the perceived level of remaining threat or, more generally, on national will to maintain military capabilities for ongoing defence or further conquest. Reconstitution completes the cycle of force projection back to generic preparedness.

Proficiency in the 10 functions demonstrates Australian military capability and intent, and constitutes an important measurement of national military competence. Since 1885, Australia has projected force nationally, regionally and internationally when governments have decided to take military action. This is Australia's military strategic culture. There have been—and will continue to be—disagreements about the resources required for Australia's defence and the importance of alliances, as well as the purpose, composition and distance from Australian shores of force projection. However, the Australian people and their governments have been—and will continue to be—at one about the need to project military force decisively and effectively whenever and wherever it is required. Thus, proficiency in force projection defines Australian defence posture, measures military competence and has to meet government and public expectations.

Practice

This monograph contains four case studies of Australian regional force projections—an evacuation contingency deployment (Fiji in 1987), a brief armed peacekeeping operation (Bougainville in 1994), an unarmed peace support intervention (Bougainville in 1997–98) and a major multinational armed stabilisation intervention (East Timor in 1999).[6] It focuses on competence at the strategic, operational and tactical levels of command. It is a critique. However, it contains empathetic and constructive criticism that makes a case for change—an important role of analytical military history.

It is reasonable to ask, 'What is meant by proficiency in the functions of force projection?' For the purposes of this monograph, proficiency is the capability and capacity for prompt, strong and smart military action that results in the strategic effects specified by the Australian Government. The underpinning of proficiency begins with maintaining generic military capability—force structure, modernisation, readiness and sustainability. There should be sufficient warning for orderly assignment of forces as well as their thorough specific force preparation. Preparations should be well-resourced, well-coordinated and well-informed by inputs, such as reconnaissance and intelligence as well as political and cultural information. These preparations (which include assembling and loading personnel and *matériel* on ships, road transport and aircraft) should be followed by protected deployment that enables personnel and their equipment and stocks to arrive with best effect—on time, fresh and ready for employment. Command and sustainment arrangements should facilitate effective, efficient, intelligent and safe employment of forces to achieve desired results. These arrangements should also facilitate a rate of effort and force rotation that maintains the required tempo of operations. After operations and campaigns, force elements should redeploy safely, and reconstitute efficiently.

This monograph sets each case study within the context of Australian military strategy and the strategic level of command, but does not comment in detail.[7] Strategic level sources are still classified and there is insufficient space in one monograph to discuss the strategic level satisfactorily as well as to examine the operational and tactical levels of command in detail.[8] Yet the absence of deep analysis of Australian political and military–strategic processes does not diminish the significance of this monograph. Within the context of force projection and the impact of the Information Age on military operations, the importance of understanding challenges facing lower levels of command has increased. Those operating at the cutting edge defeat hostile forces or create desired effects. Their success or failure often determines operational and strategic success or failure. In conventional land warfare, a divisional attack involving thousands of troops and employment of battlefield manoeuvre and significant firepower is, ultimately, a contest between opposing junior leaders and small teams. In maritime and air warfare, opposing commanders of vessels and their crews and pilots (either individually or in combination with their aircrew) decide outcomes. During land-based peacekeeping operations, junior leaders and small teams establish a deterrent presence and, guided by rules, engage hostile individuals, small teams, groups and crowds who threaten public order with carefully calibrated coercion and possibly lethal force.[9]

The Information Age has elevated lower levels of command. Since the Vietnam War, media representatives have broadcast images and stories from the tactical level instantly to a worldwide audience. Scores of commentators then analyse, explain and critique such developments. As a consequence, there can be substantial political and strategic repercussions if all does not go well at the tactical level. Tactical tipping points—the moments or short periods when tactical contests have significant political and strategic ramifications—are not new. What is new is that the media create tipping points by broadcasting tactical level setbacks or behaviour that would have gone unnoticed in earlier times.

There is also insufficient space in this monograph to discuss and compare Australia's projection of military force with allied force projection or that of other island nations. Both the United States and Britain have and continue to develop rapid joint force projection. The Americans constituted a Rapid Deployment Force in the early 1980s,[10] while the British established a joint rapid response force and a permanent joint headquarters in the late 1990s.[11] There have been differences of opinion about these initiatives.[12] This monograph neither joins this debate nor compares the proficiency and efficacy of Australian force projection to the efforts of other nations.

This monograph does, however, fill some of the gaps in the history of Australia's post-Cold War military operations, in general, and force projection, in particular. Though well covered by the media during their initial phases, Australian regional and international military operations in the late 1980s and during the 1990s have not received significant historical attention.[13] Few historians have published histories of individual peacekeeping and post-Cold War operations.[14] Aside from David Horner and the author, few have published authoritative accounts or attended to the operational and tactical levels of command in detail.[15]

The emphasis is on land force projection.[16] The navy and the air force are intrinsic mechanisms of Australian force projection of maritime and air power.[17] Navy and air force higher commands can prepare and deploy vessels and aircraft into Australia's sea and air space, the northern archipelago and the South Pacific, and around the world as long as there are secure ports and airbases to operate from and logistic resources to sustain them. The roles of maritime and air force elements are generic, well-defined and determined by the design and capabilities of individual vessels and aircraft, as well as their groupings.

The army has a number of more complex challenges. The first is to have forces equipped and rehearsed generically for warfighting as well as a range of likely contingencies. The second is to have sufficient time to conduct reconnaissance and to prepare. The third is to deploy force elements safely and effectively by land, sea and air after efficient loading. The fourth is to adapt to different and often complex and harsh operational environments. The fifth is to accomplish a variety of missions shaped by a number of stakeholders as well as to overcome or deter opponents. The sixth is to maintain a tempo of operations, level of sustainment and rotation to succeed for the duration of an operation or campaign. The seventh is to redeploy safely and reconstitute efficiently. The navy and the air force do not need the army except for securing and protecting threatened bases and providing some air defence. However, the army depends on Australian or allied maritime and air force elements, as well as commercial assets and capabilities, for force projection to hostile operational areas beyond Australian shores. Typically, land force elements rely on navy and air force elements for deployment and protection as well as for the means for sustainment, manoeuvre, additional firepower and possibly redeployment. One of the proficiency tests of Australian force projection is to synchronise maritime, land and air force elements effectively—sometimes called littoral power.[18]

This monograph briefly describes the first century of Australian force projection between 1885 and 1985 before closely examining Australia's first post-Vietnam War regional projection in 1987, Operation *Morris Dance*, two projections to the North Solomons Province (hereafter Bougainville), Operations *Lagoon* and *Bel Isi*, the eastern-most province of Papua New Guinea (PNG), in 1994 and 1997, and to East Timor in 1999 (Operations *Spitfire* and *Warden*). One of the intentions is to reveal what happened at lower levels of command when the Australian Government decided to take military action and the Defence organisation executed the functions of force projection. Another intention is to fill in parts of an operational story that authors sometimes omit. Within the framework of the 10 functions of force projection, the narrative structure of this monograph follows the generic chronology of most regional and international projections, beginning with warnings and responses, not just arrivals and subsequent employment.

Each case study does not cover all of the functions. Operation *Morris Dance* did not involve employment or sustainment of force elements. The operation was a contingency deployment that ended when forces were not required after being pre-positioned. Consequently, it does not examine whether specific force preparation, deployment and force protection arrangements increased or decreased risk after arrival. Nor does it analyse the effectiveness of force command, protection and sustainment over time. There was no force rotation or a need for well-protected and efficient redeployment. Force elements reconstituted efficiently because they returned to home bases with original personnel and *matériel*.

Operation *Lagoon* was also a brief operation. However, it was an armed peacekeeping operation that did test specific force preparation as well as other enabling functions and incorporated the additional complexities of joint and coalition operations. Operation *Bel Isi* had sufficient duration to test all of the functions of force projection over a year, not just a few days or weeks as was the case for Operations *Morris Dance* and *Lagoon*. Though unarmed, this operation was not without threats to life and property. Arrangements for force protection are still classified and are not examined here. Operations *Spitfire* and *Warden* cover all of the functions, but the emphasis in the monograph is given to those that were persistently weak on previous case studies (such as force command and sustainment).

While Australians expect that there will be risks when their governments decide to take military action, they also presume that their political, public service and military leaders will manage and minimise risk. They do not expect priorities and processes within both government and Australia's armed forces to add to the inherent dangers of military operations. These processes did increase risk for Operations *Morris Dance*, *Lagoon*, *Bel Isi*, *Spitfire* and *Warden*. Given media magnification of tactical tipping points, deficient force projection could contribute to tactical setbacks and incidents that result in significant political and strategic embarrassment. Negative consequences may only diminish

Australia's regional and international reputation during peacetime, causing temporary political problems for governments. However, if Australia goes to a substantial military contest as part of an international military emergency or has to defend the approaches to the continent in a time of war, as was the case in 1942, the consequences could be disastrous.

In summary, this monograph contributes to Australian analytical military history through describing and analysing Australia's proficiency in military force projection using case studies. It offers a new framework and narrative structure for examining Australian military intent and competence. It adds to and incorporates other accounts of contemporary regional Australian force projections, such as S.S. Mackenzie's account of the adventures of the Australian Naval and Military Expeditionary Force in 1914, Dudley McCarthy's and David Dexter's official histories of Australia's projections during the Southwest Pacific Campaign during the Second World War and two accounts by the author of operations in Bougainville and East Timor in the 1990s.[19] While the monograph describes the past, it also has potential to shape the future. C.E.W. Bean alluded to the contribution of military history and this type of monograph to the future when he said:

> How did the Australian people—and the Australian character, if there is one, come through the universally recognised test of this, their first great war? ... What did the Australian people and their forces achieve in the total effort of their side of the struggle? ... What was the true nature of that struggle and test as far as Australians who took part in it? How well or ill did our constitution and our preparations serve us in it? What were their strengths or weaknesses? And what guidance can our people or others obtain from this experience for further emergencies?[20]

ENDNOTES

[1] **force projection**: The ability to project military elements of Australia's national power within Australia's borders and beyond in response to Government requirements for military action. The functions of force projection begin with generic preparation and deployment, and end with redeployment and reconstitution back to specified generic preparedness. Adapted from US Department of Defense, 'DOD Dictionary of Military and Associated Terms', Joint Publication 1-02, Joint Doctrine Division, Washington, May 2005. See <http://www.dtic.mil/doctrine/jel/doddict/> (hereafter DOD). **deployment**: The movement of forces to and within areas of operations, including positioning forces ready for operations and battle (DOD).

[2] **military capability**: The ability to achieve specified strategic effects. It includes four major components: (1) *force structure* (numbers, size and composition of the force elements that comprise the ADF; e.g., divisions, ships, air squadrons); (2) *modernisation* (technical sophistication of forces, units, weapon systems and equipment); (3) *readiness* (the ability to provide force elements required by commanders to execute their assigned missions); and *sustainability* (the ability to maintain the necessary level and duration of operational activity to accomplish missions. Sustainability is a function of providing for and maintaining those levels of ready forces, *matériel*, facilities and consumables necessary to support military effort.) (DOD). **command and control**: The exercise of authority and direction by designated commanders over assigned and attached forces for mission accomplishment. Command and control functions are performed through an arrangement of personnel, equipment, communications, facilities

and procedures employed by commanders in planning, directing, coordinating, and controlling forces and operations (DOD).

[3] **mobilisation**: The act of preparing for war or other emergencies through assembling and organising national resources. More commonly, it is the process by which the armed forces or part of them are brought to a state of readiness for military action, including assembling, organising, training, administering personnel and pre-positioning and/or loading *matériel* (DOD).

[4] **reconnaissance**: A mission undertaken to obtain, by visual observation or other detection methods, information about the activities and resources of hostile forces as well as stakeholders, or to secure data concerning the meteorological, hydrographic, or geographic characteristics of a particular area (DOD).

[5] **force protection**: Activities, such as gathering, evaluating and communicating intelligence and employing counterintelligence and protective agents and groups, e.g. Special Forces, to protect individuals, groups and force elements from hostile interference. Force protection includes protection from the vicissitudes of operational environments, such as disease and harsh climates, through preventative health measures, clothing and equipment and conducive living conditions (New definition).
force sustainment: The science of planning and carrying out the movement of supplies and maintenance of forces through a supply chain. In its most comprehensive sense, those aspects of military operations that deal with design and development, acquisition, storage, movement, distribution, maintenance, evacuation, and disposition of *matériel*; movement, evacuation, and hospitalisation of personnel; acquisition or construction, maintenance, operation, and disposition of facilities; and acquisition or furnishing of essential services. Also logistics (DOD).

[6] Renamed Timor Leste from independence in May 2002.

[7] **strategic level**: The level at which a nation, often as a member of a group of nations, determines national or multinational (alliance or coalition) security objectives and guidance, and develops and uses national resources to accomplish these objectives. Activities at this level establish national and multinational military objectives; sequence initiatives; define limits and assess risks for the use of military and other instruments of national power; develop global plans or theatre military plans to achieve these objectives; and provide military forces and other capabilities in accordance with strategic plans (DOD).

[8] **operational level**: The level at which campaigns and major operations are planned, conducted, and sustained to accomplish strategic objectives within theatres or other operational areas. Activities at this level link tactics and strategy by establishing operational objectives needed to accomplish the strategic objectives, sequencing events to achieve operational objectives, initiating actions, and applying resources to bring about and sustain these events. These activities imply a broader dimension of time or space than do tactics; they ensure sustainment of tactical forces, and provide the means by which tactical successes are exploited to achieve strategic objectives (DOD). **tactical level**: The level at which battles and engagements are planned and executed to accomplish military objectives assigned to tactical force elements. Activities at this level focus on the ordered arrangement and manoeuvre of combat elements in relation to each other and to hostile forces to accomplish missions (DOD).

[9] **Rules of Engagement**: Directives issued by competent military authority which specify the circumstances and limitations under which Australian forces will initiate and/or continue combat engagements with other forces encountered. Australian Defence Force Publication 101, Glossary, 1994.

[10] For a short summary of the evolution of US rapid deployment forces and their command and control arrangements, visit <http://rapid-deployment-forces.iqnaut.net/>, accessed 28 July 2008.

[11] See the UK Ministry of Defence website at <http://www.mod.uk/issues/sdr/jrrf.htm> for a summary of joint rapid response forces.

[12] Paul K. Davis, *Observations on the Rapid Deployment Joint Task Force: Origins, Directions, and Mission*, Paper prepared for 23rd Annual Convention of the American International Studies Association held on 24–27 March 1982, The RAND Paper series, June 1982, available at <http://www.rand.org/publications/P/P6751/P6751.pdf>, accessed 14 November 2007; David Isenburg, *The Rapid Deployment Force: The Few, the Futile, the Expendable, Cato Policy Analysis No. 44*, The Cato Institute, Washington DC, 8 November 1984, available at <http://www.cato.org/pubs/pas/pa044.html>, accessed 14 November 2007; Keigh Hartley, 'Can the UK Afford a Rapid Deployment Force?', *Royal United Services Institute Journal for Defence Studies* vol. 127, no. 1, March 1982, pp. 18–21; and David Segal, 'Whatever Happened to Rapid Deployment?', *Armed Forces Journal*, March 1991, pp. 39–40. For a working bibliography on rapid deployment, see
<http://www.ibiblio.org/pub/academic/history/marshall/military/mil_hist_inst/d/deploy2.asc> on the University of North Carolina at Chapel Hill's iblio digital archive database, accessed 14 November 2007.

[13] Of the operations examined in this monograph, the following publications and papers merit perusal: Monica Wehner and Donald Denoon, *Without a gun, Australia's Experiences Monitoring Peace in Bougainville, 1997–2001*, Pandanus Books, The Australian National University, Canberra, 2001; Alan Ryan, '*Primary Responsibilities and Primary Risks*': *Australian Defence Force Participation in the International Force East Timor*, Study Paper, no 304, Land Warfare Studies Centre, Canberra, November 2002, available at <http://www.defence.gov.au/Army/lwsc/Publications/SP/SP_304.pdf>, accessed 14 November 2007; Alan Ryan, *From Desert Storm to East Timor, Australia, the Asia-Pacific and the 'New Age'*, Study Paper, no. 302, Land Warfare Studies Centre, Canberra, January 2000, available at <http://www.defence.gov.au/Army/lwsc/Publications/SP/SP_302.pdf>, accessed 14 November 2007; John Blaxland, *Information-era Manoeuvre, The Australian-led Mission to East Timor*, Working Paper, no. 118, Land Warfare Studies Centre, Canberra, June 2002, available at <http://www.defence.gov.au/Army/lwsc/Publications/WP/WP_118.pdf>, accessed 14 November 2007; and Kent Beasley, *Information Operations during Operation Stabilise in East Timor*, Working Paper, no. 120, Land Warfare Studies Centre, Canberra, August 2002, available at <http://www.defence.gov.au/Army/lwsc/Publications/WP/WP_120.pdf>, accessed 14 November 2007.

[14] There have been a few publications on Australian peacekeeping operations, such as (ed.) Hugh Smith, *Australia and Peacekeeping*, Australian Defence Studies Centre, Australian Defence Force Academy, University of New South Wales, Canberra, 1990; (ed.) Hugh Smith, *Peacekeeping Challenges for the Future*, Australian Defence Studies Centre, Australian Defence Force Academy, University of New South Wales, Canberra, 1993; and Peter Londey, *Other People's Wars: A History of Australian Peacekeeping*, Allen and Unwin, Sydney, 2004.

[15] See David Horner, *The Gulf Commitment: The Australian Defence Force's First War*, Melbourne University Press, Melbourne, 1992; Bob Breen, *A Little Bit of Hope: Australian Force—Somalia*, Allen and Unwin, Sydney, 1998; Bob Breen, *Giving Peace a Chance. Operation Lagoon Bougainville 1994, A Case Study in Military Action and Diplomacy*, Canberra Papers on Strategy and Defence, no. 142, Strategic and Defence Studies Centre, The Australian National University, Canberra, 2002; and Bob Breen, *Mission Accomplished. East Timor: Australian Defence Force Participation in the International Force East Timor*, Allen and Unwin, Sydney, 2001.

[16] **land power**: The ability to project military force by or from individuals and groups operating on land either on foot or from land, sea or aerial platforms, normally accompanied by application of direct and indirect fire support. Air Marshal M.J. Armitage and Air Commodore R.A. Mason, *Air Power in the Nuclear Age*, Urbana, New York, 1985, pp. 2–3.

[17] **maritime power**: The ability to project military force by or from a platform on or below water, normally the sea. **air power**: The ability to project military force by or from a platform in the third dimension above the surface of the earth. Armitage and Mason, *Air Power in the Nuclear Age*, pp. 2–3.

[18] **littoral power**: The ability to combine maritime, land and air power to project military force simultaneously on or below water, on land and in the air in a prescribed area. Armitage and Mason, *Air Power in the Nuclear Age*, pp. 2–3.

[19] See Breen, *Giving Peace a Chance. Operation Lagoon Bougainville 1994, A Case Study in Military Action and Diplomacy*; and Breen, *Mission Accomplished. East Timor: Australian Defence Force Participation in the International Force East Timor*. The story of the AN and MEF appears in S.S. Mackenzie, *The Australians at Rabaul: The Capture and Administration of the German Possessions in the Southern Pacific*, The Official History of Australia in the War of 1914–1918, Vol X, Angus and Robertson Ltd, Sydney, 1927. Accounts of Australian Second World War projections to the near region include Dudley McCarthy, *South-West Pacific Area—First Year Kokoda to Wau*, Official History of Australia in the War of 1939–1945, Series 1, vol. V, Australian War Memorial, Canberra, 1959; David Dexter, *The New Guinea Offensives*, Official History of Australia in the War of 1939–1945, series 1, vol. VI, Australian War Memorial, Canberra, 1961; and E.G. Keogh, *The South West Pacific 1941–1945*, Grayflower Productions, Melbourne, 1965.

[20] C.E.W. Bean, 'The Writing of the Australian Official History of the Great War—Sources, Methods and Some Conclusions', (read before the Royal Australian Historical Society on 22 February 1938) in *Despatch*, Journal of the New South Wales Military Historical Society, vol. XXXVI, no. 2, April/June 2001. First published in the Royal Australian Historical Society, *Journal and Proceedings*, vol. XXIV, 1938, part 2, p. 7.

Chapter 2

Australian Force Projection 1885–1985

Australia was dependent on allies for the first 100 years of its military history. From 1885 until the end of participation in the Vietnam War in 1972, they underwrote Australian involvement in regional and international military emergencies and campaigns. The Australian armed forces found it difficult to project force when allies were not in a position to help. This difficulty increased risk at tactical tipping points in 1942 on the Kokoda Track during the New Guinea Campaign and in 1966 at the battle of Long Tan in Vietnam soon after Australia deployed an independent task force. On both occasions, Australian troops prevailed against the odds, thereby obviating major political and strategic embarrassment. From 1972 until 1985, Australia did not project significant military force regionally or internationally except for some Cold War maritime and air surveillance activities. By 1985, the nation aspired to self-reliant joint force projection in defence of Australia and its interests.

The dispatch of a New South Wales contingent to Sudan in 1885 set the first benchmark for rapid deployment. There were more to follow. Australia was able to recruit, prepare and dispatch first contingents in about four weeks. Rapid deployment was not required during the Second World War. There was time for contingents to begin preparation in Australia, and then complete training and equipping after arrival and before the test of combat. During the Cold War, Australian Governments allowed less time for preparation in home bases. There was little or no preparation after arrival before employment. For Korea and Vietnam, the time to prepare for deployment returned to about four weeks. Circumstances also forced land force elements to reinforce and reorganise hastily before departure.

This chapter is a short introductory history of Australian military force projection. Australia may indeed have projected military force successfully for 100 years with the assistance of allies, but it needed good luck when taking military action alone. Over time, Governments and circumstances allowed an average of four to six weeks preparation time from official warning to the departure of initial contingents.

Projections to the Sudan, South Africa and China

The first official projection of Australian military force occurred in March 1885. In 'an example of colonial military efficiency of a high order', 750 men and 200 horses embarked in Sydney for the port of Suakin in the Red Sea to participate in the British Sudan War.[1] Impetus had come on 11 February from

Major General Sir Edward Strickland, a retired British officer living in Sydney. He proposed in a letter to the editor of the *Sydney Morning Herald* that 'Australia'—though yet to be a nation—should respond militarily to the death of Major General Charles Gordon at Khartoum on 26 January 1885.[2] Australia's first battalion group to deploy overseas arrived in the Sudan less than one month after official warning—a rapid deployment, by both historical and contemporary standards.[3]

A call to arms for another British military campaign in Africa prompted the next projection. On 3 July 1899, Joseph Chamberlain, the Secretary of State for the Colonies, sent secret cables to colonial governments in Australia asking them to consider sending contingents 'in the event of a military demonstration against the Transvaal'.[4] The British were not compromising during negotiations about the political rights of a burgeoning population of British immigrants who had settled in the South African Republic of the Transvaal after the discovery of gold. The Republic declared war on 11 October 1899.[5] In a repeat of the circumstances of the Sudan expedition, Australian men from the bush and the cities volunteered for service and quick deployment.[6] Cooperation between colonial governments, citizen committees and military authorities facilitated efficient preparation. Australian contingents arrived in South Africa in November and December 1899, fully equipped and horsed, about six weeks after enlistment. Further contingents followed at regular intervals over the next two years.[7]

In June 1900, the Australian colonies responded to another overseas military emergency.[8] British forces, accompanied by French and Russian troops, landed in northern China and advanced on Peking in order to protect members of diplomatic legations and their families who were being besieged by anti-Western members of the Society of Righteous and Harmonious Fists—nicknamed 'Boxers'.[9] Further Western incursions started a short war with China.

With forces committed to the Boer War, New South Wales and Victoria sent small contingents of sailors and marines from their permanent and volunteer naval forces to assist in China. After official warning in early June 1900, the Victorian Naval Contingent embarked in Melbourne on 31 July 1900. A 260-strong New South Wales contingent joined the Victorians on the same troop ship in Sydney, embarking on 8 August 1900, and arriving in China 38 days later. After the British had employed the Australians for six months on garrison duties, they returned to Australia in March 1901.

Observations

Projections to the Sudan, South Africa and China between 1885 and 1902 were patriotic responses to military emergencies of the British Empire. The British fostered Australian contingents in the absence of Australian capacity, capability or desire to do so. Small sizes and dispersion among British formations, as well as the predominantly mounted infantry composition of Australian force elements in South Africa, also made creating separate sustainment arrangements unnecessary.

Typically, governments disbanded contingents after redeployment. International force projection was not the first priority. Since the early days of the colonial period, generic force preparation had focused on defence of the homeland from predatory European powers.[10] The army depended on the dedication and patriotism of part-time volunteers to mobilise with their untrained compatriots to face threats to Australia's territorial sovereignty. In a manner similar to dispatching sporting teams for international competition, Australian governments, companies, institutions and citizens responded fervently with both public and private funds for projections in the service of the British Empire. In return, Australians were confident that the Empire would do the same.

Projection to Europe and the Middle East: 1914–18

On 30 July 1914, the Imperial bugle sounded again. The British Government advised secretly that war in Europe was imminent.[11] Though Australia, like the other British dominions, would be at war with Germany if Britain declared war, their contributions would be self-determined.[12] There was bipartisan support in Australia for a continental defence posture, with an implicit requirement for national projection from the eastern and southern coastal heartlands to the western and northern hinterland. However, there were differing views about the defence of the British Empire.[13] As Jeffrey Grey has observed: 'In 1914, despite all the preparations for national defence of the previous few years, the Commonwealth was ill-prepared to meet the demands of war.'[14] Years of secret warnings from the British Government and military planning by higher command staff in the army, followed by months of warnings in the press, had not equated to preparation time for force projection.[15]

After Britain declared war, the Australian Government placed the Australian Navy under the control of the British Admiralty. The government directed Brigadier General W.T. Bridges, Inspector General of the Commonwealth Military Forces, to prepare and dispatch 'an expeditionary force of 20 000 men of any suggested composition'. This force, called the first Australian Imperial Force (1st AIF), would be put 'at the complete disposal of the Home Government'.[16] Bridges raised 1st AIF in a manner that repeated the recruitment processes for Australia's participation in the Sudan, Boxer and Boer wars.[17]

The British Government prompted Australia's first regional force projection on 6 August 1914 by requesting the seizure of 'German possessions and wireless stations' in the southwest Pacific region.[18] The new Chief of the General Staff, Colonel J.G. Legge, set about raising 'His Majesty's Australian Naval and Military Expeditionary Force' (AN and MEF) immediately. Unlike the six weeks for recruitment, preparation and dispatch of the 20 000-strong 1st AIF contingent, this expeditionary force was 'to be promptly organised and despatched with the least possible delay. It was an affair of days.'[19] Legge produced his concept of operations, organisation and orders for AN and MEF in 72 hours, specifying that it would total about 1500 personnel.[20] Twice the number of men needed for 1st Battalion, AN and MEF, were already assembling at Victoria Barracks in Sydney for enlistment with only a promise of 'service abroad'.[21] After being selected, attested, clothed, armed and equipped in a week, the 1000-strong infantry component embarked with the naval contingent and other elements on 18 August 1914. This was another rapid deployment comparable to the projection to the Sudan. The AN and MEF deployed 12 days after the official warning and 'seven days after the first infantryman had been enrolled'.[22] Six days after that, the auxiliary cruiser *Berrima*, carrying 1st Battalion, assembled with several Australian navy vessels off Palm Island north of Townsville, inside the Great Barrier Reef.[23]

The AN and MEF then sailed for a final rendezvous with the flagship *Australia*, and the light cruiser *Melbourne*, at Rossel Island, located near the southeastern tip of New Guinea. In what may have been Australia's first high-level joint command conference on active service, Rear Admiral Sir George E. Patey, RN, Captain J.C.T. Glossop, RAN, Captain J.B. Stevenson, RAN, and Colonel W. Holmes, the land force commander, discussed final plans. Patey issued an operation order for the capture of Rabaul and the hinterland soon afterwards. As commander of the AN and MEF, Holmes would exercise 'a free hand in relation to all operations ashore'.[24] Holmes landed small Royal Australian Navy Reserve (RANR) patrols to search for German military forces and reinforced them when they made contact. Indigenous auxiliaries under the command of German officers quickly succumbed.[25] Medical staff on the hospital ship *Grantola* treated the few wounded Australians.[26] On 13 September 1914, the Australians hoisted the British flag at Rabaul. Thus, after the British request on 6 August, Australia had recruited a 1500-strong light infantry force, prepared and embarked it on a navy task group that then deployed several thousand kilometres into the northern archipelago. The AN and MEF had accomplished its mission for the Australian Government mission in just five weeks.

While AN and MEF projection was progressing, the Quartermaster-General's branch of the Defence Department had been working day and night to equip 1st Division, 1st AIF. Branch staff contracted Australian industry to produce a wide range of items and stripped the militia of stocks.[27] They drew on 'large quantities of army stores [that had been stockpiled] against the chance of sudden mobilisation'.[28] The 1st Division embarked after four weeks of specific force preparation. C.E.W. Bean assessed that 'no troops ever went to the front more generously equipped than the first Australian contingent', drawing attention to high quality webbing, clothing and boots.[29] Jeffrey Grey qualifies this assessment by observing that the Australians arrived in Egypt without tents and were short of 'howitzers for the artillery' and ammunition.[30] After arrival, the British army trained and sustained the 1st Division and following contingents until the 1st AIF was ready for battle in 1915.

Australia prepared and dispatched more than 330 000 troops over the next four years.[31] John Robertson assessed that 'Australia's experience in the 1914–18 war may be characterised as a great deal of slaughter with little military art'.[32] The Australian people received mostly patriotic propaganda about the conduct of the war and the activities of their men on the frontline. Only the names of the dead published in the press communicated the paucity of military art and the cost to a generation. Though journalists were present and published stories of Australian operations, there were no significant political or strategic consequences from any particular setbacks at the tactical level.

Observations

The projection of the AN and MEF into the southwest Pacific in 1914 was Australia's first regional joint force projection. The navy provided the means for deployment, force protection, sustainment, command and control support, and landing parties. The army benefited from a surfeit of fit and capable men rallying for service overseas. There was also sufficient experience within the army to make efficient arrangements for specific force preparation. These arrangements at Victoria Barracks in Sydney enabled a 1500-strong battalion group to be mobilised at very short notice. Though under-trained for conventional war, junior leaders and small teams were capable of the minor tactics required to engage and defeat lightly-armed indigenous troops commanded by German officers. After the war, Australia administered German New Guinea—a spoil of war. Australia had one less inimical European colonial power in the near region.

Generic force preparation, in the form of cooperation between government, citizens and industry, contributed to Australia's proficiency in getting sizeable forces away to fight in Europe and the Middle East on time and in good order.[33] Though the British fostered Australia's participation and the nation paid a high price in lives and national treasure, the experience enhanced the nation's military capabilities and capacities. All three Services practised force projection. A generation of Australian officers now had experience in higher-level command and staff appointments. From their ranks would come the generals and senior commanders for the Second World War. Many of them would train the next generation for combat at sea, on land and in the air. However, this was the zenith of Australia's military power for the time being. The nation was sick of war and forces were demobilised as quickly as possible.

Struggling for Self Reliance

The Second World War: 1939–45

The Second World War in general (and the year 1942 in particular) proved to be an important period for the development of Australia's strategic thinking and proficiency in force projection. Initially, Australians underwrote alliance and trade relationships, as well as racial and cultural loyalties, by projecting force to international theatres to assist Britain. After warning of a Japanese southern thrust, the Australian Government decided to pre-position forces in the national hinterland as well as in the northern archipelago. After the Japanese defeated forces that had been pre-positioned in Malaya and islands in the northern archipelago, the Australian Government decided to defend sea, air and land approaches to the homeland around New Guinea. For the first time, Australia projected force nationally to Darwin and regionally to New Guinea without substantial allied assistance. These experiences during the Second World War confirmed that Australians expected their armed forces to be proficient in national, regional and international force projection.

Australia reached a significant tactical tipping point in August and September 1942 on the Kokoda Track that ran north from Port Moresby in Papua. Good luck, rather than prompt, strong and smart force projection, helped Australian forces to prevail. Fortuitously, the USS *Lexington* raid on Japanese forces arriving in northern New Guinea, Allied maritime victories in the Coral Sea and around Midway Atoll, and a US Marine landing at Guadalcanal in the southern Solomons, as well as the Japanese deciding to conduct three major operations in the southwest Pacific simultaneously in mid-1942, took the pressure off Australian forces. These circumstances allowed Australia to reinforce Port Moresby in time to counter a Japanese advance along the Kokoda Track and a lodgment at Milne Bay west of Port Moresby.

Over-stretched Japanese lines of supply and difficult tropical climate and terrain assisted Australian forces further. However, lack of proficiency in the functions of force projection put unnecessary pressure on the tactical level of command and increased risk. The Australian Government ended up depending on fortuity and junior leaders and small teams displaying courage and tenacity at the right places, and at the right time, under the leadership of several exceptional unit and sub-unit commanders, to spare the nation from further strategic embarrassment.[34]

The Post-Second World War Period: 1946–64

There were improvements in Australian proficiency in land force projection, especially force rotation, in the 1950s and early 1960s. The Australian Government responded to a threat from Chinese-inspired communism by projecting small regular forces to participate in a US-led UN campaign in Korea and a British campaign in Malaya, and then Malaysia, to symbolise Australian resolve. However, there were persistent weaknesses in specific force preparation, deployment and sustainment of the first contingents to deploy. Land forces had to improvise and depend on circumstances, such as being given time after arrival and the goodwill of allies, to make up for these deficiencies before being committed to combat operations.

Australia expected allies to be the forward line of Australian homeland defence and to supplement the functions of force projection despite the experience of having to defend New Guinea in 1942 without substantial allied assistance. Little was done to develop autonomous logistic and higher-level communications capabilities, or to exercise joint command to enable independent projections like the AN and MEF projection in 1914. The Australian Government did not appear to expect self-reliant Australian joint force operations while British and American allies maintained a strong presence in Southeast Asia.

Indeed, Australia was still projecting land forces as it had in 1885, 1900, 1914, 1940 and 1942; and light infantry battalions supported by field artillery remained at its core. The change for the Cold War was that land forces were not comprised of rallying volunteers already possessing many of the skills and attributes of soldiers. A relatively small group of officers and men, who spent years in regimental service, maintained Australia's capability and capacity for land force projection.

The projections of the first 20 years following the Second World War confirmed that the Australian people expected their armed forces to operate in the Southeast Asian archipelago and beyond to protect Australian interests and bolster alliance relationships. However, the British were about to withdraw east of the Suez. As a result, British grand strategy, cultural and racial ties, historical obligations or mutual self-interest would not prompt Australian military action. Australia would have to depend solely on American military power in Southeast Asia. This historic parting of the ways from the mother country was symbolised by the divergence of British and Australian policies over supporting the Americans in Vietnam.

The Vietnam War: 1965–71

The initial projections of a 1000-strong 1st Battalion, Royal Australian Regiment Group (1 RAR) group in 1965 and of an independent 4500-strong task force to Vietnam in 1966 exposed problems with force projection that echoed deficiencies evident in 1942 (New Guinea), 1950 (Korea) and 1955 (Malaya). The Americans assisted the 1 RAR group in 1965. However, they were not in a position to do so for the task force in 1966. A seven-month military planning embargo (from August 1965 until March 1966) imposed by the government crippled tactical training and logistic preparations for the task force and, according to the official historian, Ian McNeill, 'important matters were overlooked'.[35] These matters increased risk and put unnecessary pressure on those working at the tactical level of command.[36] This accumulation of risk could have resulted in Australia losing a tactical contest at Long Tan near the Australian task force base in August 1966 that would have had significant political and strategic consequences.[37]

Australian operations in Vietnam continued for another six years. Aside from a two-battalion sized operation outside Phuoc Tuy province in 1968 that also almost ended in military disaster, operations involved a slow, inconclusive attrition of Viet Cong guerrilla units in Phuoc Tuy province.[38] The army became proficient in the mechanics of force rotation. Battalion groups shed their national servicemen on return from Vietnam and most regular personnel moved on to other appointments in the army. Concurrently, other battalion groups reconstituted and prepared for their next tours of duty.

Post-Vietnam War Period: 1972–85

Australia's participation in the Vietnam War ended almost 100 years of involvement in British and American campaigns until participation in the Gulf War in 1991. Even before the end of the Vietnam campaign, Australia's forward defence posture had begun a transition to 'defence-in-depth' of the Australian mainland. The withdrawal of the British east of Suez, the end of the volatile Sukarno era in Indonesia, the Nixon Doctrine enunciated in Guam in 1969 and a relatively benign near region after the end of the Vietnam War contributed (by the early 1970s) to a shift in Australian Government policy away from regional and international force projection.[39]

The election of the Whitlam Labor Government in 1972 ended selective conscription and finalised Australia's withdrawal from Vietnam.[40] Though it did not initiate the demise of the forward defence policy, the Whitlam Government confirmed its end and began a process of 'monumental change'.[41] David Horner suggests that the Australian Government then began a 'reorganisation [that] revolutionised the way Defence conducted its business'.[42] Prime Minister Gough Whitlam appointed his Deputy, Lance Barnard, as his initial Minister for Defence. Barnard found Sir Arthur Tange, the Department's Secretary, to be a willing and forceful organisational reformer.[43] Since his appointment in 1970, Tange had not been able to persuade Coalition Governments to approve changes that he and other senior public servants, as well as some senior military officers, considered overdue.[44] After consolidating both past and contemporary views, and with an eye on arrangements in Britain and the United States, Tange presented his recommended changes, *Australian Defence: Report on the Reorganisation of the Defence Group of Departments* (the Tange Report), to Barnard on 15 November 1973.[45] His intentions were structural, strategic and economic.[46] The structural objectives were to integrate 'the various aspects of defence' by abolishing the three Service departments with their separate ministers and bureaucracies. A diarchy, comprised of a Chief of the Defence Force Staff (CDFS) and the Secretary, would lead and manage a new consolidated department simultaneously. The report also recommended fresh strategic thinking, based more firmly on Australia's 'new world situation'.[47]

The Labor Government accepted the Tange Report. The major weakness of these reforms, from a military perspective, was that the CDFS did not have a headquarters or staff to orchestrate the functions of force projection with the three Services.[48] Moreover, a Chief of Joint Operations and Plans had insufficient authority or staff to summon the three Services for joint planning, or to synchronise Service capabilities on behalf of the CDFS. In effect, the CDFS had statutory authority, but not the means to exercise it.

The 1975 *Strategic Basis* Paper 'was explicit that there was no requirement for the maintenance of Australian military forces for conflict in South-East Asia' and that 'there were no military threats to Australia or the prospect of major assault'.[49] In 1976, a newly-elected government issued a Defence White Paper, *Australian Defence*, that explained Australia's changed strategic circumstances and emphasised force projection into the 'neighbourhood' rather than 'some distant or forward theatre'.[50] The ANZUS Treaty partners began conducting the *Kangaroo* series of exercises in 1974, 1976 and 1979. David Horner described exercise scenarios during this period as 'a window into the nature of the threat that the ADF [Australian Defence Force] was preparing to counter'.[51] There were no scenarios based on offshore counterinsurgency or expeditionary operations. Initial exercises in the 1970s simulated conventional operations that in some ways replicated Korean War scenarios of offensive and defensive operations on land, with accompanying close air support. The navy simulated battles like those fought in the Coral Sea in 1942 and the air force fought off notional encroachments of Australian airspace by hostile military aircraft and provided air cover for the navy. By the early 1980s, land force elements exercised to defend small incursions by hostile forces intent on sabotaging Australia's mining infrastructure in the northwest (*Kangaroo 83*) and the navy and the air force exercised in the northern sea and air approaches to the continent.

Small contingents left Australia in support of UN overseas operations. None were urgent, large scale or particularly dangerous. Similarly, force elements from each service operated offshore as tokens of support and demonstrations of resolve as part of Cold War surveillance operations.[52] Several hundred ADF personnel, mostly from the army, served in support of the PNG Defence Force (PNGDF) after independence in 1975. The Government had wound this effort back by 1985.

The ADF was not 'a truly joint force' by 1985. It lacked joint doctrine and clearly enunciated and practised joint command arrangements.[53] However, this situation was about to change. The CDFS, General Phillip Bennett, had begun to strengthen ADF joint command and control arrangements.[54] Bennett formed Headquarters Australian Defence Force (HQ ADF) in September 1984 to give the military–strategic level of command capacity to direct the three Services for joint and single Service operations. The parliamentary Joint Committee on Foreign Affairs and Defence tabled a supportive report, *The Australian Defence Force: its Structure and Capabilities*, in October 1984.[55] A year later, Bennett dropped the word 'Staff' from his title, leaving him with a more commanding designation of Chief of the Defence Force (CDF). He established a two-star position for strategic-level joint operations and plans, and another for military strategic policy and military inputs into force development.[56] Later, he added a three-star position of Vice Chief of the Defence Force (VCDF), who was to act as a chief of staff at HQ ADF with responsibilities for both policy development, and operations and planning functions. He also included a Joint Logistics Section at HQ ADF, in order to link both departmental and Service logistic organisations.

Bennett initiated staff processes for the establishment of environmental commands. In effect, he gave the three senior Service combat commanders environmental titles (Maritime, Land and Air) and placed them under his command for ADF operations. Simultaneously, these officers reported to their Service chiefs for raising, training and maintaining their combat forces. From 1984, the CDF, through his nominated joint force commanders, would command ADF operations. Bennett's initiatives, like those of Sir Arthur Tange in 1972, were the beginnings of a new era of Defence reform that would either enhance or detract from national, regional and international force projection.

ENDNOTES

[1] E.J.H. Howard in Foreword to Ralph Sutton, *Soldiers of the Queen: War in the Soudan*, New South Wales Military Historical Society and The Royal New South Wales Regiment, Sydney, 1985.

[2] Kenneth S. Inglis, *The Rehearsal: Australians at War in the Sudan 1885*, Rigby Publishers, Adelaide, 1985, pp. 15–16.

[3] The contingent received two weeks specific force preparation (13 February–3 March 1885) after official warning, arriving in the Sudan 27 days later.

[4] Kenneth S. Inglis in Preface of Laurence M. Field, *The Forgotten War: Australian involvement in the South African Conflict of 1899–1902*, Melbourne University Press, Melbourne, 1979.

[5] Robert L. Wallace describes the lead-up to the declaration of war in 'The Boer War, 1899–1902', in (ed.) Ralph Sutton, *For Queen and Empire: A Boer War Chronicle*, 75th Anniversary Commemorative Edition, New South Wales Military Historical Society, Sydney, 1974, p. 18.

[6] The most comprehensive account of Australian participation in the Boer War is Craig Wilcox, *Australia's Boer War*, Oxford University Press, Melbourne, 2002.

[7] Field, *The Forgotten War: Australian involvement in the South African Conflict of 1899–1902*, Appendix C, Details of Colonial Contingents.

[8] See Bob Nicholls, *Blue Jackets and Boxers*, Allen and Unwin, Sydney, 1986.

[9] James J. Atkinson, *Australian Contingents to the China Field Force 1900–1901*, New South Wales Military Historical Society and The Clarendon Press, Sydney, 1976, p. 11–18.

[10] For a discussion on Australian threat perceptions, see John Mordike, *An Army for a Nation: A history of Australian military developments 1880–1914*, Allen and Unwin in association with The Directorate of Army Studies, Department of Defence, Sydney, 1992.

[11] C.E.W. Bean, *The Story of ANZAC, Official History of Australia in the War of 1914–1918*, vol. 1, Angus and Robertson, Sydney, 1939, p. 25.

[12] Bean, *The Story of ANZAC, Official History of Australia in the War of 1914–1918*, pp. 1–2.

[13] See Mordike, *An Army for a Nation, A history of Australian military developments 1880–1914*, for a description of a debate between 'imperialists' and 'Australianists'.

[14] Jeffrey Grey, *The Australian Army, The Australian Centenary History of Defence*, vol. I, Oxford University Press, Melbourne, 2001, pp. 37–39.

[15] For information on these warnings, see Grey, *The Australian Army, The Australian Centenary History of Defence*, pp. 34 and 39.

[16] Bean, *The Story of ANZAC, Official History of Australia in the War of 1914–1918*, pp. 28–29.

[17] Bean, *The Story of ANZAC, Official History of Australia in the War of 1914–1918*, p. 34.

[18] See Bean, *The Story of ANZAC, Official History of Australia in the War of 1914–1918*, p. 36; and S.S. Mackenzie, *The Australians at Rabaul: The Capture and Administration of the German Possessions in the Southern Pacific, The Official History of Australia in the War of 1914–1918*, vol. X, Angus and Robertson Ltd, Sydney, 1927, p. 5.

[19] Bean, *The Story of ANZAC, Official History of Australia in the War of 1914–1918*, p. 23.

[20] Bean, *The Story of ANZAC, Official History of Australia in the War of 1914–1918*, p. 23.

[21] Bean, *The Story of ANZAC, Official History of Australia in the War of 1914–1918*, p. 23.

[22] Bean, *The Story of ANZAC, Official History of Australia in the War of 1914–1918*, p. 28.

[23] The light cruiser *Sydney*, the supply ship *Aorangi*, the submarine tenders *Protector* and *Upola*, and two submarines, the AE 1 and AE 2.

[24] Mackenzie, *The Australians at Rabaul: The Capture and Administration of the German Possessions in the Southern Pacific, The Official History of Australia in the War of 1914–1918*, p. 34.

[25] Mackenzie, *The Australians at Rabaul: The Capture and Administration of the German Possessions in the Southern Pacific, The Official History of Australia in the War of 1914–1918*, p. 73.

[26] The capture of Rabaul cost the Australians six killed and four wounded: two of those killed were officers in command, apparently victims of German instructions to their indigenous subordinates to shoot officers first.

[27] Australia had 'factories which had been set up after 1910 to manufacture military equipment'. Grey, *The Australian Army, The Australian Centenary History of Defence*, p. 39.

[28] Bean, *The Story of ANZAC, Official History of Australia in the War of 1914–1918*, p. 63.

[29] Bean, *The Story of ANZAC, Official History of Australia in the War of 1914–1918*, p. 63.

[30] Grey, *The Australian Army, The Australian Centenary History of Defence*, p. 39.

[31] Grey, *The Australian Army, The Australian Centenary History of Defence*, p. 67. Grey nominates a figure of 331 000 men who served overseas during the First World War.

[32] John Robertson, *Australia at War 1939–1945*, William Heinemann, Melbourne, 1981, p. 1.

[33] Bean, *The Story of ANZAC, Official History of Australia in the War of 1914–1918*, p. 5.

[34] See Bob Breen, 'Australian Military Force Projection in the late 1980s and the 1990s: What happened and why.' PhD Thesis, The Australian National University, Canberra, 2006, pp. 23–31.

[35] Ian McNeill, *To Long Tan: The Australian Army and the Vietnam War 1950–1966, The Official History of Australia's involvement in Southeast Asian Conflicts 1948–1975*, Allen and Unwin in association with the Australian War Memorial, Sydney, 1993, p. 191.

[36] Australian Army, Contingency Planning paper 'Lessons Learnt from Operation Hardihood: The Deployment of the First Australian Task Force to South Vietnam in 1966', Annex B, undated, p. 4. This paper appears to be an annex to a parent document that focused on logistics aspects of the deployment of 1 ATF. Probably written in 1971 for a CGS Exercise as part of a presentation by Major General G.F.T. Richardson CBE, Quartermaster General, 'Logistics Aspects of Operation Hardihood', AWM 101, item [10]. Copy held by author.

[37] Breen, 'Australian Military Force Projection in the late 1980s and the 1990s: What happened and why', pp. 32–52.

[38] See Ian McNeill and Ashley Ekins, *On the Offensive: The Australian Army in the Vietnam War 1967–1968. The Official History of Australia's involvement in Southeast Asian Conflicts 1948–1975*, Allen and Unwin in association with the Australian War Memorial, Sydney, 2003.

[39] David Horner, *Making of the Australian Defence Force, The Australian Centenary History of Defence*, Volume V, Oxford University Press, Melbourne, 2001, pp. 50–51.

[40] The previous Gorton and McMahon Governments had begun withdrawing Australian troops in 1971. By November 1972, remaining troops numbered 128 and Defence planners had no role for them beyond November 1972.

[41] Eric Andrews, *The Department of Defence, The Australian Centenary History of Defence*, vol. V, Oxford University Press, Melbourne, 2001, p. 208.

[42] Horner, *Making of the Australian Defence Force, The Australian Centenary History of Defence*, p. 46.

[43] Sir Arthur Tange became Permanent Secretary on 2 March 1970. He had been aware of defence issues for many years and sought to bring about reform to its structure and management. The Tange Reforms had their origins in recognition that the Defence Department was an amalgam of interests rather than an entity. Andrews, *The Department of Defence, The Australian Centenary History of Defence*, pp. 192–93.

[44] One of the most farsighted senior military officers to recognise the need for a unified, joint ADF was General Sir John Wilton. His role in beginning the reform process in the 1960s is described in a biography, David Horner, *Strategic Command: General Sir John Wilton and Australia's Asian Wars*, Oxford University Press, Melbourne, 2005, chapters 17 and 20. Also Andrews, *The Department of Defence, The Australian Centenary History of Defence*, pp. 183–96.

[45] Sir Arthur Tange, 'Australian Defence: Report on the Reorganisation of the Defence Group of Departments.' Presented to the Minister of Defence, November 1973, Department of Defence, Canberra, 1973.

[46] Andrews, *The Department of Defence, The Australian Centenary History of Defence*, p. 200.

[47] Andrews, *The Department of Defence, The Australian Centenary History of Defence*, p. 200.

[48] Andrews, *The Department of Defence, The Australian Centenary History of Defence*, p. 204.

[49] Andrews, *The Department of Defence, The Australian Centenary History of Defence*, p. 210.

[50] Department of Defence, *Australian Defence*, White Paper presented to Parliament by the Minister for Defence, the Hon. D.J. Killen, November 1976, Australian Government Publishing Service, Canberra, 1976, p. 10.

[51] Department of Defence, *Australian Defence*, p. 67.

[52] Operation *Gateway* (1980–89) was Australia's contribution to Western surveillance during the last decade of Cold War. Long range P-3C *Orion* aircraft and navy vessels maintained surveillance operations in the Indian Ocean and the Strait of Malacca. Australian submarines conducted patrols as part of US Cold War deterrence and surveillance operations against Soviet submarines. The army maintained an infantry company group at Butterworth airbase in Malaysia to protect allied aircraft.

[53] Horner, *Making of the Australian Defence Force, The Australian Centenary History of Defence*, p. 73.

[54] Horner, *Making of the Australian Defence Force, The Australian Centenary History of Defence*, p. 62.

[55] Joint Committee on Foreign Affairs and Defence, *The Australian Defence Force; its Structure and Capabilities*, Australian Government Printing Service, Canberra, October 1984.

[56] The terms 'one-star', 'two-star', 'three-star' and 'four-star' corresponded to joint positions that could be filled by equivalent ranks in the three Services. For example, the term 'one-star' equated to the ranks of Commodore (navy), Brigadier (army) and Air Commodore (air force), and 'two-star' equated to Vice Admiral (navy), Major General (army) and Air Vice Marshal (air force).

Chapter 3

Lead Up to Operation *Morris Dance*

Australia's defence posture was changing during the years before the conduct of Operation *Morris Dance* in May 1987. The Defence Minister, Kim Beazley, began a renewed effort to clarify Australia's military strategy in February 1985. He appointed Paul Dibb, an academic at the Strategic and Defence Studies Centre at The Australian National University and former Deputy Director of the Joint Intelligence Organisation (JIO) and Head of the National Assessments staff, as a 'Ministerial Consultant'. He issued terms of reference for him to examine and report on the content, priorities and rationale for defence forward planning and to advise on what capabilities were appropriate for Australia's present and future defence requirements.[1] Dibb presented his report in 1986.[2] He advocated projecting credible military power nationally and regionally.[3] He recommended a self-reliant and 'layered' national defence strategy that would defend the approaches to the Australian national hinterland.[4] For that, the Australian Defence Force (ADF) needed to be capable of projecting military force both nationally—from the southern and eastern coastal heartlands to the western and northern coastal hinterlands—and offshore. He clarified what capabilities each Service needed within the context of credible contingencies, putting first priority on defending Australian territorial sovereignty through national force projection and pre-positioning force elements and military infrastructure in Australia's northern and western hinterland.[5] He also incorporated regional and international force projection by leaving open 'an option to make modest military contributions in support of our more distant diplomatic interests and the military efforts of others'.[6]

The Dibb Report set the scene for and informed the White Paper, *The Defence of Australia 1987*.[7] It explained Australia's strategic posture for defending sea and air approaches to the mainland: a blueprint for defence-in-depth as well as national and regional force projection.[8] The ADF needed to be 'able to track and target an adversary and able to mount sea and air operations throughout the area [of direct military interest] [as well as have] range, endurance, and mobility, and independent logistic support'.[9] The two 'fundamental elements' of this posture were maintaining and developing capabilities for the independent defence of Australia and its interests, and promoting strategic stability and security in Australia's area of direct military interest.[10] It summarised strategic intentions with the following words:

Australia's combined air, land and sea forces can secure our continent against any possible aggressor. Equally, those forces will have the capacity to support regional security too. They will be well-suited to supporting Australia's regional role. Long range ships, submarines and aircraft, and highly mobile ground forces, will enable us to play our proper role in the region, and if necessary, beyond it.[11]

From the perspective of force command, Dibb supported an increase in the power of the CDF over the Service chiefs.[12] He wrote that 'a framework of functional commands should be developed so that peacetime arrangements more closely reflect the Joint Service requirements for credible contingencies'.[13]

In the same month that Dibb released his report, the CDF, General Sir Phillip Bennett, issued a directive to the Service chiefs and the three environmental commanders.[14] The CDF would command the Services through Headquarters Australian Defence Force (HQ ADF) and appoint joint force commanders for operations.[15] The Service chiefs and the environmental commanders (Maritime, Land and Air commanders) would be the enablers of national, regional and international force projection. They would sometimes command operations that predominantly favoured one environment and the dominant use of a particular Service's force elements. Generically, the army would continue to maintain 3rd Brigade in Townsville at high readiness for deployment. The navy and the air force would also keep selected vessels and aircraft on short notice to move.

General Peter Gration succeeded Bennett in April 1987. He inherited Bennett's aspirations for the CDF to command Australia's joint and single Service operations. He also found himself putting Bennett's recent directives into practice for an urgent regional force projection. As had been the case with the Espiritu Santo secessionist rebellion in the emerging South Pacific nation of Vanuatu in mid-1980, a political crisis arose quickly and unexpectedly—this time in Fiji.[16] On 14 May 1987, Lieutenant Colonel Sitiveni Rabuka, Chief of Operations, and an armed and masked group of Republic of Fiji Military Forces (RFMF) soldiers walked into the chamber of the Fijian parliament while it was in session and escorted the newly-elected Prime Minister, Dr Timoci Bavadra, and all of the members of his government at gunpoint to waiting trucks. Members of the RFMF then drove them to Queen Elizabeth Barracks and put them into protected accommodation.[17] Rabuka announced that he was temporarily assuming control of both the Fijian Government and the RFMF. This was a polite, firm but bloodless coup accompanied by assurances that it would not presage violence and that everyone in Fiji should remain calm and go about their business as normal. Patrick Walters, reporting first-hand from Suva, described it 'as probably the most polite coup in history' and 'was expected as much as one in Canberra would be'.[18]

In response to these events, the Fijian Governor General, Ratu Sir Penaia Ganilau, declared a state of emergency and stated that he had taken over executive power under the provisions of the constitution. The commander of the RFMF, Brigadier Epeli Nailatikau, who was in Australia at the time, told journalists that he would fly back to Fiji and take command of the RFMF. For their parts, the Australian Prime Minister, Bob Hawke, the Australian Opposition Leader, John Howard, and the New Zealand Prime Minister, David Lange, deplored what Hawke described simply as, 'the first military coup against an elected government in the South Pacific'.[19] Hawke, Howard and Lange dismissed military intervention to restore the Bavadra Government. Lange left open a military response option however by suggesting that New Zealand would consider participating in a regional military response to 'a cry from a legitimate government'.[20]

At midnight on 14 May 1987 Rabuka announced in a radio broadcast that he had suspended the Fijian Constitution, abolished the position of Governor General and also suspended the commander of the RFMF and his chief of staff. He would brook no opposition to the coup. In the interim he had appointed a Council of Ministers that included the former Prime Minister, Ratu Sir Kamisese Mara, and members of his government that had been defeated at elections in April. He emphasised that he was taking action 'in the national interest' in order to 'prevent further disturbance and bloodshed' after 'monitoring events of the past few weeks'.[21] He called out the 5000-strong Fijian reserve forces to report for duty.

The coup was the culmination of many years of growing tension between Fijians and Indian immigrants.[22] During the colonial period, the British had sponsored the migration to Fiji of large numbers of Indian workers and their families to perform the hard manual labour required in the sugar cane fields. These Indian labourers settled in the country, raised families and within a couple of generations were integrated into most areas of the economy as well as into society. This migration progressively altered the demographic balance in Fiji and enhanced Fiji's economic performance. By the mid-1980s, Indians slightly outnumbered Fijians, precipitating concern among many members of the Fijian population about their political and economic future in their own country.[23]

In the mid-1980s, the Leader of the Opposition party, Dr Timoci Bavadra, a Fijian, built a political coalition from a range of so-called 'left' and 'centre' groups of Indians and Fijians. He mobilised this coalition to win a four-seat majority at the elections in April 1987. Bavadra's Cabinet was comprised of ministers from the Fijian and Indian communities, but 19 of his government's 28 members were Indians. His coalition replaced the long-serving conservative government of Ratu Sir Kamisese Mara (comprised mostly of Fijian representatives from leading families) that had been in power for 17 years since Fiji's independence in 1970. The election of the Bavadra Government would be the first test of the depth and resilience of Fiji's democracy as well as the resolve of the Australian and New Zealand Governments to intervene in the region when democracy was threatened by traditional elites who assumed that power would always belong to them.

Although the probability of a change of government had been recognised for some time, the result came as a surprise and shock to many, especially members of the hardline Fijian nationalist 'Taukei' Movement. They began a series of demonstrations and activities designed to disrupt and put pressure on the new government.[24] This led to a rising sense of tension and uncertainty in the country, as well as considerable emotive speculation that there would be a civil war. These were the disturbances and bloodshed that Rabuka alluded to in his justification of the coup in his radio broadcast to the nation on 14 May 1987.

The RFMF was a bastion of Fijian interests and possibly their final protection if they were threatened by the Indian majority. The RFMF was an institution that emanated from a long martial history. The role of Fijian males was to be warriors. The British drew on this warrior culture during the Second World War to recruit large numbers of Fijian males into the British armed forces.[25] Fijian men found military service lucrative and amenable. Upon war's end, a significant number enlisted in both the British Army and the post-independence RFMF. While the Fijian police was comprised of many Indians and lightly armed, the RFMF was predominantly comprised of Fijians and was heavily armed.[26]

With an increase of UN peacekeeping operations in the Middle East after the war in 1973, successive Fijian Governments offered RFMF units for overseas service. This had the advantages of reducing the cost of the RFMF, providing employment for hundreds of Fijian men and earning additional foreign exchange. In the late 1970s and the 1980s, the RFMF had two 600-strong infantry battalions permanently deployed on UN missions in the Sinai and southern Lebanon.

By the mid-1980s a significant proportion of the Fijian male population had served as short service enlistees or Reservists with the RFMF. This service had given them operational experience with the United Nations in the conduct of low-intensity operations in the midst of a civilian population. Overseas deployments extended the political awareness of many past and present officers and men. They had observed first hand the role of the Israeli Defence Force in maintaining law and order. Thus, by the mid-1980s the RFMF was quite competent and confident in the conduct of internal security operations. After several tours of duty with the United Nations, many men had returned to civilian employment, and family and village life. Many joined (or were sympathetic to) the Taukei Movement as economic, social and political tensions between Fijians and Indians increased during the 1980s.

In the uncertain and increasingly violent climate after the election of the Bavadra Government, Lieutenant Colonel Sitiveni Rabuka, the third most senior officer in the RFMF, was able to draw on nationalistic and ethnic sentiments among members of the RFMF and their opposition to the ascendancy of Indian interests in the Fijian economy and society. The disruptive protests by the Taukei Movement gave him reason to suspend civilian government in the interests of public safety. He spoke of an assassination plot against Indian Cabinet Ministers by anti-government elements.[27] He had achieved surprise and was now able to draw on Fijian loyalties to secure support from members of the police force and government departments to acquiesce to his demands for a new constitution and form of governance that would favour Fijian interests.

On 15 May 1987 Rabuka had warned the local media not to stir up opposition to the coup.[28] He ordered a series of raids on newspaper offices and radio studios after they had expressed concern about the coup's legitimacy and speculated on a range of responses. During the night of 15 May, armed troops closed Fiji's two newspapers (the *Fiji Times* and the *Fiji Sun*) and its radio station. Groups of troops also confronted Australian and other Western journalists and warned them that, if they wrote or broadcast any more negative stories about the coup, they would be arrested and expelled from Fiji. Soldiers arrested Hugh Rimington, a journalist working for Australia's Macquarie Network, presumably for taking umbrage.[29] By this time, Western and regional condemnation of the coup was uniform. The United States and Britain joined Australia, New Zealand and regional countries such as Papua New Guinea and Vanuatu, as well as other Commonwealth nations in calling for the restoration of democratic governance.[30] However, these governments were silent, ruled out or equivocated about military intervention to restore the Bavadra Government. The editorial in the *Sydney Morning Herald* concluded that, in absence of a firm commitment for regional military intervention, 'the Fijian coup now seems irreversible' and, while acknowledging that Prime Ministers Bob Hawke and David Lange had not ruled out military action if requested, the only defensible pretext for Australia and New Zealand projecting military force into Fiji would be humanitarian—'a total breakdown of law and order'.[31]

ENDNOTES

[1] Kim C. Beazley, *Terms of Reference, Review of Australia's Defence Capabilities*, 13 February 1985, in Paul Dibb, *Review of Australia's Defence Capabilities*, Report to the Minister for Defence by Mr Paul Dibb, Australian Government Publishing Service, Canberra, 1986, p. xv. See also Paul Dibb, Covering letter to Defence Minister K.C. Beazley, March 1986, in Paul Dibb, *Review of Australia's Defence Capabilities*, p. i.

[2] Paul Dibb, *Review of Australia's Defence Capabilities*, Report to the Minister for Defence by Mr Paul Dibb, Australian Government Publishing Service, Canberra, 1986.

[3] Dibb, *Review of Australia's Defence Capabilities*, p. 149 and p. 175.

[4] Dibb, *Review of Australia's Defence Capabilities*, p. 44 and p. 51.

[5] Dibb, *Review of Australia's Defence Capabilities*, parts 3–6 and 7–8, and parts 1 and 2 and pp. 113 and 149.

[6] Dibb, *Review of Australia's Defence Capabilities*, p. 43.

[7] Department of Defence, *The Defence of Australia 1987*, Australian Government Publishing Service, Canberra, 1987.

[8] Department of Defence, *The Defence of Australia 1987*, pp. 31–32. **posture:** a combination of capability and intent. Australian Defence Force Publication, 101, glossary, 1994.

[9] Department of Defence, *The Defence of Australia 1987*, preface, p. vii, and p. 3.

[10] Department of Defence, *The Defence of Australia 1987*, p. vii. According to *The Defence of Australia 1987*, the area of direct military interest included Australia, its territories and proximate ocean areas, Indonesia, Papua New Guinea, New Zealand and other nearby countries in the southwest Pacific. It stretches over 7000 kilometres from the Cocos Islands to New Zealand and the islands of the southwest Pacific and 5000 kilometres south to 'the Southern Ocean'. (p. 2.)

[11] Department of Defence, *The Defence of Australia 1987*, An Introduction by the Minister for Defence, Australian Government Publishing Service, 1987, p. 5.

[12] Dibb, *Review of Australia's Defence Capabilities*, p. 99.

[13] Dibb, *Review of Australia's Defence Capabilities*, p. 99.

[14] General Sir Phillip Bennett, CDF Directive 5/87, 12 March 1987. Described by David Horner in *Making of the Australian Defence Force*, pp. 62–63.

[15] The Service chiefs could command single Service operations, though the likelihood of significant projections of force not involving at least two Services was remote, unless the means for deployment and sustainment of land force elements were contracted to commercial agencies, or allies provided strategic lift and means for sustainment. Larger projections would also require the application of firepower and deterrent presence of all three Services.

[16] A secessionist Francophile rebellion broke out on the island of Espiritu Santo on 28 May 1980, two months before the New Hebrides was to be granted independence from Britain and France on 30 July. The newly-elected Prime Minister, Father Walter Hadye Lini, called on members of the South Pacific Forum to quell the rebellion and declared a state of emergency. With independence still two months away, France put 100 paratroopers on standby in New Caledonia while Britain had 200 Royal Marines already located at Port Vila. In the end military action to quell the rebellion was taken by force elements from the PNG Defence Force, facilitated by Australian military logistics support and coordination. For a comprehensive account, see Matthew Gubb, *Vanuatu's 1980 Santo Rebellion—International Responses to a Microstate Security*, Canberra Papers on Strategy and Defence, no. 107, Strategic and Defence Studies Centre, The Australian National University, Canberra, 1994.

[17] Patrick Walters, Mary Louise O'Callaghan and Ross Dunn, 'Former Fiji PM in Coup Cabinet', *Sydney Morning Herald*, 15 May 1987, p. 1.

[18] Walters, O'Callaghan and Dunn, 'Former Fiji PM in Coup Cabinet', *Sydney Morning Herald*, 15 May 1987, p. 8.

[19] Quoted in Walters, O'Callaghan and Dunn, 'Former Fiji PM in Coup Cabinet', *Sydney Morning Herald*, 15 May 1987, p. 1.

[20] Staff correspondents in Suva, 'Ratu Kamisese Mara involved in Coup', *The Australian*, 16 May 1987, p. 1.

[21] Staff correspondents in Suva, 'Ratu Kamisese Mara involved in Coup', *Australian*, 16 May 1987, p .4. Also Rex Gardiner, publisher of *Fiji Times*, report of an interview with Lieutenant Colonel Rabuka, *Australian*, 15 May 1987, p. 4.

[22] See (ed.) Sahendra Prasad, *Coup and Crisis: Fiji—A Year Later*, Arena Publications, Sydney, 1988, for a description of the causes and consequences of the coup.

[23] Peter Hastings, 'Uneasy Past, Uncertain Future', *Sydney Morning Herald*, 15 May 1987, p. 8. Hastings quoted population figures of 347 000 Indians and 333 000 Fijians.

[24] On 24 April 1987 the Taukei Movement organised a demonstration that resulted in the RFMF being placed on full alert with a riot squad on standby. P. Clements, 'Coups and the Fiji Military', *Peacekeeping & International Relations*, vol. 30, issue 1–3, January–March 2001, p. 5.

[25] See R. Howlett, *The History of the Fiji Military Forces 1939–45*, Government Printer, Suva, 1948.

[26] Hastings, 'Uneasy Past, Uncertain Future', *Sydney Morning Herald*, 15 May 1987, p. 8.

[27] See (ed.) Prasad, *Coup & Crisis: Fiji—A Year Later*, p. 220–24; and Kenneth Bain, *Treason at 10: Fiji at the crossroads*, Hodder & Stoughton, Melbourne, 1989, p. 96.

[28] Rex Gardiner, publisher of *Fiji Times*, report of an interview with Lieutenant Colonel Rabuka, 15 May 1987, *Australian*, 15 May 1987, p. 4.

[29] Patrick Walters and Mary Louise O'Callaghan, 'Rabuka: Fijians must rule the rest', *Sydney Morning Herald*, 16 May 1987, p. 1.

[30] Walters and O'Callaghan, 'Rabuka: Fijians must rule the rest', *Sydney Morning Herald*, 16 May 1987, p. 1. See also James Oram and Brian Woodley, 'Fijian Soldiers stop our writers; papers closed', *Weekend Australian*, 16–17 May 1987, p. 5; and Peter Hastings, 'Paias Wingti attacks Fiji coup', *Sydney Morning Herald*, 18 May 1987, p. 6.

[31] Editorial, *Sydney Morning Herald*, 16 May 1987, p. 28.

Chapter 4

Responses to Crisis

Circumstances in Fiji began to change quickly over the weekend of 16–17 May. On Saturday an estimated crowd of 3000 Indians conducted a protest in the capital, Suva, and there were reports of protests elsewhere. Indian leaders called for an indefinite general strike until the Bavadra Government was restored to power. A strike would paralyse the economy, disrupt the supply of food, fuel and power and increase racial tension considerably.[1] A journalist smuggled out a letter from the beleaguered Dr Timoci Bavadra calling for Australian and New Zealand intervention to restore democracy in Fiji and reinstate his government.[2] New Zealand's Prime Minister, David Lange, now had 'a cry [for help] from a legitimate government'. Fiji's Chief Justice and all the Supreme Court Justices declared Lieutenant Colonel Sitiveni Rabuka's suspension of the constitution illegal. A political confrontation was shaping up between Rabuka and his Council of Ministers on the one hand (who represented traditional Fijian elites), and the Governor General and the judiciary on the other (who represented the rule of law, the constitution and democracy). On the streets and in townships throughout Fiji, a more bare-knuckled confrontation between Indians and Fijians appeared to be on the horizon.

The *Sun-Herald* in Melbourne warned of a coming crisis with the headline, 'Fiji Set to Erupt—Fear of Racial Bloodbath'.[3] In continuing efforts to muzzle critical media comment on the coup, Rabuka ordered Fijian soldiers to detain another Australian journalist, Frank Walker, at gunpoint.[4] Other Australian newspapers were less strident about eruptions of racial violence, but also suggested that, until the political future of Fiji was resolved, violence would increase.[5] For his part, Australian Liberal Senator Robert Hill, who was attending an international conference in Suva, pointed out that the only delegates concerned about the coup were from Central and South America, and they had left Fiji immediately. He observed that all other delegates and tourists at the convention hotel appeared to be untroubled and were enjoying themselves.[6]

This was the Hawke Government's first major regional political crisis. Australian Prime Minister Bob Hawke recalled later that he found 'an amusing excess of enthusiasm' for intervening militarily in Fiji's affairs by his Defence Minister, Kim Beazley, and acting Foreign Minister, Senator Gareth Evans, whom he described as 'two Rambos'. He laughed off their suggestions for using a navy helicopter to pluck Bavadra from the New Zealand High Commission, to where it was rumoured he had escaped.[7] Hawke commented that the look on the face of the Chief of the Defence Force (CDF), General Peter Gration, when this proposal was discussed, was sufficient alone to persuade him that this course of action was folly.[8]

By Sunday 17 May 1987 the Australian Government was on the record as condemning the coup as undemocratic, but at the same time ruling out a military response to restore the Bavadra Government. By coincidence, the Commander in Chief of the RFMF, Brigadier Ratu Epeli Nailatikau, was in Australia at the time of the coup, having attended a ceremony in Perth where the Australian Government handed over patrol boats to the Government of Papua New Guinea (PNG) as part of the South Pacific Defence Cooperation Program. Apparently, confidential discussions took place with him over the possible redeployment of the RFMF troops located in the Middle East back to Fiji.[9] The Fiji Governor General did not support this redeployment.[10] The prospect of complicating the situation with the return of supposedly 'loyalist' troops, let alone the logistical effort required to do so at short notice, would also have been enough to scuttle this response option. After dismissing military options, Mike Steketee, senior political commentator for the *Sydney Morning Herald*, reported that the Australian Government's strategy was to strongly condemn the coup, encourage international pressure for a return to democracy in Fiji and to refuse to extend diplomatic recognition.[11] Paul Kelly, Steketee's counterpart at *The Australian*, reported that the Hawke Government was mobilising opinion and not the military.[12]

The British Commonwealth connection gave countries in the region a mechanism for both consultation and leverage in Fiji. Hawke would pursue this avenue subsequently.[13] The South Pacific Forum was another mechanism for intervening in the Fijian crisis. Its annual meeting, due to take place at the end of June 1987, was a possible forum for consolidating a regional response under Australian and New Zealand leadership. There appeared to be no political advantages for elected governments in the South Pacific to condone or ignore a successful military coup in the region.[14] At dawn on Monday 18 May 1987, groups of Fijian soldiers conducted raids on the hotel rooms of several Australian journalists and took them into custody at gunpoint.[15] *The Australian* headline was 'Tension Mounts'. Malcom Brown, reporting from Suva, wrote, 'At 12.55 p.m. Fijians started bashing Indians', adding that Indians had begun to set sugar cane fields on fire.[16]

Events in Fiji since the coup became news on the evening of 14 May had not escaped the notice of the Australian Defence Force (ADF) tactical level of command in Townsville. Major Gary Stone, Second-In-Command, 1 RAR, the battalion in 3rd Brigade that was on standby for emergencies, asked the Brigade Major, Major Peter Pursey, on Friday 15 May to make enquiries about whether he should be preparing the 154-strong Advance Company Group (ACG) to protect and coordinate an evacuation of Australian nationals from Fiji, should the need arise.[17] The battalion had an obligation to keep the ACG on seven days' notice to move. Stone assessed that the situation in Fiji was volatile and troops might be needed immediately. Pursey called back and told Stone that Brigadier Mick Harris, Chief of Staff at the newly renamed Land Headquarters in Sydney, had directed that notice to move for the ACG should not be reduced, and no preparations were to be made. Furthermore, Stone was to discourage any activity or rumour that might suggest Australia was preparing troops for intervention into Fiji.[18] At the time, Hawke, Beazley, the Defence Secretary, Alan Woods, and Gration, as well as the three Service chiefs were heading for Perth to attend a ceremony to hand over a patrol boat to PNG as part of the Pacific Patrol Boat program on Saturday 16 May 1987.

Colonel Adrian D'Hage, Director Joint Operations and Plans, Headquarters Australian Defence Force (HQ ADF), wrote later:

> It was apparent within HQ ADF that if, as a result of the coup, civil disorder in Fiji was to break down, the Australian Government would wish to take appropriate steps to safeguard Australian citizens.[19] There was a paramount requirement not to be seen to be interfering in the internal affairs of another sovereign country, counter-balanced by an undisputed obligation of providing protection for Australians overseas.[20]
> ... Both the Government and the ADF were faced with the difficulty of planning an operation without wishing to invite media speculation as to the probable tasks and preparation of a military force.[21]

Thus, there were competing priorities of obeying international law and meeting obligations to Australian citizens, as well as allowing the ADF enough time to prepare if there were signs that the situation in Fiji was deteriorating. In secrecy, staff at HQ ADF considered options on Saturday 16 May for evacuating 4000–5000 Australian nationals from Fiji based on assessments of the situation from the Joint Intelligence Organisation (JIO) and the Department of Foreign Affairs and Trade (DFAT). After Beazley, Gration and Woods had returned to Canberra from Perth on Sunday 17 May, staff from JIO briefed them 'at around midnight', prompting Beazley to direct that 'formal options for the evacuation of Australian nationals be developed'.[22]

On Monday 18 May 1987, staff at HQ ADF developed maritime and air options for evacuation operations. They were based on assumptions of cooperation from Fijian authorities and military and police forces. There were concerns, however, that civil unrest might close roads needed by evacuees to move to airports or wharves. The Joint Planning Committee (JPC) convened later that afternoon to design Operation *Morris Dance*. Committee members included an option of employing Australian troops to keep routes open to airports and wharves, and to secure evacuation points. Air Vice Marshal Peter Scully, the Assistant Chief of the Defence Force (Operations) chaired the JPC. Membership was inter-departmental and included the Chiefs of Staff of Maritime, Land (also called Field Force Command at the time) and Air Commands and representatives from the Service offices (navy, army, and air force) in Canberra.[23]

On Tuesday 19 May 1987, James Oram, a journalist reporting for *The Australian* in Fiji, wrote that the country was 'at a flashpoint after a bridge was bombed, cane fields were set on fire and brawls erupted between Fijians and Indians in the streets of Suva [the capital]'.[24] The day before, his colleague, Brian Woodley, had confirmed that all of the RFMF Reserves had been called out to patrol the streets in response to the planned beginning of a national strike.[25] Matthew Gubb wrote later that shots were heard as the Indians went on strike, bringing the sugar industry to a standstill.[26] The editorial in *The Australian* warned that Fiji could sink into anarchy, autocracy or civil war if there was no early return to constitutional government. Steketee offered: 'Australia might have to swallow hard and, as it did on the case of the Indonesian take over of Timor, accept reality and extend de facto recognition, followed sometime later by formal diplomatic recognition'.[27]

Interestingly, Steketee revealed that officials at DFAT were not only drawing up plans for economic sanctions against Fiji but also crafting a 'RAN evacuation plan', with five navy ships already on standby in Fijian waters.[28] Though Hawke had rejected military intervention to restore the political situation, he remained cognisant of his government's obligations to Australians located in Fiji and to the expectations of allies, such as New Zealand and the United States, that Australia would take the lead in any evacuation operation.[29] However, this recognition did not include allowing for military preparation. Hawke and Beazley were reluctant to give permission in case such preparations were misinterpreted as a military intervention, rather than an evacuation operation.[30] Possibly, whoever was briefing Steketee on the Government's intentions was creating a media story that military planning was only for emergency evacuation operations.

By Tuesday 19 May 1987, events in Fiji had the potential to overtake the methodical workings of the Australian Government's crisis machinery and the ADF planning process. The JPC had no authority to issue warning orders to the Services to be prepared to make force elements available to the CDF for evacuation operations in Fiji. Orders could only be issued with the authority of the CDF, after consultation with the Chiefs of Staff Committee (COSC). The COSC, augmented with the Secretary and additional senior ADF officers and defence officials, met on the morning of 20 May 1987. While members of COSC considered an appreciation of the situation by members of the JPC, New Zealand announced that a New Zealand Defence Force group was on standby to evacuate 1800 New Zealand nationals if they were endangered by increasing civil unrest.[31] The media was broadcasting images of crowds setting buildings on fire and looting, as well as Fijian troops bashing Indians with rifle butts to break up increasingly violent demonstrations against the coup.

Members of COSC preferred an evacuation by civil aircraft coordinated by Australian High Commission staff in Fiji. However, Gration concluded 'In [my] view, the situation had already deteriorated to such an extent that it was presently a questionable course.'[32] The COSC put aside the option of deploying an infantry company to assist with an evacuation for the time being: 'Until Government had made a decision [about conducting an evacuation], no higher state of readiness order was to be issued to the ODF [Operational Deployment Force], and planning was to be confined to Army Office in Canberra'.[33]

This order was carried out to the letter after Pursey, on behalf of Brigadier Peter Arnison, Commander 3rd Brigade, asked Harris once again for permission to reduce the notice to move for the ACG in light of the New Zealand announcement and the apparent worsening situation in Fiji. Harris ordered him emphatically not to initiate any activity at 1 RAR that might spawn speculation about Australia intervening with military force.[34]

Political sensitivity about being discovered preparing troops in Townsville should be seen in light of maritime tensions between Fiji and Australia at the time. Fijian military officers supporting the coup 'had become suspicious of Australian military intentions' and, on the evening of Monday 18 May 1987, a Fijian patrol boat, HMFS *Kira*, had challenged HMAS *Stalwart*, a supply ship, at sea.[35] At 1.00 p.m. Tuesday 19 May, the Fijian Naval Division Commander informed the Australian High Commission in Suva that Australian ships berthed in Suva had overstayed their diplomatic clearances and, if they did not sail immediately, their presence would be construed as a hostile act. Feelings were running high between two normally cooperative and friendly navies. Technically, the Fijian coup leaders in the RFMF were threatening action against Australian ships. That night, Fijian authorities formally challenged HMAS *Sydney*, a frigate berthed in Suva, for not having a diplomatic clearance. All Australian ships departed from Fijian waters in the early hours of 20 May to avoid an escalation of tensions over their presence in Fijian ports.[36]

By this time there had been a mix of positive and negative developments in Fiji as violence increased and the Governor General, whom Queen Elizabeth had told to stand firm, negotiated with Rabuka and his Council of Ministers.[37] One unhelpful event had occurred when an Indian man hijacked an Air New Zealand 747 jet on the tarmac at Nadi Airport early on Tuesday 19 May 1987. This situation distracted planners in both Australia and New Zealand, and interrupted negotiations. Fortunately, the hijacker surrendered to authorities at 1.30 p.m. local time. At 4.00 p.m. the Governor General addressed the Great Council of Chiefs in an effort to achieve a compromise that would facilitate a reconciliation process towards drafting a new constitution and conducting new elections. The prospects of Bavadra and members of his coalition being released increased when the Governor General agreed to swear in Rabuka's Council of Ministers as a new Council of Advisors until the conduct of a new election in what was reported as a 'secret compromise'.[38] At 10.00 p.m. soldiers released Bavadra and his colleagues. Bavadra did not ease tensions. He angrily told waiting media representatives that he was still the Prime Minister and that Rabuka should be tried for treason.[39] It now remained to be seen whether Bavadra's release and the Governor General's secret compromise would cool or inflame tensions between the Indian and Fijian communities, and also whether the newly-promoted Colonel Rabuka and his RFMF forces were controlling Suva's streets.

Later on the morning of Wednesday 20 May, the ADF strategic and operational levels of command issued the first formal orders for Operation *Morris Dance*. The first order was to assign army landing craft to HMAS *Tobruk*, the navy's heavy landing ship that was alongside at the Garden Island fleet base in Sydney.[40] At 1.00 p.m. the Chief of the General Staff (CGS), Lieutenant General Laurie O'Donnell, directed Harris, who was acting Land Commander at the time, to put landing craft and crews as well as a detachment of communications personnel under command of the officer commanding the ship's 15-strong army detachment, who was aboard HMAS *Tobruk*.[41] Land Headquarters staff gave crews from Chowder Bay on Sydney Harbour and a detachment of signallers from Holsworthy in Sydney, who were not on any formal notice to move for offshore deployment, four hours' warning to get themselves, their craft and vehicles as well as their equipment on board.[42] At 9.00 p.m. the Maritime Commander, Rear Admiral Peter Sinclair, signalled that he would exercise 'full command' over all maritime force elements assigned to Operation *Morris Dance*.[43] This action conformed to General Sir Phillip Bennett's March directive and sidelined O'Donnell and Chief of the Naval Staff (CNS), Vice-Admiral Mike Hudson, from operational command of HMAS *Tobruk* and its embarked army elements. At 2.00 a.m. on 21 May 1987, Gration's staff issued a directive to the environmental commanders for the conduct of Operation *Morris Dance*.[44] He did not nominate a joint force commander because Cabinet had not decided whether there would be an evacuation and, if ordered, whether it would be by sea or air. Gration issued a further directive 30 minutes later to the Chief of the Air Staff, Air Marshal Jim Newham, to assign aircraft to the Air Commander, Air Vice Marshal Ted Radford, thus completing the removal of all of the Service chiefs from the operational command over force elements assigned to Operation *Morris Dance*.[45]

In reality, however, each Service chief was still involved because Gration's directives, informed by Bennett's March directive, obligated them to provide logistic support.[46] Accepting that logistic support is a function of command, the joint force commander—either the Maritime Commander or Air Commander—would have to be supported by a joint logistic component commander once Gration decided on who would command the operation. However, there was no mechanism for appointing a joint logistic commander or for assigning the effort of logistic force elements or infrastructure from the Services to a joint force commander for offshore operations. Thus, Gration had to include the Service chiefs in support of Operation *Morris Dance*, using their processes and procedures as well as logistic support assets, such as supply depots, distribution agencies, bases and airfields.

None of the orders on 20 May or the early morning of 21 May 1987 authorised any reduction in the notice to move for the ACG, despite the increased readiness of navy vessels and aircraft to conduct evacuation operations with army landing craft embarked on HMAS *Tobruk*.[47] For his part, Harris once again reinforced his orders with an insistent Arnison on 20 May prohibiting any preparations in 3rd Brigade.[48] For their parts, Gration and Woods, briefed Beazley and the Acting Foreign Minister, Gareth Evans, after the COSC meeting on 20 May, about options for evacuation, but did not include reference to employing an ODF infantry company.[49]

Cabinet reportedly met on the morning of 21 May 1987 and decided that Australia should have troops on standby at sea for evacuation operations.[50] According to Gration, the Maritime Commander, Rear Admiral Peter Sinclair, prompted his sudden decision to embark the ACG on ships as part of Australia's 'contingency deployment' to the waters off Fiji after he assessed that there would be insufficient numbers of personnel from ships' companies to coordinate an evacuation of several thousand people.[51] He asked Gration to make troops available to assist. As a result, seven days after the coup and one day after again prohibiting any specific force preparation, Harris directed Arnison by telephone to have the ACG ready to deploy by air to Norfolk Island by that afternoon in preparation for transfer to HMAS *Tobruk* and HMAS *Success* on their way to Fiji.[52] This was the only location *en route* to transfer an infantry company with vehicles and equipment to ships.[53]

Reflecting the Hawke Government's assessment of the Fijian situation or possibly only his own, Evans commented to the media that there might be a 20 per cent likelihood that law and order in Fiji could break down completely.[54] This quantification suggests that Evans may have been echoing a JIO assessment as well as that of the High Commission in Fiji or that it was his personal assessment derived from information from military and diplomatic sources.

Serious rioting erupted during the night of 21 May 1987, and there was the prospect of more violence in the coming days. The Great Council of Chiefs was taking time to agree to the Governor General's arrangements for an interim government. The release of members of the Bavadra Government did not appear to have helped ease the violence. Gangs of Fijians went on the rampage, injuring scores of Indians, looting and vandalising their shops and smashing glass windows. They attacked Indians at random in frenzied assaults. James Oram reported that Fijian troops had fired at praying protesters.[55] Australian journalists described 20 May as Suva's bloodiest day and that rioting appeared to be at a turning point—either it had peaked and would subside, or it would increase.[56] Milton Cockburn, reporting for the *Sydney Morning Herald*, revealed that the Australian Cabinet would be finalising evacuation plans for Australians from Fiji on Thursday 21 May 1987.

Meanwhile, Stone and his men had arrived at the Royal Australian Air Force (RAAF) base in Townsville in the early morning dark (at 5.00 a.m.) on Thursday 21 May in anticipation of a 6.30 a.m. departure. However, the loading of their stores and vehicles (which had arrived at the base several hours earlier) was not proceeding satisfactorily. After four C-130 *Hercules* transport aircraft had arrived later than expected, ground staff discovered that there were insufficient ramp pallets or experienced air movements specialists to load the aircraft efficiently.[57] In the haste to make up time, ground staff loaded the 1 RAR duty officer's vehicle with a full fuel tank, the wrong way round, instead of a Landrover that had been pre-prepared for air transportation.[58]

After receiving maps of Fiji 30 minutes before final boarding, the contingent began lifting off one and a half hours later than orders had specified. Three aircraft departed at 7.30 a.m., 8.15 a.m. and 8.50 a.m. After take-off at 8.30 a.m., the other aircraft that was transporting Stone and his headquarters staff had to return to Townsville. The crew discovered a leakage of fuel from the 1 RAR duty officer's vehicle. If this leak had not been detected, the fuel may have been ignited in flight from sparks from an electrical fault or some other source of combustion. Air force crew were also to discover a small Butane gas stove in a Non Commissioned Officer (NCO)'s pack leaking in this aircraft after its next take-off—undiscovered, it would have exploded at altitude with 'catastrophic' consequences.[59] The owner had packed the stove in his pack 36 hours before in anticipation of a road trip to a training area, not a high-altitude air move to an operation in the South Pacific, and had forgotten about it. Stone's aircraft took off a second time, but had to return again when crew discovered another Landrover fuel leak. Stone and his headquarters staff finally departed for Norfolk Island at 9.30 a.m,[60] arriving four hours after the first aircraft had landed. Major Vince Walsh, a liaison officer from Land Headquarters, who had arrived at Norfolk Island the day before, met him.[61] Walsh, who had not been issued independent secure communications equipment prior to his departure from Sydney, was communicating and coordinating activities as well as reporting back to Land Headquarters through the local telephone exchange. All was not going well.

The navy had not been able to provide a liaison officer to the contingent who could have advised on what lay ahead for the transfer of personnel, vehicles and stocks to HMAS *Success* and HMAS *Tobruk* at Norfolk Island. Already tired, troops unpacked containers and redistributed their contents by hand into smaller and lighter loads because the army's storage containers were too heavy to be lifted full' by the navy's *Wessex* helicopter.[62] The helicopter flew the contingent's stores from shore to ship as slung loads. Lieutenant Colonel John P. Salter wrote later that, 'had the storage arrangements aboard HMAS *Success* been known, [that particular container] would not have been used'.[63] Small civilian lighters, crewed by Norfolk Islanders, ferried the two Landrovers.[64] 'It was only the clemency of the weather that made the job possible.'[65] 'This was a difficult task and it was surprising that a craft did not capsize.'[66]

HMAS *Tobruk* arrived offshore at 10.00 p.m. on Thursday 21 May 1987. Utility helicopters picked the contingent up from shore and transferred them to the ship in the dark. This transfer was another risky activity because the helicopters 'were not equipped for night flying over water, which made height extremely difficult to judge'. Gubb, attributing an anonymous source in Maritime Headquarters, added that, 'with the exception of the senior pilot, the air crews were not current for flying their helicopters at night'.[67] After the weary infantrymen arrived, 'reception on HMAS *Tobruk* was slow, with individuals having to unpack and store weapons, ammunition, pyrotechnics and hexamine in separate stowage, on an unfamiliar ship, in the dark early hours of the morning'.[68]

There was another risky transfer of personnel two days later at sea. HMAS *Tobruk* was due to be present at a meeting of representatives from Pacific Forum countries in Apia, the capital of Samoa. As a consequence, the contingent, many of whom had been suffering from sea sickness, had to be transferred to other vessels in the Operation *Morris Dance* task group on 26 May—a very windy day.[69] Helicopter load masters winched down troops from hovering helicopters onto rolling decks in challenging conditions; a first time for the soldiers, UH-1B helicopter pilots and their loadmasters as well as for the crews from HMAS *Parramatta* and HMAS *Adelaide*. During this transfer, three helicopters became unserviceable and another crashed onto the deck of HMAS *Tobruk*.[70] Fortunately, no one was injured.

Norfolk Island had surgical facilities (including a hospital) which could have been used in case of any accidents and injuries during the transfer from shore to ship. However, during the transshipment of troops at sea, there was no surgeon, anaesthetist or surgical facilities on any of the ships in the Operation *Morris Dance* task group.[71] Given his expectation of an unopposed evacuation, Gration had assessed a surgical capacity as unnecessary.[72]

Hindsight should not disguise the potentially difficult task that would have faced Stone and his men if the situation in Fiji had deteriorated further and he had been ordered to protect as well as to assist Australian High Commission staff to coordinate an evacuation of 4000–5000 frightened people. His orders from Land Headquarters specified that Stone and his 105 infantrymen had 'to control, coordinate and administer personnel for evacuation; provide escorts for movement of civilian groups; marshal civilians at concentration points; provide communications on shore; defend Australian assets [in Fiji] and provide support to AUSCOM FIJI [Australian High Commission]'.[73] Land Headquarters, presumably in consultation with O'Donnell's staff at Army Office in Canberra, had elaborated on General Gration's supplementation of a maritime contingency deployment by specifying generic evacuation tasks that would be expected of the company group during a protected evacuation—a worse case scenario that Gration was not anticipating.[74]

Salter, Stone's commanding officer, wrote later that higher levels of command had not appreciated 'the complexity of this [overall] task'.[75] He assessed that only one of the tasks specified in Stone's orders could have been attempted by the depleted ACG. A minimum of two additional company groups would have been required before an evacuation operation could have been attempted. Only one follow-on company had been put on 24 hours' notice to move from Townsville after the ACG had left.[76] He opined: 'The [evacuation] task will only be required when law and order has broken down. The spectre of 1000 people of mixed race [presumably Indians fleeing violence] attempting to get a seat on an aircraft designed for 200 should be imagined.'[77] The unserviceability of helicopters in transit had also reduced the capacity of the task group to transfer troops from ship to shore (to nine soldiers at a time in two helicopters), thus making rapid concentration of force impossible.[78] For his part, if Gration had received information that Australian troops might have to operate in more dangerous circumstances, he would have ordered the deployment of more of them to create a deterrent presence.[79] With the benefit of hindsight, the difficulties the three Services encountered in deploying Stone's contingent suggested that rapid reinforcement at sea or on the ground in Fiji would have been problematic.

The situation in Fiji stabilised rather than deteriorated during the deployment phase of Operation *Morris Dance*, as Gration had anticipated, and there was no evacuation. Indeed, hundreds of nationals, who had wished to leave Fiji, flew out on commercial aircraft with the assistance of Fijian authorities.[80] Stone and his men were back in Australia by 7 June 1987, 15 days after they had flown to Norfolk Island. Their adventures would not go down in Australian military history as a benchmark for joint force projection. It was now up to the ADF to examine what went wrong and apply the lessons—thankfully, these important lessons had manifested without mission failure, loss of life or serious injury.

ENDNOTES

[1] Patrick Walters, 'Indians could strangle the economy', *Sydney Morning Herald*, 18 May 1987, p. 6.

[2] Tony Stephens, Patrick Walters, Malcom Brown and Mary Louise O'Callaghan, 'Judges Challenge Rabuka', *Sydney Morning Herald*, 18 May 1987, p. 1.

[3] Correspondents, 'Fiji Set to Erupt—Fear of Racial Bloodbath', *Sun Herald*, 17 May 1987, p. 1.

[4] Correspondents, 'Fiji Set to Erupt—Fear of Racial Bloodbath', *Sun Herald*, 17 May 1987, p. 2.

[5] James Oram and Brian Woodley (in Suva), 'Fijian Soldiers stop our writers; papers closed', *Weekend Australian*, 16–17 May 1987, p. 17.

[6] Danielle Robinson, 'Robert Hill unperturbed by coup', *Sydney Morning Herald*, 15 May 1987, p. 4.

[7] Robert J. Hawke, *The Hawke Memoirs*, William Heinemann Australia, Melbourne, 1994, pp. 329–30.

[8] Hawke, *The Hawke Memoirs*, pp. 329–30.

[9] Mike Steketee, 'Why Canberra accepts Rabuka's regime as a fact of life', *Sydney Morning Herald*, 19 May 1987, p. 1.

[10] Steketee, 'Why Canberra accepts Rabuka's regime as a fact of life', *Sydney Morning Herald*, p. 1.

[11] Steketee, 'Why Canberra accepts Rabuka's regime as a fact of life', *Sydney Morning Herald*, p. 1.

[12] Paul Kelly, 'Hawke mobilises opinion instead of the military', *The Australian*, 18 May 1987, p. 1.

[13] Hawke, *The Hawke Memoirs*, p. 330.

[14] See Matthew Gubb, *The Australian Military Response to the Fiji Coup: An Assessment*, SDSC Working Paper, no. 171, Strategic Defence Studies Centre, The Australian National University, November 1988.

[15] See Tony Stephens, 'Reporter: Rifle at nose persuasive', *Sydney Morning Herald*, 18 May 1987, p. 5; and James Oram, 'Dictatorship tightens its grip in dawn raids, *The Australian*, 18 May 1987, p. 4.

[16] Malcom Brown, 'An ugly scrimmage in Fiji', *Sydney Morning Herald*, 18 May 1987, p. 1.

[17] Gary J. Stone in interview with author, 17 May 1997. See G.J. Stone, personal diary entry of 15 May 1987 (copy held by author). Lieutenant Colonel John P. Salter, CO 1 RAR, was in northwest Australia attending an exercise at the time.

[18] Stone in interview with author, 17 May 1997.

[19] Colonel Adrian S. D'Hage, 'Operation *Morrisdance*: An Outline History of the Involvement of the Australian Defence Force in the Fiji Crisis of May 1987', *Defence Force Journal*, no. 80, January/February 1990, p. 4.

[20] D'Hage, 'Operation *Morrisdance*: An Outline History of the Involvement of the Australian Defence Force in the Fiji Crisis of May 1987', p. 8.

[21] D'Hage, 'Operation *Morrisdance*: An Outline History of the Involvement of the Australian Defence Force in the Fiji Crisis of May 1987', p. 8.

[22] D'Hage, 'Operation *Morrisdance*: An Outline History of the Involvement of the Australian Defence Force in the Fiji Crisis of May 1987', p. 6.

[23] D'Hage, 'Operation *Morrisdance*: An Outline History of the Involvement of the Australian Defence Force in the Fiji Crisis of May 1987', pp. 5–7. D'Hage describes the 'High Command Planning Sequence' in these pages.

[24] James Oram, 'Bomb, brawling push Fiji to the brink', *The Australian*, 19 May 1987, p. 1.

[25] Brian Woodley, 'Fiji troops called out for general strike', *The Australian*, 18 May 1987, p. 1.

[26] Gubb, *The Australian Military Response to the Fijian Coup: An Assessment*, p. 5.

[27] Steketee, 'Five RAN ships on Standby', *Sydney Morning Herald*, 19 May 1987, p. 2.

[28] Steketee, 'Five RAN ships on Standby', *Sydney Morning Herald*, 19 May 1987, p. 2.

[29] See Alan Fewster, 'Hawke rules out 'Rambo-like' military action', *The Australian*, 19 May 1987, p. 8; and Gubb, *The Australian Military Response to the Fijian Coup: An Assessment*, pp. 1 and 8.

[30] General Peter C. Gration in interview with author, 19 August 2005.

[31] JPC Report 2/87, 'Appreciation of the Situation in Fiji', 19 May 1987, 87–22646, Defence Archives, Queanbeyan. Australian Associated Press report, quoted in *Sydney Morning Herald*, 21 May 1987, p. 10.

[32] COSC Minute 27/87 (Agendum 16/87 refers), Meeting Wednesday 20 May 1987, paragraph 19. Defence Archives, Queanbeyan.

[33] COSC Minute 27/87 (Agendum 16/87 refers), Meeting Wednesday 20 May 1987, paragraph 19. Defence Archives, Queanbeyan.

[34] Brigadier Brian R. Dawson to author, 29 September 2004. Dawson was a member of the operations staff at Land Headquarters and recalled being in the operations room when Harris spoke with Pursey and told him forcefully not to reduce the notice to move for the ACG and not to make preparations.

[35] D'Hage, 'Operation *Morrisdance*: An Outline History of the Involvement of the Australian Defence Force in the Fiji Crisis of May 1987', p. 7.

[36] D'Hage, 'Operation *Morrisdance*: An Outline History of the Involvement of the Australian Defence Force in the Fiji Crisis of May 1987', pp. 7–8.

[37] Yvonne Preston, 'The Queen to GG: stand firm', *Sydney Morning Herald*, 18 May 1987, p. 6.

[38] Tony Stephens, Patrick Walters and Mary Louise O'Callaghan, 'Secret deal: timetable to end coup', *Sydney Morning Herald*, 19 May 1987, p. 1; and Peter Hastings, Colonel Rabuka's coup has succeeded', *Sydney Morning Herald*, 20 May 1987, p. 1.

[39] Herald Reporters, 'I'm still PM says freed Bavadra', *Sydney Morning Herald*, 20 May 1987, p. 1.

[40] HMAS *Tobruk*, known as a Landing Ship Heavy, was the first purpose-built major amphibious ship in the navy. The vessel was commissioned in 1981 and designed to carry troops (350–550), vehicles and stores, and put them ashore without the aid of port facilities.

[41] Signal was issued at 10.24 a.m. on 20 May 1987. Annex A to *Morrisdance Post Action Report*, p. A-1, Attached to Air Vice Marshal P.J. Scully, Assistant Chief of the Defence Force (Operations), Operational [sic] *Morrisdance* —Post Action Report, 15 December 1987, 87–25649. Defence Archives, Queanbeyan.

[42] D'Hage, 'Operation *Morrisdance*: An Outline History of the Involvement of the Australian Defence Force in the Fiji Crisis of May 1987', p. 9. The communications detachment almost did not make it. They arrived soon after *Tobruk* had sailed and were loaded on *Success*.

[43] Maritime Headquarters Signal, 201050ZMAY87. Annex A to *Morrisdance Post Action Report*, p. A-2. Copy held by author.

[44] General Peter C. Gration, CDF Directive 16/1987, 201206ZMAY87, Annex A to *Morrisdance Post Action Report*, p. A-2. Copy held by author.

[45] General Peter C. Gration, CDF Directive 18/1987, 201227ZMAY87. Annex A to *Morrisdance Post Action Report*, p. A-2. Copy held by author.

[46] General Peter C. Gration, CDF Directive, 5/87, 12 March 1987, paragraph 5d. See also General Peter C. Gration, CDF Directive 17/1987, 201230ZMAY1987, which ordered Chief of the Air Staff to provide support to Air Commander Australia 'as required'; and CDF Directive 18/1987, 201230ZMAY87, which ordered the Chief of the General Staff to provide logistic support to Land Commander Australia, 'as required'. Annex A to *Morrisdance Post Action Report*, p. A-2. Copy held by author.

[47] On 20 May 1987 air force aircraft were on 12 hours notice to move for an air evacuation (Annex A to *Morrisdance Post Action Report*, p. 9). On 20 May, the Maritime Commander had vessels sailing off Fiji and HMAS *Tobruk* was about to sail from Sydney. (Annex A to *Morrisdance Post Action Report*, p. 8.)

[48] Gary J. Stone in interview with author, 17 May 1997.

[49] COSC Minute 25/87.

[50] Gubb, *The Australian Military Response to the Fijian Coup: An Assessment*, p. 6.

[51] Gration in interview with author, 19 August 2005.

[52] Stone in interview with author, 17 May 1997. Brigadier Brian R. Dawson to author, 29 September 2004.

[53] Gration in interview with author, 19 August 2005.

[54] Australian Associated Press, 'Evans sets risk factor for evacuation', *Weekend Australian*, 23 May 1987, p. 4.

[55] James Oram, 'Troops fire at group of praying protesters', *The Australian*, 20 May 1987, p. 9.

[56] Patrick Walters, Mary Louise O'Callaghan and Malcom Brown, 'Suva's bloodiest day: chiefs delay decision on interim government', *Sydney Morning Herald*, 21 May 1987, p. 1.

[57] Lieutenant John P. Salter, 'Post Deployment Report', p. 9.

[58] Salter, 'Post Deployment Report', p. 9.

[59] Salter, 'Post Deployment Report', p. 9.

[60] Land Headquarters, Operations Log entry, 12 20 PM, 23 May 1987, 291–K1-9, NAA, Sydney.

[61] LHQ Situation Report 2/87, 212300ZMAY87.

[62] Gubb, *The Australian Military Response to the Fijian Coup: An Assessment*, p. 15.
[63] Salter, 'Post Deployment Report', p. 9.
[64] Salter, 'Post Deployment Report', p. 10.
[65] Gubb, *The Australian Military Response to the Fijian Coup: An Assessment*, p. 15.
[66] Salter, 'Post Deployment Report', p. 10.
[67] Gubb, *The Australian Military Response to the Fijian Coup: An Assessment*, p. 15.
[68] Salter, 'Post Deployment Report', p. 10.
[69] The navy task group comprised three warships (HMAS *Sydney*, HMAS *Adelaide* and HMAS *Parramatta*), four patrol boats (HMAS *Cessnock*, HMAS *Dubbo*, HMAS *Townsville* and HMAS *Wollongong*) and two support vessels (HMAS *Stalwart* and HMAS *Success*). Salter, 'Post Deployment Report', p. 11.
[70] See Gubb, *The Australian Military Response to the Fijian Coup: An Assessment*, p. 13; and Salter, 'Post Deployment Report', p. 11.
[71] Salter, 'Post Deployment Report', p. 7.
[72] Gration, Annotations.
[73] Salter, 'Post Deployment Report', p. 14. Salter quoted these tasks from Land Headquarters' operation order for Operation *Morris Dance* (LANDCOM OPORD 1).
[74] Gration in interview with author, 19 August 2005.
[75] Salter, 'Post Deployment Report', p. 16.
[76] Annex A to *Morrisdance Post Action Report*, p. A-5.
[77] Salter, 'Post Deployment Report', p. 16.
[78] Salter, 'Post Deployment Report', p. 15.
[79] Gration in interview with author, 19 August 2005.
[80] Paul Dibb, Annotations.

Chapter 5

Lessons and Observations

The Australian Defence Force (ADF) strategic level of command was eager to learn from Operation *Morris Dance*. It was a rare opportunity for the ADF to practise offshore joint force projection. Air Vice Marshal Peter Scully had acted quickly. On 3 June 1987 he wrote to the Service chiefs and environmental commanders stating that 'we need to analyse the potential strengths and weaknesses that became obvious throughout the operation'. He requested them to submit reports 'to provide differing perspectives of ADF actions in relation to Operation "MORRISDANCE". ... The reports are to highlight observed strengths and weaknesses and contain recommendations for improvements in planning processes, liaison, command arrangements and control measures within the ADF.'[1]

The Deputy Exercise Director, Joint Exercise Planning Staff, who had been informed by reports from Headquarters Australian Defence Force (HQ ADF) staff, the three Services and the three environmental commanders, submitted a consolidated report on Operation *Morris Dance* four months later in October 1987.[2] He focused on the strategic level of command.[3] As a consequence, his report would not inform Chiefs of Staff Committee (COSC) about the difficulties encountered by those working at the tactical level. Rather, the report evaluated higher level processes of planning, command, control, communications and administration.

The Post Operation Report concluded that strategic and operational level planning processes had neither complied with doctrine nor worked well. The interaction between HQ ADF and the three Service headquarters in Canberra demonstrated that General Sir Phillip Bennett's recent directives had not yet streamlined ADF joint planning process. This was unsurprising considering that extant processes had been untested for over 20 years, and that the new arrangements (only announced two months before) had been neither rehearsed nor practised. The report recommended that HQ ADF should issue 'a Planning or Initiating Directive' to advise subordinate headquarters quickly and comprehensively on what planning data was needed to develop military response options for the government.[4]

While the author of the report recognised correctly that 'the government may not make decisions on military options in the timeframe desired by HQ ADF' and that 'when a government decision is made, a rapid response by the ADF will be expected', he did not highlight that political leaders imposed strict secrecy during the Fiji crisis that prohibited the Chief of the Defence Force (CDF) issuing planning directives or warning orders, and would most likely do the same during future crises.[5] The lesson was not that the CDF should issue 'Planning Directives' or 'Warning Orders' as early as possible—this was well understood by military officers—but that it was unlikely that he would warn the ADF until the government was prepared to advise the public about its military intentions. As Operation *Morris Dance* demonstrated, after the Prime Minister and Cabinet made their decision to project force, they expected the ADF to do so quickly.

The author of this report assessed that assignment of force elements from the Service chiefs to the CDF and environmental commanders was 'a cumbersome process. ... The [Bennett] directives do not make clear whether this assignment is to be through the Service Chiefs of Staff or direct.'[6] He went on to observe that 'the "either/or" command arrangements' that envisaged the Maritime Commander or the Air Commander commanding Operation *Morris Dance*, depending on whether the Chief of the Defence Force (CDF), General Peter Gration, ordered an air or sea evacuation, had

> resulted in a deal of 'ad hoc' co-ordination at lower levels, especially in the provision of administrative support, and contributed to the general comment of 'interference' and overlaps in actions taken and direction given by HQ ADF and Service Offices [in Canberra] ... the whole process was unnecessarily complicated.[7]

There was room for improvement for liaison between participating government departments and the ADF. Remarkably, HQ ADF quickly established liaison with the Department of Foreign Affairs and Trade (DFAT), but included neither the office of the Minister for Defence nor the Department of Prime Minister and Cabinet.[8] The passage of classified information was impeded by a lack of secure telephone and facsimile links between departments, ministerial offices and HQ ADF. There was also no independent military radio communication between Australia and its High Commission in Fiji or between the ADF liaison officer on Norfolk Island, Major Vince Walsh, back to Australia or to deploying ships and aircraft.[9]

Command and control was further complicated because each Service chief of staff had responsibilities to provide logistic support through environmental commanders to deployed force elements.[10] Scully did not include representatives from Joint Logistics Branch, the Surgeon General and Financial Management Branch in initial planning. There was no 'integrated joint logistic planning and coordination'.[11] There was no joint logistic desk officer on duty in the control centre at HQ ADF, and there were no air supply arrangements made for spare parts or mail.[12]

The final major concern was arrangements for intelligence support. Major Mike Dennis, who was assigned to Major Gary Stone as a Joint Intelligence Organisation (JIO) liaison officer, did not have independent secure communications back to Australia or to Fiji. Understandably, intelligence agencies were not used to providing analytical and predictive support for offshore evacuation operations. For Operation *Morris Dance*, there might have been violent interference from hostile groups within the RFMF and nationalistic Fijian organisations; yet Australian intelligence services did not appear to be in a position to identify and monitor this threat. Certainly, Stone was not included as a recipient of intelligence of this kind and assumed, possibly incorrectly, that there was none.[13] The author of the post-operations report offered:

> Experience from Operation MORRISDANCE confirmed the requirement to establish the intelligence system at the outset of any operation, possibly even before the involvement of the ADF has been confirmed and before command and control arrangements have been settled. ... There are still grey areas in the practical coordination of intelligence requirements, management of assets and division of responsibilities between the strategic and operational intelligence agencies.[14]

Under the heading 'Intelligence' in his tactical level report, Lieutenant Colonel John P. Salter (Stone's commanding officer) had written that, 'in the event of a requirement to deploy ashore', Stone would have appreciated information from Special Forces, who might have deployed ahead of them, as well as information on New Zealand intentions in order to avoid 'considerable confusion'.[15] The Maritime Headquarters report highlighted the need to know the intentions of other interested countries and, by implication, their intelligence operations as well as their evacuation plans.[16] Interestingly, JIO denied access to intelligence staff from the Service officers to briefings on Operation *Morris Dance*—an unhelpful demarcation according to the Army Office report.[17]

Concerns about the problems encountered at the tactical level with coordination, joint procedures for deployment and logistic support appeared to be confined to lower levels of command. Colonel Ian Ahearn, Colonel (Plans) at Land Headquarters, assessed that the ADF lacked the 'capability at the operational level to coordinate the operational deployment of a small joint force'.[18] Walsh and Stone echoed this assessment in their reports.[19] Ahearn's colleague at Land Headquarters, Colonel John Bertram, Colonel (Administration), added that, despite orders from Land Headquarters earlier in 1987:

> 3rd Brigade had, and still has, shortfalls in their maintenance stocks and there were delivery times of between 45 days and 4 months for demands for supply. ... This [situation] tends to highlight a major concern with the AJSP (Army Joint Support Plan) for PLAN BENEFACTOR—[the plan

that specified arrangements for rapid deployment and sustainment of the ODF [Operational Deployment Force].][20]

Gration responded to the difficulties identified during Operation *Morris Dance* by modifying ADF command and control. In future, he would exercise command through his HQ ADF staff directly to a joint force commander for operations and not involve the Service chiefs except in an advisory capacity.[21] This change had the potential to simplify processes in Canberra and streamline the transfer of strategic guidance to the operational and tactical levels of command.

Observations

The conduct of Operation *Morris Dance* confirmed that the Australian Government, in general, and the Defence Department in particular, still had some way to go to synchronise joint force projection to promote regional stability and security in a time of crisis. The first challenge was to contemplate military action in secret, yet also allow the tactical level of command to take prudent preparatory action. The second was to streamline government and ADF crisis machinery in areas, such as inter-departmental liaison and consultation, planning, force assignment and communication of strategic intent. The third was to specify command and joint logistics support arrangements early and include logisticians in initial planning. The fourth was to anticipate contingencies with relevant training and acquisition of specialist equipment, including secure communications equipment, and to keep quantities on hand for short notice deployments. The fifth was to specify intelligence arrangements early enough to facilitate early warning, force protection and timely responses to threats. The sixth, and by no means the least challenge, was to get the operational and tactical levels of command from the three Services working together more effectively and practising rapid deployment of land force elements by air and sea.

One of the features of Operation *Morris Dance* was the different perceptions and attitudes of the strategic and tactical levels of command. Gration had a first hand understanding of the Australian Government's intent while he advised political leaders and senior departmental officials on military response options. He also had the benefit of JIO and DFAT assessments of the situation in Fiji as well as information broadcast by the media. He based his assessment of the dangers that lay ahead in Fiji on these inputs and sought to calibrate Australia's initial military response carefully to accommodate political sensitivities in Australia and in Fiji, as well as more generally in the South Pacific. Prime Minister Bob Hawke had to decide on the blend of military and political imperatives, while Gration managed the risks and delivered Hawke's specified strategic effects.

Salter and Stone based their assessments of the dangers that lay ahead in Fiji on media reports and their preference to be prepared for worse case scenarios. They found it difficult to accept Gration's risk management of Operation *Morris Dance* for several reasons. The first was that they felt that they could be trusted to keep secrets and to make prudent preparations without public exposure.[22] The second was that staff at Army Office, Land Headquarters and HQ 3rd Brigade—the operational level of command—interpreted Gration's strategic intent and complicated what he intended to be a simple contingency deployment. Orders issued to Salter and Stone via the operational level of command assumed that an evacuation would have to be commanded on the ground by an army commander and his headquarters rather than by a naval officer aboard a ship. Yet Gration's intention was the opposite. He envisaged army personnel acting as evacuation marshals in conformity to a naval plan that would be worked out in consultation with Stone at sea on the way to Fiji—a process reminiscent of the successful deployment of the Australian Navy and Military Expeditionary Force (AN and MEF) to the southwest Pacific to capture German military radio stations and Rabaul in 1914. The third reason was that Salter and Stone wished to prepare, deploy and operate as they and their men had been organised and trained. Downsizing and leaving their machine guns and grenade launchers behind is an anathema to infantrymen, who prefer to operate with familiar and trusted teams and individuals around them, and weapons at their disposal to both defend themselves and win military contests.

Salter and Stone relied on media reports in the absence of intelligence reports. Arguably, they should have been given the same intelligence as Gration and members of COSC to balance what they were seeing broadcast in the electronic media and reading in the print media. It was useful to view and read first-hand reports from journalists close to the action, but journalists had a tendency to emphasise the more dramatic elements of what they were observing so as to engage their audiences and readers. Salter and Stone would have benefited from more objective, analytical and predictive information from the Australian High Commission in Fiji and any other sources that were informing COSC. In 1987 there appeared to be no intent, mechanisms or facilities in the ADF for the tactical of command in Townsville or elsewhere to receive highly-classified intelligence or copies of diplomatic cables in a timely way.

Gration's assessment of how the situation in Fiji would play out was vindicated by events. From a strategic perspective, he had delivered a short-notice maritime evacuation option close to Fiji for the government just in case events had not unfolded as they did. From an operational and tactical perspective, there had been too many risks. The processes and procedures for regional force projection were understandably rusty after a 15-year pause in offshore operations since the end of Australia's military participation in the

Vietnam War in 1972. However, there were systemic weaknesses in all of the enabling functions of force projection that increased risks unnecessarily.

Conclusion

The ADF was still evolving into a joint defence force in the late 1980s. Operation *Morris Dance* was a short notice deployment in response to an unexpected and volatile political situation. None of the Services had rehearsed jointly for political emergencies and consequent evacuation operations in the near region. This small-scale projection was a valuable 'wake up call'. Operation *Morris Dance* confirmed historical precedents that Australian Governments would expect the ADF to project military force offshore at short notice in an emergency.

Political volatility in the South Pacific suggested that there would be a need for more carefully calibrated regional projections of Australian military force in the future. Matthew Gubb's summary is apt:

> A final point well illustrated by the Vanuatu case [Espiritu Santo Rebellion in 1980] is the ultimate reliance of beleaguered microstates on rapid and decisive military assistance from one or two capable friends, rather than multilateral aid. The ease and speed with which unlawful elements can overwhelm a microstate government means that if external assistance is to be provided at all, then, as a rule, it must be provided extremely rapidly.[23]

ENDNOTES

[1] Air Vice Marshal Peter J. Scully, Operation *Morrisdance*—Post Action Report, ACOPS BS2487/1987, 3 June 1987, 87-22646, Defence Archives, Queanbeyan.

[2] Anon, *Operation Morrisdance—Post Action Report*, undated. Attached to Scully, Operational (sic) '*Morrisdance*—Post Action Report', 15 December 1987, 87/25649, Defence Archives, Queanbeyan.

[3] Anon, *Operation Morrisdance—Post Action Report*, undated. Attached to Scully, Operational (sic) '*Morrisdance*—Post Action Report', p. 2.

[4] Anon, *Operation Morrisdance—Post Action Report*, undated. Attached to Scully, Operational (sic) '*Morrisdance*—Post Action Report', p. 5.

[5] Anon, *Operation Morrisdance—Post Action Report*, undated. Attached to Scully, Operational (sic) '*Morrisdance*—Post Action Report', p. 6.

[6] Anon, *Operation Morrisdance—Post Action Report*, undated. Attached to Scully, Operational (sic) '*Morrisdance*—Post Action Report', p. 7.

[7] Anon, *Operation Morrisdance—Post Action Report*, undated. Attached to Scully, Operational (sic) '*Morrisdance*—Post Action Report', p. 7.

[8] Anon, *Operation Morrisdance—Post Action Report*, undated. Attached to Scully, Operational (sic) '*Morrisdance*—Post Action Report', p. 9.

[9] Anon, *Operation Morrisdance—Post Action Report*, undated. Attached to Scully, Operational (sic) '*Morrisdance*—Post Action Report', p. 9. Also Annex D to *Morrisdance Post Action Report*, p. D-1.

[10] Anon, *Operation Morrisdance—Post Action Report*, undated. Attached to Scully, Operational (sic) '*Morrisdance*—Post Action Report', p. 8.

[11] Anon, *Operation Morrisdance—Post Action Report*, undated. Attached to Scully, Operational (sic) '*Morrisdance*—Post Action Report', p. 12.

[12] Annex C to *Morrisdance Post Action Report*, p. C-4.

[13] Gary J. Stone in interview with author, 17 May 1997.

[14] Anon, *Operation Morrisdance—Post Action Report*, pp. 13–14.

[15] John P. Salter, '1 RAR Post Action Report—Operation MORRIS DANCE', 1 RAR 611-10-1 (2), 24 July 1987, p. 15. Copy included in Colonel R.J. Breen, *Compendium of Operational Lessons from Africa and the Arch of instability 1987-2000*, Land Headquarters, February 2004.

[16] Anon, *Operation Morrisdance—Post Action Report*. Annex C to *Morrisdance Post Action Report*, p. C-3.

[17] Anon, *Operation Morrisdance—Post Action Report*. Annex C to *Morrisdance Post Action Report*, p. C-7.

[18] Colonel Ian F. Ahearn, Colonel (Plans), Field Force Command, Minute to Chief of Staff, Brigadier Mick J. Harris, 2 October 1987, 291-K1-11, NAA: Sydney.

[19] Major Vince Walsh, LAND COMD LO—NORFOLK ISLAND Minute 291/87, R553/1/1, 28 May 1987, 291-K1-11, NAA: Sydney. Walsh was a liaison officer who witnessed transshipment of personnel, vehicles and stores from air force C–130 *Hercules* transport aircraft to navy ships moored at Norfolk Island during the deployment phase of Operation *Morris Dance*. Also Gary J. Stone, Interview with author, 17 May 1997; and Stone, OP MORRIS DANCE Commander's diary, 21 May–7 June 1987. Copy held by author.

[20] *Plan Benefactor* was a contingency plan for short notice deployment of 3rd Brigade in emergency situations. Colonel John F. Bertram, 'Lessons from OP 'MORRISDANCE', Minute COL (ADMIN) 5/87, 2 June 1987, 291-K1-11, NAA: Sydney.

[21] General Peter C. Gration in interview with author, 19 August 2005.

[22] Stone in interview with author, 17 May 1997.

[23] Matthew Gubb, *Vanuatu's 1980 Santo Rebellion—International Response to a Microstate Security*, Canberra Papers on Strategy and Defence, no. 107, Strategic Defence Studies Centre, The Australian National University, Canberra, 1994, p. 77.

Chapter 6

Lead-Up to Operation *Lagoon*

After Operation *Morris Dance*, Australia's next force projection into the near region occurred in October 1994. Sir Julius Chan, the newly-elected Prime Minister of Papua New Guinea (PNG), was taking the initiative on the Bougainville Crisis, a war with secessionists in Bougainville that had begun in the late 1980s.[1] He had started negotiations with Australia in May 1994 when, as Foreign Minister, he had consulted his Australian counterpart, Senator Gareth Evans.[2] Chan's plan depended on Australia providing diplomatic, logistic and other specialist military support for the deployment of a South Pacific peacekeeping force to Bougainville to provide a secure environment for a peace conference.

The agreed trigger for convening a peace conference was the submission of a report from an Australian delegation that had visited Bougainville in response to reports of human rights abuses by the PNG Defence Force (PNGDF). Senator Stephen Loosely, head of the delegation, presented his report in Parliament on 8 June 1994.[3] It contained a timetable for a peace process that would begin with community consultations and culminate with a peace conference later in the year. The report recommended that a South Pacific peacekeeping force provide security for the conference venue and delegates. In his formal reply to Loosely's report in Parliament, Evans signalled:

> Australia could play a role in supporting a small regional peace keeping force, established to facilitate a peace process: this has not been put to us as a detailed proposal, and we await further elaboration of the concept. We would certainly consider any such proposal very sympathetically.[4]

On the same day that Loosely tabled his report, Defence Minister Robert Ray approved a plan for Operation *Lagoon*. The plan envisaged a Fijian-led South Pacific Peace Keeping Force (SPPKF) assembling and training in Fiji and deploying from there to Bougainville via Honiara, the capital of the Solomon Islands.[5] In the covering minute to the plan, the Chief of the Defence Force (CDF), Admiral Alan Beaumont, wrote to Ray:

> I am confident we could mount the operation successfully given the appropriate political climate, but because of the ADF's supporting role, the RFMF [Republic of Fiji Military Forces] would be key players; without them we would be on shaky ground militarily. ... You might note it would require approx[imately] three weeks from receiving your approval

to proceed until all arrangements were in place to commence the conference.⁶

Beaumont had set an ambitious timetable, presumably on advice from his Assistant Chief of the Defence—Operations (ACOPS), Major General Jim Connolly. For the time being, the only persons officially aware of this plan were six officers at Headquarters Australian Defence Force (HQ ADF), Beaumont, Ray, and probably Evans. It remained as a contingency plan, untested by wider analysis from staff at HQ ADF or subordinate headquarters. The need to keep the Operation *Lagoon* plan a secret from staff at HQ ADF as well as the environmental commanders and their senior staff was puzzling. Evans had talked freely to the media and in Parliament in June 1994 about Australia supporting a small-scale, short-time deployment of a SPPKF to Bougainville. Chan was reported later to have undertaken some personal lobbying during a tour of South Pacific island countries, canvassing participation in a SPPKF.⁷ These indicators that a force projection was in the offing did not prompt HQ ADF to begin contingency planning with subordinate headquarters, who would have to plan and execute Operation *Lagoon*. For their part, subordinate headquarters, such as Land Headquarters, HQ 1st Division and HQ 3rd Brigade, did not take their cue from Evans' statements to conduct any contingency planning either. Lieutenant General John Baker, who was Vice Chief of the Defence Force (VCDF) at the time, commented later that Ray was not as keen as Evans about supporting Chan's initiative in Bougainville. Accordingly, he gave no encouragement to Beaumont to begin more comprehensive planning with lower levels of command.⁸

On 27 August 1994, PNG foreign affairs officials, following Chan's direction, met Bougainvillean secessionist leaders at Tambea in the Solomon Islands and signed the Tambea Accords. The PNG Government and the Bougainville Revolutionary Army (BRA) agreed to pursue a peace process that would involve deployment of a SPPKF into Bougainville. This was a clear signal to Australia that more detailed planning was now urgently required. Australian diplomats met in Canberra during the following days to decide on the way ahead. Chan gave further impetus to the Bougainville peace process on 30 August, soon after being appointed Prime Minister. He used his inaugural speech to state that he would lead negotiations for peace in Bougainville with secessionist leaders. Five days after the Tambea Accords were signed, and two days after Chan's announcement of his intentions, Beaumont had still not issued a warning order to subordinate levels of command. He advised Ray on 2 September that he would continue planning in secret.⁹ Ray may have directed Beaumont to wait for formal agreements between the PNG Government and the Bougainvillean secessionists on the conduct and location of the peace conference before issuing a warning order. In any event, time shortened for subordinate headquarters to plan, check and organise, and for logisticians to anticipate and pre-position supplies.

Chan met with the secessionist military commander, General Sam Kauona, at Honiara on 2 September 1994. They signed *Commitment for Peace on Bougainville* the next day. The document contained arrangements for a ceasefire, nomination of Arawa as the peace conference site, a schedule for the peace process and the tasks that would be required of the SPPKF (including the creation of a secure environment in three neutral zones and collection of arms at those zones prior to transporting delegates to Arawa). There would be a ceasefire from midnight on 12 September and the peace conference was planned to begin on 10 October. They scheduled discussions for raising the SPPKF on 9 September in Nadi, Fiji.

Chan's insistence that the peace conference would begin on 10 October caught his own and the Australian Government by surprise. When he first proposed this timetable late in August, his advisers and departmental officials, as well as the Australian High Commission in Port Moresby, had advised him that it was unworkable.[10] However, Chan maintained his position: the conference would begin no later than 10 October. The Australian Defence Force (ADF) now had less than six weeks to prepare and deploy a SPPKF comprised of contingents from Fiji, Tonga and Vanuatu to Bougainville.

Beaumont nominated the Land Commander, Major General Peter Arnison, as his lead joint commander for Operation *Lagoon*. His staff sent a copy of the *Lagoon* contingency plan to Arnison's staff three days later on 5 September. By then, Arnison had sent his senior planning officer, Lieutenant Colonel Justin O'Connor, to the Gulf of Carpentaria to brief Brigadier Peter Abigail, Commander, 3rd Brigade, about Operation *Lagoon*, in anticipation of him becoming the combined force tactical commander. After the briefing on 5 September, O'Connor told Abigail and two of his senior staff that he would be convening a planning conference on 9 September to consider a planning directive that was being developed by staff at HQ ADF. Abigail insisted that his Brigade Major, Major David Morrison, attend. O'Connor later tried to dissuade Morrison from attending because it was not time for the tactical level of command to be involved.[11] Morrison insisted and went. He recalled:

> I think it was very opportune that I was there. This was the first time all of the 'doers' met for Operation *Lagoon*. The navy, the air force and the movers [probably 11 Movement Control Group] were in the loop. There were about 12 officers there who represented organisations that would have to make things happen. The meeting opened with a briefing from the Land Commander, General Arnison, followed by some intelligence people and then [Lieutenant Colonel] Bob Shoebridge told us about what had been happening in Canberra. I had no idea that HQ ADF had known about this operation for months and that very little real planning had gone on, especially in the logistics and administrative areas.[12]

Beaumont's draft planning directive went well beyond providing strategic guidance. It specified tasks for Arnison and then went on to include operational and tactical details. After a day of deliberation, the members of O'Connor's planning group produced notes for a concept for operations and a draft directive to Abigail. In this draft, Arnison directed Abigail to present a concept for operations on 15 September to the staff at Land Headquarters so it could be refined before transmission to HQ ADF for approval. Arnison had given Abigail and his staff a significant challenge because they knew very little about the situation in Bougainville, Rules of Engagement (ROE) for a combined force, or the potential threat to the SPPKF. Morrison recalled later:

> I left Sydney with a very loose draft directive [from Arnison] for the Commander [Abigail], my notes from the meeting and some other loose paperwork that I had managed to gather. At this stage everything about this operation was loose.[13]

Morrison flew back to Townsville to find that Abigail had returned from the field to meet him and find out what Operation *Lagoon* was all about. Even with the sketchy information they had, Abigail knew he had to begin developing concepts and anticipating what would be required to support the SPPKF.[14] Offsetting the tight deadlines and gaps in information, Abigail, Morrison and Major Ian Hughes, Abigail's senior logistic staff officer, were used to producing plans and getting 3rd Brigade into action at short notice. The brigade was on an operational footing from Exercise *Swift Eagle* and had benefited from preparing and dispatching the Medical Support Force to Rwanda several weeks before.[15]

Abigail and his staff were well into tactical level planning by the time Colonel Gordon Hurford, Director Joint Operations and Plans, HQ ADF, and Colonel Phil McNamara, Colonel (Operations), Land Headquarters, were finalising a planning directive for Beaumont to sign.[16] Hurford and McNamara were having difficulty keeping subordinate headquarters informed of latest developments. The outcomes of a meeting in Nadi, Fiji, on 9 September 1994, that specified arrangements for assembling and training the SPPKF, were communicated quickly to HQ ADF for incorporation into Beaumont's planning directive. However, planning had already begun at Sydney and Townsville, based on earlier advice. As quickly as tactical level staff planned some aspect of the operation, changes arrived from HQ ADF.

After several days of intensive work, Abigail and Morrison flew to Sydney on 15 September 1994 to brief Arnison's staff. Abigail argued for a substantial increase to the size of the combined force. He assessed that the SPPKF should comprise 390 South Pacific troops supported by 250 ADF personnel, not including the crews of support ships HMAS *Tobruk* and HMAS *Success*. After Abigail's briefing, planners began refining his concept to incorporate information from the most recent draft of Beaumont's planning directive and other sources.[17]

Morrison noticed that, like the planning meeting on 9 September, there were no logisticians or engineers attending to comment on whether operational concepts were logistically sound.[18]

Coincidentally, planning at Land Headquarters was going ahead as another round of diplomatic negotiations began in Suva, Fiji. This situation replicated the coincidence of the first planning meeting on 9 September being held on the same day as the meeting of participating nations in Nadi. Once again, decisions that were made at the strategic level in Suva did not inform Land Headquarters planning until later. As a consequence, changes had to be made to the plans. Defence legal officers and officials developed important documents, such as the Status of Forces Agreement (SOFA) and ROE, without information on the operational plan and vice versa.[19]

Planners at Land Headquarters decided to pre-position a reconnaissance group in Townsville and put its members on a short notice to move. Staff at HQ ADF would not authorise anyone to deploy offshore until the Australian Cabinet had approved Operation *Lagoon*. Colonel Sevenaca Draunidalo, the nominated Fijian tactical ground force commander, was the reconnaissance leader. Colonel Feto Tupou, a Tongan officer nominated to command a liaison headquarters, and a Ni Vanuatu representative, Colonel Sevle Takal, would accompany him. Representatives from 3rd Brigade, HMAS *Tobruk*, Land Headquarters and Air Headquarters, as well as a representative from the Australian High Commission in Port Moresby, Lieutenant Colonel Gary Young, and an interpreter, who would join the reconnaissance group in Port Moresby, were to comprise the remainder of the group.[20] In anticipation of the Australian Cabinet approving Operation *Lagoon* on 19 September, Arnison put Draunidalo and his team on 12 hours notice to move from 6.00 p.m. on 18 September. At this stage, no decision had been made in Canberra on whether Abigail should go on the reconnaissance.

Planners at Land Headquarters also decided on 18 September to send liaison officers to Fiji, Tonga and Vanuatu to keep abreast of events as contingents were formed and their support requirements became known. Abigail telephoned Lieutenant Colonel Ray Martin, Commanding Officer (CO) of 1st Battalion, the Royal Australian regiment (1 RAR), that afternoon, directing him to have three officers ready to move the next day. Most of Martin's officers were on local leave or about to depart Townsville on leave after Exercise *Swift Eagle*. He went down to the 1 RAR Officers' Mess and nominated three of the officers he found there having a late afternoon beer. The next afternoon, Abigail briefed Major John Cronin and Captains Greg Ducie and Steve Grace. Cronin flew to Fiji, Ducie to Tonga and Grace to Vanuatu; none of them spoke the local language or had been to the South Pacific before.[21] Arguably, the Defence Intelligence Organisation (DIO), the Department of Foreign Affairs and Trade (DFAT) or HQ Special Forces should have provided officers or officials with the relevant language and cultural skills. Higher levels of command left 3rd Brigade to 'make do'.

Meanwhile, the navy was preparing for participation in Operation *Lagoon*.[22] Beaumont had ordered the Maritime Commander to provide sea transport, command and control afloat, and aviation and medical support. On 16 September, the Maritime Commander, Rear Admiral Don Chalmers, issued a warning order to HMAS *Success* and HMAS *Tobruk*, appointed the CO of HMAS *Success*, Captain Jim O'Hara, Royal Australian Navy (RAN), to command the group and designated HMAS *Tobruk* to be Abigail's headquarters afloat. Two lieutenant commanders assisted O'Hara to exercise command as well as to fulfil his duties as Abigail's maritime advisor. Arnison had operational control of navy vessels. This was the first time that navy vessels had been placed under control of a joint commander.[23]

Land Headquarters staff sent the concept of operations for *Lagoon* to HQ ADF on 16 September 1994. Despite almost doubling the numbers of troops from early estimates, acting CDF, Lieutenant General John Baker, and Major General Connolly supported Abigail's concept of operations. Subsequently, Senator Robert Ray approved the concept on 18 September and Cabinet approved a joint Defence–DFAT submission the next day, allocating A$5.2 million to Defence in supplementary funds. Though the political outcomes were problematic, the peace conference at Arawa represented the best chance of beginning a negotiated settlement of the Bougainville Crisis since the failure of the Endeavour Accords (brokered by New Zealand in 1990).

In the days before and after Cabinet approval, the ADF operations network worked well. Connolly's staff in Canberra and Arnison's staff in Sydney trusted each other to exchange drafts of documents, to question any aspect of planning and to offer advice. The smooth working relationships between HQ ADF and Land Headquarters were also reflected in the relationships further down the chain of command between McNamara's staff and Abigail's staff. Morrison recalled that he was in constant contact with O'Connor and his staff, and occasionally received useful and informative telephone calls from Lieutenant Colonel Robert Shoebridge at HQ ADF. The operations staffs at the strategic, operational and tactical levels of command were working harmoniously through a line of experienced army officers who knew each other well.

Intelligence, Communications and Logistic Support

While operational planning was running smoothly within tight deadlines, the equivalent processes for intelligence, communications and logistics were not synchronising well. Tactical level effects would be important. The Australian intelligence community in general, and intelligence assets and capabilities deployed to Bougainville in particular, had to anticipate any threats to members of the ADF personnel, SPPKF, or delegates to the conference. Urgent messages had to be transmitted quickly for timely decision-making, especially in response to any threat. For example, DIO had to identify any armed groups on Bougainville intending to disrupt the peace process by harming peacekeepers or delegates. Intelligence had to be communicated efficiently up and down the chain of command so that commanders could monitor a threat, take evasive action or neutralise it. For their part, ADF logisticians had to deploy sufficient stocks and set up a supply chain to provide basic commodities (such as rations, water and ammunition) and other consumables (such as spare parts), as well as logistic services (such as catering, maritime and air transport, medical support and mail).

Secrecy at HQ ADF stymied operational level intelligence planning from June to September 1994. DIO and other agencies did not warn intelligence staff at Land Headquarters that the ADF might be going to support a regional peace support operation in Bougainville. Lieutenant Colonel Roger Hill, the senior intelligence analyst at Land Headquarters, took the initiative. He and his staff briefed Arnison and key operations, communications and logistic staff on the situation in Bougainville every week after Sir Julius Chan became PNG's Prime Minister. Hill felt that it was his duty to keep his commander informed about unstable areas of the near region. He was also aware that Senator Gareth Evans was talking about the ADF supporting a SPPKF in Bougainville.[24] Despite these briefings, Arnison did not authorise contingency planning.

After Beaumont issued his warning order for Operation *Lagoon* on 2 September 1994, Hill and his staff developed an intelligence collection plan targeting all armed antagonists in Bougainville and submitted it to intelligence agencies in Canberra and elsewhere. Intelligence support for Operation *Lagoon* could not follow the doctrine of conventional warfare. There was no specified enemy, but there were several ill-defined threats. This meant that ADF intelligence personnel and assets should gather information on the PNG defence and police forces, and their intelligence services, as well as Bougainvillean secessionist groups and their political and military allies and opponents. Hill based his assessment on the premise that, despite none of these groups declaring publicly that it was their intention to disrupt the peace process by attacking peacekeepers or delegates, there were rogue elements from each group capable of taking violent or destructive action without authorisation from their superiors.[25] During this time, Hill received no intelligence guidance from higher headquarters or agencies in Canberra. Neither Arnison nor members of his operations, communications or logistic staff requested specific intelligence. This ambivalence, accompanied by an inference that intelligence was an irrelevant contributor to a peacekeeping operation, did not augur well for force protection for Operation *Lagoon*.

Representatives from intelligence agencies at the strategic, operational and tactical levels did not meet during the initial planning phase for Operation *Lagoon* in early September. Consequently, there were no intelligence arrangements or procedures worked out for the operation.[26] This meant that there was no shared assessment of what intelligence elements should be deployed to support either Arnison as the lead joint commander or Abigail as the combined force commander. If a threat arose quickly and unexpectedly, there was no shared understanding of how information would be passed in a timely way to these two key decision-makers. In effect, the ADF intelligence community decided that, aside from convening a Bougainville Crisis Action Team on 6 September within the ADF Intelligence Centre (ADFIC) in Canberra to advise Connolly, it would be 'business as usual'.

'Business as usual' meant that intelligence agencies would continue to operate independently, in compartments and in great secrecy. Hill and his staff were unable to influence the provision of intelligence to their commander or direct agencies to do so. For example, he knew from ADF peace support operations in Somalia and Rwanda that human intelligence constituted the most effective way to anticipate threats to ADF personnel. DIO staff ignored his requests for them to recruit a human intelligence network in Bougainville while there was time to do so. Lieutenant General John Baker commented later that it would have taken several years, not a few weeks, to set up a human intelligence network in Bougainville, adding that Defence had no authority to do so: PNG was a sovereign nation and one of Australia's important neighbours.[27] There also appeared to be no coordination between Defence intelligence agencies and other government departments with intelligence-gathering capabilities. This lack of coordination and mutual trust was not unusual at the time.[28]

Undaunted, Hill reminded his superiors and agencies in Canberra that interpreters as well as liaison officers would be required to go ashore in support of South Pacific commanders and ADF support personnel. He recommended that they be directed to gather intelligence to protect Bougainvillean delegates. Frustrated with the lack of response, he and his staff established their own small Bougainvillean human intelligence network through informal contacts.[29]

For Operation *Lagoon* HQ ADF staff directed Hill to deal only with ADFIC, which was under Connolly's command. This one-off arrangement ensured that staff who reported to Connolly would decide what information Arnison's intelligence staff would receive. As a consequence, Hill was unable to access certain types of data and information directly, losing the capability to interpret and advise Arnison independently. Hill also lost authorisation to task intelligence agencies. Arnison would have to depend on Connolly and his staff. Unfortunately, these *ad hoc* arrangements did not result in either agreed procedures for reacting to a crisis or an independent secure communications link from ADFIC directly to Abigail and his staff.

In summary, DIO and other intelligence agency support for Operation *Lagoon* was plugged in at the strategic level for Connolly and his staff through ADFIC.

However, Arnison and Abigail, the operational level and tactical level customers, were not connected. Their intelligence staffs were making their own arrangements. All intelligence would be passed using the same frequencies as operational and logistic information. Thus, intelligence gathered at the tactical level in Bougainville would compete with other communications traffic to be received further up the chain by Arnison's staff, and then by ADFIC. Similarly, intelligence gathered at the strategic level and coordinated through ADFIC would compete with other traffic being filtered down to Abigail and his staff in Bougainville.

Logistic Preparations

While the ADF intelligence community made tenuous arrangements for Operation *Lagoon*, ADF logisticians entered the planning cycle. Secrecy at HQ ADF had not only left logisticians in subordinate headquarters and at Logistic Command in Melbourne in the dark until early September, but also logisticians within HQ ADF itself. This resulted in some internal friction. Colonel Hurford, Director, Joint Operations and Plans at HQ ADF, gave Captain Russ Sharp, RAN, Director Joint Logistic Operations and Plans at HQ ADF, a copy of the contingency plan for Operation *Lagoon* in the first week of September 1994. Sharp commented later:

> It took us precisely 60 minutes to work out that it [the plan] was unachievable. We made representations that it had to change but initially they fell on stony ground. It was not until the operators at the operational level [at Land Headquarters] made the self-same observations to the strategic level [HQ ADF] that our views became legitimate and the force structure changed.[30]

By 9 September, when the South Pacific Forum delegations who had expressed an interest in participating in Operation *Lagoon*, met in Nadi, logistic support planning at HQ ADF had been underway for several days.[31] There were many more questions than answers. There was no strategic concept for operations to guide logisticians. Beaumont's planning directive was still in draft form and its approval was a week away. Issues like the structure of the force, duration of the operation, modes of transport to be used and the locations of forward mounting and operating bases were critical prerequisites for any meaningful logistic preparation.

It was not until 13 September 1994 that Connolly submitted the final draft of Beaumont's planning directive to the acting CDF, Lieutenant General John Baker, for signature. By this time, Abigail and his staff in Townsville had already begun to develop a concept for delivery to Land Headquarters on 15 September. In effect, Abigail was working without logistic guidance from above and Sharp was working without operational and tactical guidance from below.

Guided by a draft of Beaumont's planning directive, but still without Abigail's input, Sharp convened an administrative planning group in Canberra on 13 September 1994 to set some parameters and identify all of the questions that would need to be answered in order to sustain Operation *Lagoon*.[32] Sharp decided that, given the short duration of the operation, the combined force was to be self-sufficient. Lieutenant Colonel Tony Ayerbe, the acting Colonel (Operations) at HQ Logistic Command, who had attended Sharp's planning meeting on 13 September, signalled to Land Headquarters that there were significant problems concentrating stores in Townsville in time to meet the operational timetable. He suggested that HMAS *Tobruk* load in Sydney, closer to the issuing depots and the freight terminal at the newly-designated Defence National Supply Distribution Centre (DNSDC) at Moorebank.[33]

Ayerbe's suggestions did not please Hughes at HQ 3rd Brigade.[34] Ultimately, he would be responsible to Abigail for the administration and supply arrangements for Operation *Lagoon*. He wanted stores to be concentrated in Townsville, checked by the people who would use them, accounted for by his staff and then loaded on HMAS *Tobruk* under his supervision. Since returning from Exercise *Swift Eagle*, Hughes and his staff had been confirming the brigade's stock levels to identify what items needed to be ordered in. One of the early challenges was concentrating stores for setting up and supporting the peace conference. Arnison supported Hughes's views over those of Ayerbe on where stocks should be concentrated and loaded. An expensive concentration of stocks in Townsville began—a rerun of the deployment of a battalion group to Somalia in January 1993.[35]

Hughes directed his staff to raise requests for hundreds of beds, and other accommodation stores, as well as office furniture, tentage, office equipment and stationery. He recalled:

> The concern I had was whether we could get sufficient stores in on time. We were told early in the piece that we would be responsible for setting up and supporting the entire conference. We did not have time to debate the issue or seek clarification of exact requirements. I had staff working long hours ordering all of these items. They did a great job and all the stuff came into 2 Field Log Battalion [located in Townsville].[36]

On 16 September 1994 Sharp sent a copy of his strategic concept for logistics to Land Headquarters. However, guidance from the strategic level to the operational level did not have much impact on planning and preparations in Townsville. Hughes had closely monitored the development of Abigail's concept. By the time his proposals had been approved at Land Headquarters on 15 September and at HQ ADF on 17 September, Hughes had submitted all demands for stocks for Operation *Lagoon*, including his best guess at the requirements for the South Pacific contingents. Time would have run out for delivery if he had waited for guidance from above.[37] It was too late to get information from Cronin, Ducie and Grace on the logistic status of South Pacific contingents. They would leave Townsville on 19 September.

In addition to meeting the logistic requirements of the operation in Bougainville, Hughes also had to organise support for the administration and training of the South Pacific contingents in Townsville. It had been difficult supporting the administration and training of troops for service in Rwanda while units were in Townsville preparing for Exercise *Swift Eagle* six weeks before in the Gulf of Carpentaria. Fortunately, South Pacific contingents and Australian personnel not based in Townsville would arrive while 3rd Brigade units were away on leave after Exercise *Swift Eagle*. Abigail and Hughes decided to use vacant facilities and the close training areas of 1 RAR and some of their administrative personnel to prepare the SPPKF. Fortunately, Major Colin Chidgey and his staff from a force preparation and support unit had arrived in Townsville already, to prepare a training program for the SPPKF in conjunction with a 10-man New Zealand Army training cadre. He and his staff had a very good feel for what was happening in Townsville because they had prepared the Medical Support Force for Rwanda and had worked with the brigade before hand.[38]

In summary, by the third week of September all intelligence and logistic support planning had happened without detailed guidance, information or coordination. There had been no reconnaissance to inform anyone's deliberations. At the tactical level, the intelligence staff at 3rd Brigade, guided by Hill's staff at Land Headquarters, had made *ad hoc* arrangements to collect intelligence and had produced substantial quantities of information on Bougainville for their commanders and staffs. At the operational level, Hill's intelligence staff at Land Headquarters waited in vain for strategic guidance, orders and advice on intelligence gathering and reporting procedures from ADFIC.[39] Hughes's logistic staff at 3rd Brigade had taken the initiative to ensure that stores were ordered in time.

Reconnaissance and Planning

Operation *Lagoon* was now about to enter a reconnaissance phase that would precipitate another round of rushed planning, hasty gathering of resources, robust negotiations and last-minute organising. There was some debate among Australian officials in Canberra about whether Abigail should go on a reconnaissance scheduled for 21 September 1994.[40] There was a desire among Australian diplomats to keep public exposure of Australian involvement in Operation *Lagoon* to a minimum. The aim appeared to be to minimise Australia's profile in the peace process in general, and the command role of the ADF in Operation *Lagoon* in particular. However, DFAT officials did recognise that Abigail needed to have a first-hand understanding of the political situation in

Port Moresby and Bougainville, as well as the operational environment around Arawa (where the conference would be conducted) and the neutral zones.[41] In the end, Abigail accompanied Tupou, Draunidalo and Takal on the condition that he adopted a low profile and did not answer questions or discuss any political issues during meetings.[42]

The information gathered during the reconnaissance on 20–22 September proved to be crucial. Abigail, Draunidalo and Tupou worked out that they needed more troops and more UH-60 *Black Hawk* helicopters, and that the SPPKF should undergo a minimum of a 10-day training period to prepare for operations in Bougainville. In two days, Abigail came up with requirements that ADF planners had been unable to anticipate over the previous four months or during the three weeks after Chan and Kauona had signed the Honiara Agreement on 2 September 1994. The reconnaissance also allowed Abigail and his contingent commanders to make a collegial assessment of the challenges facing them and to establish mutual respect. Indeed, without Abigail's diplomacy and his ability to win the respect of Draunidalo and Tupou soon after meeting them, Fiji and Tonga may not have participated in Operation *Lagoon*.[43] Abigail and his Fijian, Tongan and Ni Vanuatu commanders had also met and established contact with PNG civil and military authorities as well as Bougainvillean antagonists.

On 20 September, the day that Abigail departed with the SPPKF reconnaissance team, HQ ADF issued an instruction and Land Headquarters issued an order. This was the day after Cabinet approval for Operation *Lagoon*.[44] Reconnaissance had not informed any of these documents. However, they constituted Abigail's higher level guidance. He convened his first planning meeting for the combined force on 24 September, after returning from his visit to PNG. The problem faced by Abigail and his staff was how to integrate guidance that was contained in several disparate documents. The Ceasefire Agreement provided neither legal coverage nor guidance on important issues. The PNG Government and the Bougainvillean secessionists had signed it, but neither the Australian Government nor the governments of the South Pacific contingents had endorsed it. The governments of Australian and PNG had signed the SOFA that gave legal cover, but was silent on many of the important issues related to creating a secure environment. The ROE contained protocols for search and detention of persons and use of force, but these rules had not been agreed to in the SOFA or the Ceasefire Agreement. Consequently, it was left to Abigail to decide what powers of search, arrest, detention and application of force the SPPKF would have in the neutral zones—a potentially career-shortening position to be in if anything went wrong.[45] Abigail's mission was 'to provide a secure environment for the conduct of a Bougainville Peace Conference, and to provide security and movement for selected delegates'.[46]

There was no explanation of what constituted a delegate or the criteria that would be used to identify delegates requiring security that would most likely include transport, emergency medical support, accommodation and meals. Estimates of the numbers of delegates who might attend the peace conference varied from 500 to 1500. The rush to achieve a starting date of 10 October obviated orderly conference registration. Flexibility became a key concept because it was very difficult to predict the way the peace conference would unfold. Threats to security could emerge in many different ways. Abigail and his staff decided that the SPPKF should not operate at less than platoon strength so as to maintain national identity and also to deter ambush. The planning staff anticipated as many contingencies as they thought might occur and how the combined force would respond.[47] There was also concern that the combined force might have to provide last-minute logistic support to set up conference facilities if PNG Government preparations for the conference did not go according to plan. The major outcome from Abigail's planning was a tactical concept for operations founded on guidance from higher headquarters, information gathered during his reconnaissance and his detailed mission analysis that identified many enabling tasks. The concept focused on creating a secure environment by maintaining strict neutrality, a deterrent presence and reducing any tension between participants during the conference.

Meanwhile, Captain Jim O'Hara handed command of HMAS *Success* over to his Executive Officer, and moved to Townsville at Abigail's invitation on 23 September 1994. O'Hara reported simultaneously to two senior officers—Chalmers, who maintained technical and administrative control, and Abigail, who had operational control. Abigail decided to exercise operational control of navy vessels through O'Hara, not directly to the officers commanding ships. There was some controversy about these command and control arrangements at the time.[48] O'Hara reported later that, 'this indirect method of command, utilising the component method, worked well'.[49]

Specific Force Preparation

On 25 September 1994, the first warning signs that preparations were not going according to plan emerged. The Fijians were going to be late.[50] Abigail would not be able to promise that the SPPKF would be ready for movement from Townsville to Arawa until at least 7 October. This would leave insufficient time to deploy and secure neutral zones if the conference began on 10 October. Chan had to be persuaded to postpone the start of the peace conference until at least 15 October. This would allow for 10 days' pre-deployment training and sufficient time to secure neutral zones and set up the conference site.

Beaumont briefed Ray on 26 September.[51] He pointed out that there were critical safety and legal issues at stake that could cause major problems later if the SPPKF was deployed without sufficient training. The ADF had a duty of care to ensure that all troops could handle their weapons safely, had complied with the medical countermeasures against malaria and other tropical diseases, and were thoroughly briefed and rehearsed in the use of ROE and Orders for Opening Fire. There was also a legal requirement to brief troops on the principles of peacekeeping, the Geneva Conventions and the Laws of Armed Conflict. The South Pacific contingents needed thorough training in helicopter operations, including night deployment. Not to do so would risk the lives of South Pacific soldiers as well as Australian aircrew. There was also a requirement to conduct command-post exercises and other training, to ensure that all components of the combined force could work together cohesively and thoroughly understood the mission. Not to do so might risk the lives of those in the field and the lives of Bougainvilleans, as well as those needing urgent medical evacuation. Finally, Beaumont wrote that, unless there was training in how to use the night vision equipment, radios and other technical equipment, expensive breakage or malfunctions could occur. While issues of safety, legal obligations and expensive breakages were significant, less tangible justifications for the 10-day training period, such as the cohesion and morale of the force, were also crucial and made sense. Beaumont emphasised to Ray that a minimum of seven days was required to prepare the site at Arawa, and to deploy and secure neutral zones. Time was needed to coordinate the withdrawal of PNGDF forces and to assure local Bougainvilleans of the SPPKF's neutrality and goodwill. Things could go wrong if the PNGDF withdrawal was rushed and SPPKF forces were not settled in before the peace conference began.

Unfortunately, pre-deployment training got off on the wrong foot after the Fijian contingent arrived on 28 September. The ADF had not paid enough attention to culture, ceremony and status. Several officers among the South Pacific contingents were members of prominent families or nobility in their home countries. There were no formal welcoming ceremonies for them as individuals or for their contingents as participants in a historic regional combined operation. The 'business-like, deadline-conscious' ADF staff appeared to ignore the importance of welcoming ceremonies, church services and after hours socialising among the South Pacific contingents.[52] The Pacific Islanders found the assumption by Chidgey's staff that they would conform to Australian doctrine and adhere to a 'minute-by-minute' training timetable set up by Australians and New Zealanders without prior consultation quite patronising.[53]

Deployment

Meanwhile, the maritime component of the combined force was coming on line. HMAS *Tobruk* berthed in Townsville on 28 September 1994. However, despite the efforts of the CO, Commander John Wells, and staff at Maritime Headquarters to seek guidance and advice, there was no information available from the army as to the logistic requirements. Logistic staff at both Land Headquarters and HQ Logistic Command did not appear to have briefed their naval counterparts at Maritime Headquarters on logistic requirements before HMAS *Tobruk* sailed from Sydney. In effect, the first orders Wells would receive, about the role his ship would play and its load, came from O'Hara in Townsville after Wells arrived. Loading now became a 'hand to mouth' activity reminiscent of the deployment of a battalion group to Somalia in 1993, some 10 months before.[54] Over the next few days, stores accumulated on the Townsville wharf as the ship's army staff developed a loading plan 'on the run' in conjunction with Hughes and his 3rd Brigade staff. In an early indication of the communications problems awaiting the operation, naval communications staff discovered that the portable Inmarsat telephone installed by Land Headquarters communications staff was not suited to being on a ship. The Inmarsat was normally ground-based and depended on a small dish (pointing up at the satellite in stationary orbit) being used to transmit the signal. The rolling of a ship and its movement through the water meant that the Inmarsat dish was not stable and able to keep its direction.[55]

By the end of September there was still no news of whether Chan would postpone the start date of the conference. By this time, the South Pacific contingents had begun pre-deployment training and administration in Townsville.[56] Staff at HQ ADF issued final ROE for Operation *Lagoon* the night before training began.[57] Training in these ROE was going to be rushed even if the full 10-day period was allowed. Specific force preparation in Townsville was still predicated on the start date for the conference being postponed until 15 October. If Chan did not agree, there would be some difficulty completing sufficient training in time. There were also indications that the PNG Government had not allowed sufficient time to put basic infrastructure, such as accommodation, food preparation areas, sanitation services, electrical power and a clean water supply in place for the conference. Because there was no clear division of responsibility, the ADF might be left with the blame for providing insufficient logistic support and amenities to facilitate the conduct of the conference.

ENDNOTES

[1] See Anthony J. Regan, *The Bougainville Conflict: Origins and Development, Main Actors, and Strategies for Resolution*, Mimeo, Port Moresby, 1996.

[2] Classified source, 94 26303, Defence Archives, Queanbeyan.

[3] Australian Parliament, *Bougainville: A Pacific Solution, Report of the Visit of the Australian Parliamentary Delegation to Bougainville 18–22 April 1994*, Australian Government Publishing Service, Canberra, 1994.

[4] Australian Parliament, Government Response by Senator the Hon Gareth Evans QC, Minister for Foreign Affairs, to the *Report of the Parliamentary Delegation to Bougainville*, 8 June 1994, p. 4 (copy held by author). Evans went on to send further supportive signals through the media on 22 June when he told an interviewer on Radio Australia that there was a proposal for a peacekeeping operation in Bougainville on the table and that Australia was prepared to give transport and logistic support. A copy of the transcript of the Radio Australia interview with Senator Gareth Evans on 22 June 1994 is located in 94 26303, Defence Archives, Queanbeyan.

[5] HQ ADF, 'Outline Plan for OP Lagoon', CDF 160/1994, 8 June 1994, 94 26303, Defence Archives, Queanbeyan.

[6] Admiral Alan L. Beaumont, Cover note on 'Outline Plan for OP Lagoon', CDF 160/1994, 8 June 1994, 94 26303, Defence Archives, Queanbeyan.

[7] Papua New Guinea Government, Gabriel Dusava, Secretary PNG Department of Foreign Affairs and Trade Circular: *Outcome of Bougainville Peace Conference*, 16 October 1994, 94 26303, Defence Archives, Queanbeyan.

[8] General John S. Baker in interview with author, 30 August 2005.

[9] Admiral Alan L. Beaumont, 'Op Lagoon Planning', CDF 258/1994, 2 September 1994, 94 26303, Defence Archives, Queanbeyan.

[10] Classified source, 94 26303, Defence Archives, Queanbeyan.

[11] Major David L. Morrison in interview with author, 24 October 1997.

[12] Morrison, Interview. Lieutenant Colonel Robert W. Shoebridge, SO1 Land Operations, HQ ADF.

[13] Morrison, Interview. Lieutenant Colonel Robert W. Shoebridge, SO1 Land Operations, HQ ADF.

[14] Brigadier Peter J. Abigail in interview with author, 18 March 1997.

[15] Lieutenant Colonel Ian K. Hughes in interview with author, 23 October 1997.

[16] Colonel Phil J. McNamara in interview with author, 31 October 1997.

[17] The other information incorporated into the concept came from documents produced by the Assistant Defence Attaché, Lieutenant Colonel Gary Young, and his planning team in Port Moresby, reports from Colonel David J. Hurley, who had been sent to assist the PNG Government with its planning and intelligence reports on the Bougainville Crisis. (Morrison in interview with author, 24 October 1997.).

[18] Morrison in interview with author, 24 October 1997.

[19] Lieutenant Colonel Garth J. Cartledge, 'Op Lagoon—Legal Post Operation Report', 16 November 1994, p. 2, 94/26461, Defence Archives, Queanbeyan.

[20] Land Headquarters, 'Members of the Recon Gp': LHQ OPS SIG E3L/I4S, 160557ZSEP94, K94 01325, NAA, Sydney.

[21] Major John O. Cronin in telephone discussion with author, 31 December 1997.

[22] Captain Jim S. O'Hara, RAN, 'Op Lagoon POR Maritime Aspects', 24 October 1994, 98 18173, Defence Archives, Queanbeyan.

[23] Commodore (formerly Captain) Jim S. O'Hara, RAN, in interview with author, 13 November 1996.

[24] Lieutenant Colonel Roger A. Hill in interview with author, 31 October 1997.

[25] Hill in interview with author, 31 October 1997.

[26] Hill in interview with author, 31 October 1997.

[27] Baker in interview with author, 30 August 2005.

[28] Baker in interview with author, 30 August 2005.

[29] Hill in interview with author, 31 October 1997.

[30] Captain Russ W. Sharp in interview with author, 19 March 1997.

[31] Planning documents are filed on 94-27354, 'Operation *Lagoon*—ADF Support to Bougainville Peace talks—Joint Log Ops and Plans Aspects', Defence Archives, Queanbeyan.

[32] HQ ADF, 'Notes from JAPG held on 13 September 1994', 15 September 1994, 94 27354, Defence Archives, Queanbeyan.

[33] Hughes in interview with author, 23 October 1997.

[34] Hughes in interview with author, 23 October 1997.

[35] See Bob Breen, *A Little Bit of Hope, Australian Force—Somalia*, Allen and Unwin, Sydney, 1998, Chapter 2: Ramping Up and Getting There.

[36] Hughes in interview with author, 23 October 1997.

[37] Hughes in interview with author, 23 October 1997.

[38] Hughes in interview with author, 23 October 1997

[39] Hill in interview with author, 31 October 1997.

[40] Abigail in interview with author, 18 March 1997.

[41] Classified source, 94 26303, Defence Archives, Queanbeyan.

42 Abigail in interview with author, 18 March 1997.

43 Abigail in interview with author, 18 March 1997.

44 HQ ADF, OPS OPSINST 34/94, 20 September 1994, 94 26303, Defence Archives, Queanbeyan. LHQ, OPORD 53/94, DTG 200546ZSEP94, K01357, NAA, Sydney.

45 Abigail in interview with author, 18 March 1997.

46 Major General Peter M. Arnison, 'Directive to 47054 Brigadier P.J. Abigail, Combined Force Commander—Op Lagoon', LCAUST Directive 27/1994, 22 September 1994, 94 26303, Defence Archives, Queanbeyan.

47 Eventually they were to be tabulated for use at Combined Headquarters and in the field to guide commanders on the responses expected of them. Copy held by the author.

48 Abigail in interview with author, 18 March 1997; and O'Hara, RAN in interview with author, 13 November 1996.

49 O'Hara, 'POR—Maritime Aspects', p. 3.

50 Major General J.M. Connolly, 'Brief to Minister by ACOPS Situation at 1600 hrs 25 September 1994', 94 26303, Defence Archives, Queanbeyan.

51 Beaumont. 'Brief to Defence Minister Robert Ray—Preparation of the SPPKF', 26 September 1994, 94-26303, Defence Archives, Queanbeyan.

52 Major L. K. Qusiadranituragu, 'A Report on the Bougainville Assignment', 25 October 1994. Copy held by author.

53 Qusiadranituragu, 'A Report on the Bougainville Assignment', 25 October 1994. Copy held by author.

54 Breen, *A Little Bit of Hope, Australian Force—Somalia*, chapter 2.

55 Lieutenant Colonel Gary J. Allan, Post Operation Report (POR) LHQ CIS—OP Lagoon, CIS OPS 2/66/95, 30 January 1995, Annex N, p. 3, K94-01440, NAA, Sydney.

56 Numbers in contingents: Fiji (232); Tonga (107 including crew of patrol boat); and Vanuatu (47). There were therefore a total of 386 South Pacific personnel.

57 An extract from the ROE reads: 'The policy of the Combined Force is Reduce Tension ... avoid the use of force and provocation. Force may not be applied except in self-defence. ... Unit self-defence is an inherent right of Combined Force [element] to spontaneously defend themselves or designated entities against actual armed attack (hostile acts) or immediate threats of armed at[tac]k (hostile intent). No mines/graduated response. End contacts ASAP'. Included in Land Headquarters, 'Post Operation Support for Operation *Lagoon*—Combined Force Peace Support Operations on Bougainville, PNG', October 1994', LCAUST 137/94, 28 November 1994, K94-01325. Copy held by author.

Chapter 7

Conduct and Aftermath of Operation *Lagoon*

On Saturday 1 October 1994, after renewed pressure from inside the Government of Papua New Guinea (PNG) and from Australia for him to postpone the start date of the conference, PNG's Prime Minister, Sir Julius Chan, appealed directly to Australian Prime Minister Paul Keating to insist that the Australian Defence Force (ADF) deploy the South Pacific Peace Keeping Force (SPPKF) prior to the start date of 10 October. Chan pointed out that the deployment time could be reduced if troops were moved by air rather than by sea. He called for a substantial advance party to be deployed to Arawa by 8 October to establish a presence. Keating contacted the Australian Defence Minister, Senator Robert Ray, soon after a conversation with Chan and told him to instruct the ADF to have the SPPKF on Bougainville before the peace conference started on 10 October.[1]

Confirmation that the peace conference would start on 10 October had a significant impact. Pre-deployment training stopped.[2] HMAS *Tobruk* had to be loaded with personnel and stores in less than 24 hours. At around this time, HMAS *Tobruk*'s ship's army detachment staff assessed that there was too much stock on the wharf. The ship would be overloaded and possibly 'bulk out'.[3] Captain Jim O'Hara's only option was to load HMAS *Success* with the stores that would not fit aboard *Tobruk*. Unfortunately, both ships bulked out before all stores could be loaded. HMAS *Tobruk* was also 200 tonnes over its authorised weight limit. Commander John Wells advised O'Hara of the final weight only five hours before the vessel was due to sail. He and Wells spent the next hours calculating the risk in allowing her to sail on schedule.[4] Any delay would result in the SPPKF not getting on the ground in Bougainville in time to set up the peace conference venue and protect delegates. O'Hara analysed the weather forecasts for the voyage to Bougainville. Fortunately the weather was on the side of Operation *Lagoon*—calm conditions. O'Hara and Wells accepted the increased risk and HMAS *Tobruk* sailed on schedule.

While HMAS *Tobruk* and HMAS *Success* were at sea, the main body of the combined force flew out on 6 October in Australian and New Zealand C-130 *Hercules* transport aircraft. To satisfy Chan's request, a 100-strong advance party flew directly to Buka Island airfield from Townsville to meet up with four *Black Hawk* helicopters and two *Caribou* transport aircraft that had been pre-positioned there to fly them to Arawa by 8 October. HMAS *Tobruk* arrived in Honiara, the capital of the Solomon Islands, on 7 October 1994. Brigadier Peter Abigail, his staff, the main force of the SPPKF and the ADF logistic support force were aboard by 2.00 a.m and HMAS *Tobruk* sailed from Honiara at 5.00 a.m. on 8 October. The previous 24 hours had been a tiring period for all personnel. The cramped conditions and the general excitement at finally being inbound to Bougainville were not conducive to catching up on lost sleep.[5]

HMAS *Tobruk* anchored in Arawa Bay at 5.30 a.m. on 9 October. This arrival, less than 24 hours before the start of the conference, meant that neutral zones had not been secured, the conference site was not set up and administrative support for the conference was not in place. Planners had assessed that it would take seven days to achieve these objectives. The 100-strong advance party had been working without rest since arriving the day before to secure the conference site and set up facilities, but there was still much to do.[6] Troops on HMAS *Tobruk* now had 12 hours to do what they could during the daylight hours of 9 October.

Just to add to the challenges facing Abigail and his headquarters,

> when [HMAS] *Tobruk* berthed alongside Loloho Jetty, a combination of high hills surrounding the berth, the metal cranes, warehouses and ship ore loading facilities on and adjacent to the jetty resulted in the loss of both HF [High Frequency] and VHF [Very High Frequency] communications. Without SATCOM [satellite communications], HQ Combined Force would have had no strategic or tactical communications, other than UHF [Ultra High Frequency], for approximately 16 hours.[7]

The origins of these problems lay in disjointed planning. Like logistics, communications planning for Operation *Lagoon* had followed a divided approach; vertically between each level of command and horizontally between each Service. At the strategic level, the mechanism for joint planning, the Joint Communications Planning Group sponsored by the Director General of Joint Communications and Electronics, had not met. If it had, subsequent problems would have been reduced.[8] There would have been one point of contact for allocating and clearing frequencies with PNG authorities. As it was, the combined force depended on Inmarsat terminals to provide telephone, facsimile and data services back to Australia that were 'subject to congestion due to the uncontrolled access to the overall system'.[9]

At the operational level, 'there was poor information flow from all parties', according to one navy report.[10] A Land Headquarters report noted some army and navy coordination problems that resulted in late arrangements for the distribution of cryptographic equipment and an unnecessarily large number of communications and cryptographic plans.[11] At the tactical level, Abigail's senior communications officer, Major Bill Teece, was not appointed at the outset as the Chief Communications Officer to develop a joint communications plan and bid for additional equipment. This left each Service to make separate communications arrangements for Operation *Lagoon*.[12] Also at the tactical level, HMAS *Tobruk* had not received a substantial update 'to its communications fit' for two years and its HF receivers and transmitters continually broke down and took some time to repair.[13] Army signallers rigged army RAVEN tactical radios on HMAS *Tobruk*'s flag deck that enabled Abigail and his staff to communicate with Australian radio operators who were with SPPKF platoons, giving Abigail a good understanding of the progress of South Pacific contingents. There were persistent problems communicating between army RAVEN equipment and non-RAVEN equipment being operated by the navy and the air force.[14]

Force Employment

The consequences of putting the tactical level of command under pressure were now beginning to show on the ground and offshore in Bougainville. Communications capabilities were limited from the beginning. There had been no time to test the satellite communications (SATCOM) equipment that had been fitted to HMAS *Tobruk*. Communications managers had not anticipated the impact of the infrastructure around Loloho on communications. The crash in communications was a great source of frustration for General Peter Arnison who was trying to command Operation *Lagoon* from Victoria Barracks in Sydney.[15] It was during this time that three Bougainvillean gunmen opened fire on a PNG Water Board party. The gunmen fled after firing a volley of shots, leaving the workers unharmed. This was a hasty 'hit and run' attack—an unsettling start for the SPPKF's first day in Arawa. The sound of shots, and then a noisy clearance operation by the PNG Defence Force (PNGDF), involving use of hand grenades and automatic fire, frightened several hundred Bougainvilleans in the vicinity, who had gathered for the conference, as well as the inhabitants of a nearby displaced persons camp. However, there appeared to be an immediate loss of confidence in the SPPKF. Word of the incident and PNGDF retaliation soon got around those who had already gathered for the conference, and over 600 Bougainvilleans in the camp who were normally protected by the PNGDF.[16]

The withdrawal of PNGDF troops from the outskirts of Arawa had also caused problems on the roads leading to the conference site at the Arawa High School. Locals began approaching members of the SPPKF with reports that groups of armed young men were intimidating and robbing people coming to the conference. Colonel Feto Tupou convened an emergency meeting of the Ceasefire Committee at the Arawa High School at 5.15 p.m. on 9 October to discuss these reports and the shooting incident. Mr Nick Peniai, a representative from the North Solomons Interim Authority, informed the meeting that the optimism present when delegates began arriving in Arawa had been replaced by fear. The robberies, intimidation, shooting incident and the ill-disciplined PNGDF response had lowered the morale of those gathered for the conference and the inhabitants of the Arawa displaced persons camp.[17]

These incidents put Tupou, Colonel Sevenaca Draunidalo and the SPPKF in an awkward situation. Criminal gangs had become emboldened by the PNGDF withdrawal. The displaced persons and the hundreds of delegates gathering in the Arawa area were at risk, especially at night. Peniai called for a curfew and regular patrols to ensure security. The Rules of Engagement (ROE) for Operation *Lagoon* permitted the questioning (but not detention) of persons behaving suspiciously. The ROE were silent about the confiscation of weapons in the neutral zones. There was also no provision for curfews or interventions to protect the lives and property of Bougainvilleans if they were assaulted or robbed. The expectation of ordinary Bougainvilleans was that the SPPKF was there to protect them during the conference. In reality, the SPPKF was not authorised to enforce full control over neutral zones or anywhere else in Bougainville. Peacekeepers were there to maintain a deterrent presence during the conference. The ROE of 'presence' would be insufficient to deter criminals from going about their business. The SPPKF may have had the right mission, but it did not have robust ROE to achieve it. The difficulty in controlling armed groups on the ground was emphasised on the day the conference opened when one of the Australian *Sea King* helicopters returned from a routine reconnaissance mission with two bullet holes in its tail section. O'Hara reported stirringly that, 'this was the first occasion [that] the RAN [Royal Australian Navy] had incurred battle damage since the Vietnam War'.[18]

Later that day, one of Abigail's attached intelligence officers informed him that the PNGDF had set an ambush, supported by Australian-supplied *Claymore* anti-personnel mines, on the main route into Arawa. Local PNGDF forces appeared to be using the conference as an opportunity for payback. Abigail told the local commander to abandon the ambush site and move his troops out of the area.[19] As dangers increased, ADF communications capabilities decreased. Communications between Arnison and Abigail and their staffs were breaking down or overloaded. Lieutenant Colonel Steve Ayling, a communications staff officer with Headquarters Australian Defence Force (HQ ADF), reported that the Inmarsat satellite, through which most communications were being sent, was overloaded and there was also congestion elsewhere in the Defence network.[20]

End of the Conference

Colonel David Hurley, who was attending the conference as an advisor to the PNG Government, assessed that it was Chan's intention to press on with the conference even if senior Bougainvillean secessionist leaders did not attend. Chan planned to garner sufficient signatures from attending delegates to make progress towards a settlement and to undermine support among Bougainvilleans for hard-line Bougainvillean secessionist leaders.[21] A group of PNGDF soldiers assured non-attendance by firing at a secessionist liaison team, seriously wounding one member.[22] Chan still had several days to bring the PNGDF into line and to make further overtures to the secessionist leadership. He decided to end the peace conference the next day, blaming the non-attendance of senior secessionist leaders for his decision.[23] Subsequently, his representatives signed a document with moderate Bougainvillean delegates.[24]

The SPPKF redeployed by sea and air in 72 hours, continuing a tradition of well-executed Australian military withdrawals begun at Gallipoli in 1915. In the months after the peace conference was abandoned, the campaign by the PNGDF to find a military solution in Bougainville continued. The post-conference agreement signed between the PNG Government and a delegation of moderate Bougainvilleans did not result in the sustained renewal of a peace process. Indeed, the leader of the moderates, Theodore Miriung, was subsequently murdered.

Observations

From the perspective of force projection, there are many observations to make about the seven weeks of intense diplomatic and military activity associated with Operation *Lagoon*. Though its duration was brief, *Lagoon* exercised all of the functions of force projection except force rotation.[25] For the first time Australia had responsibility for a multinational peace support operation. The ADF was in command and there were no major allies present to command, protect or sustain.[26] More complex than Operation *Morris Dance*, Operation *Lagoon* tested Australia's self-reliance and begged the comparative question: 'Had the ADF improved its capacity and capability for regional force projection in the seven intervening years between *Morris Dance* and *Lagoon*?'[27]

Operation *Lagoon* was always going to be a dangerous, politically sensitive operation with risks for Australia's standing in the South Pacific. The tactical level of command had been put under pressure from the day Admiral Alan Beaumont issued his warning order on 2 September 1994—there had been insufficient 'thinking time'. Neither Arnison nor Abigail had sufficient time to gather information, work through contingencies or develop tactical plans, supported by mature logistic, communications and intelligence plans that were also informed by reconnaissance. Repeating the circumstances of the battalion group deployment to Somalia the previous year, logistic planning, gathering supplies and loading of ships had been disordered and rushed.[28] Guiding documents from HQ ADF and Land Headquarters were either largely irrelevant by the time they were signed or had been produced in isolation of each other. There were contradictions and gaps. All higher-level documents had been produced without the benefit of reconnaissance.

Land Headquarters reported to HQ ADF that the operation had been

> conducted without casualties or incidents, without wasting resources, and with all agencies informed of events in a secure and timely manner. ... The joint planning and execution of OP Lagoon was highly successful. ... The joint command arrangements worked well.[29]

Members of COSC proudly assessed that:

> Overall, the planning and conduct of the Operation were most successful. All objectives were satisfied with no modification to the strategic Concept of Operations being required, although the ADF plan was amended to satisfy additional PNG Government and BRA [Bougainville Revolutionary Army] requirements. This Operation validated ADF doctrine as flexible and appropriate for mounting and conducting coalition operations of this type.[30]

From the perspective of proficiency in force projection, Operation *Lagoon*, like Operation *Morris Dance*, left room for improvement. The ADF in general, and the army in particular, had yet again increased risk for the tactical level of command. Beaumont and his staff did not deliver timely warning or particularly effective guidance. Their directions were late and contained some unworkable and logistically unsound tactical details, or left gaps in important areas. The army's logistic support system was again unable to meet tight deadlines and load ships efficiently. HMAS *Tobruk* was at risk during its voyage to Bougainville. Reforms within the Defence intelligence community begun by then Major General John Baker, inaugural Director of the Defence Intelligence Organisation (DIO) in the late 1980s, had still not resulted in unity of purpose, efficient communications and best tactical-level effect where it counted. The behaviour of members of the PNGDF in Bougainville could have resulted in not only the loss of Bougainvillean lives but also the lives of members of the SPPKF.

There appear to be two explanations for not using warning time more efficiently. The first is that Beaumont, like his predecessor, General Peter Gration, did not appear to be confident that contingency planning for a peace operation in Bougainville could be kept secret outside a small compartment of officers within HQ ADF. The second was that senior officers at lower levels of command would not pre-empt strategic guidance, even after media reports suggested that an operation was on the horizon. The ADF depended on a hierarchical process and sequential planning. For his part, Baker commented later that the Australian Government often prohibited military planning when it considered its options. He offered that Beaumont, like any Chief of the Defence Force (CDF), was often not authorised to take any action to prepare the ADF that might pre-empt diplomatic and political processes and considerations.[31]

There were three major penalties for keeping secrets at HQ ADF from June until September 1994. The first was that the strategic-level contingency plan for Operation *Lagoon* was developed without the benefit of inputs from a range of specialists. Nor was there any input from those in subordinate headquarters staffs who had access to relevant and up–to-date information. Consequently the HQ ADF *Lagoon* plan was logistically unsound and contained insufficient detail on a number of aspects, including arrangements for joint communications and intelligence, to be useful for subordinate headquarters. The second penalty was rushed planning. This led to a number of aspects of the operation being overlooked, some joint arrangements not being well defined, and individuals (especially at the tactical level in Townsville) being put under additional pressure.[32] The third penalty was that short notice put the army logistic and movements system off-balance and forced an expensive concentration of stocks in Townsville and impromptu ship loading.

Sequential hierarchical planning processes make sense when there is time to follow them. However, planning for Operation *Lagoon* showed that, when time was tight, these processes did not work satisfactorily for the tactical level of command. Parallel planning became a matter of necessity. Commanders and staff took action to assemble and prepare personnel and *matériel* based on draft documents, telephone discussions between headquarters staff and individual initiative rather than as a result of reacting to signed instructions that authorised action and allocated resources. For example, staff members at Land Headquarters were well into developing a concept of operations 48 hours before Baker signed a planning directive. Abigail was writing his concept for operations on the day the CDF issued his planning directive. Beaumont issued an operation instruction on the same day that Arnison issued his concept for operations. None of these documents were informed by reconnaissance, so all were redundant by the time Abigail returned from his visit to PNG on 20–22 September 1994.[33]

Further analysis of decision-making at HQ ADF revealed that there were inbuilt problems:

> The ADFCC [Australian Defence Force Command Centre] can be viewed as a distributed decision making environment where parts of a problem are solved by different people. For the most part, decision-making occurs outside formal meetings, and so meetings become a means to inform of decisions, rather than a forum to make decisions. This phenomenon can lead to delays in conveying decisions and information to a wider audience. Many members of the Immediate Planning Group felt the majority of meetings fulfilled a briefing rather than a planning and decision- making role. A core group of senior ADFCC staff effectively formed an 'Executive Immediate Planning Group' which appeared to do

more of the planning and decision making than the larger Immediate Planning Group.

Several Inter-Departmental Committee [IDC] members were unable to make immediate decisions and often had to refer to their superiors. This was time consuming and disruptive to the IDC process. ... Rarely were liaison officers from the relevant departments present in the ADFCC.[34]

Brigadier Rod Earle, Director General Army Operations Support, criticised the HQ ADF planning process. On 3 November 1994, he wrote that planning guidance from HQ ADF lacked clear military objectives and a strategic 'end state'. He criticised Beaumont's planning directive as being a mixture of tasks and constraints that 'did not provide the essential strategic parameters for the operation to the Lead Joint Force Commander [Arnison] resulting in an inefficient planning cycle'. He went on to point out that the use of the phrase 'maintain a presence' required specific definition for it to constitute guidance for those tactical commanders who were to allocate troops to each task.[35] Higher headquarters putting pressure on 3rd Brigade to develop concepts for operations at short notice with little guidance was not new. The development of concepts and the hard work of mounting and dispatching force elements at short notice had fallen to 3rd Brigade in May 1987 for Operation *Morris Dance*, in December 1992 for Operation *Solace* in Somalia, and in July 1994 for Operation *Tamar* in Rwanda.

Once again HQ ADF staff did not facilitate sufficient tactical-level reconnaissance. The day after Cabinet approved Operation *Lagoon* on 19 September, a small group (that included Abigail) left for PNG and Solomon Islands. Combat and logistic commanders from the SPPKF were unable to see the Loloho wharf area or Arawa until they arrived the day before the conference began. They had no time to achieve situational awareness. Chan may have forced the combined force into rushed deployment for political reasons. It was the ADF, however, that ignored the old military adage that 'time spent in reconnaissance is seldom wasted'.

There was no separation of liaison and reconnaissance functions. From the point of view of liaison, the two-day visit to PNG by Abigail and his South Pacific contingent commanders enabled them to meet for the first time and to develop plans and mutual understandings. By the end of the visit, they had developed some rapport and a common approach. This high-level liaison resulted in Fiji confirming its commitment of forces to the SPPKF.[36] Furthermore, the reconnaissance party also met stakeholders in Port Moresby, Arawa and Honiara. This gave them the opportunity to hear from key protagonists, and to make personal and professional assessments of the issues they raised. The visit also provided the first opportunity for Abigail, Draunidalo, Tupou and Colonel Sevle

Takal to assure PNG officials and Bougainvillean groups in person about their commitment to neutrality.

From the point of view of reconnaissance, the visit enabled Abigail and his three senior subordinate commanders to assess the security environment on Bougainville first hand. They found it to be more benign than their intelligence briefing in Australia had suggested.[37] This first-hand experience enabled them to understand the nature and extent of subsequent security operations. It also enabled them to assess security and control requirements for the four prospective neutral zones. However, because of a restriction on numbers, Abigail's commanders and operations and logistic staff were not able to conduct liaison and reconnaissance in each of the neutral zones, including at the site of the conference at Arawa, or to meet key locals and ascertain each area's particular security requirements. Thus, in strict military terms, this activity was more like a top-level liaison visit than a reconnaissance that would inform specific force preparation.

More thorough reconnaissance may have revealed the need for more troops on the ground. Even though Abigail was able to convince higher levels of command that he needed 390 combat troops rather than the original number of 120 specified in the Ceasefire Agreement, the force structure for Operation *Lagoon* was neither sufficient to accomplish its mission nor was it allowed enough time to coordinate security and movement of delegates, especially in light of apparent PNGDF intentions to ambush secessionist leaders. A security force of 390 personnel, comprising an *ad hoc*, under-trained headquarters and eight under-strength platoons proved inadequate. Furthermore, the combined force did not have time to employ force multipliers, such as liaison, human intelligence and technical surveillance, as well as high-level and low-level communications, to offset the lack of numbers to cover the main routes to the conference site.

There were several negative consequences of shortening the period of collective preparation, training and team-building before deployment and rushing movement to Bougainville. Abigail was not satisfied with the standards his regional troops had achieved for offshore deployment. There was a lack of cohesion and mutual confidence among the contingents. Deployment became more complex, expensive and tiring. Rushed deployment allowed insufficient time to verify with conference organisers those delegates who warranted protection from the SPPKF. PNGDF intelligence operatives in plain clothes infiltrated the conference site, and secessionist leaders had no confidence that the SPPKF would protect them.[38]

Operations began on Bougainville only 48 hours before Prime Minister Julius Chan opened the peace conference. Criminals intimidated conference delegates and accompanying family members and friends as well as curious locals, because SPPKF troops did not have time to establish themselves in designated neutral zones or around Arawa. Though thwarted, rogue PNGDF elements were able to set up an ambush undetected after the arrival of the SPKKF, and subsequently to engage a BRA liaison group and wound one of its members. These incidents verified that the SPPKF was not in a position to guarantee security or properly support the conference for its brief duration. Sam Kauona, the secessionist military commander, described Operation *Lagoon* as the 'poorest example of "peacekeeping duties" ever undertaken in the history of peacekeeping in the world.'[39]

The logistic system once again proved, as it had for the battalion group in Somalia the year before, to be unresponsive to a deployed force.[40] This was disappointing when considering that the execution phase of the operation only lasted a little over a week and that all force elements were supposed to be self-sufficient in all classes of supply. O'Hara was particularly critical of the logistic system in general, and HQ Movement Control at HQ Logistic Command in particular. He reported that, shortly after arrival in the waters off Bougainville, the *Sea Hawk* helicopter embarked on HMAS *Success* was grounded due to a defective fuel pressure gauge. Despite several signals from HMAS *Success* and O'Hara's headquarters staff to Australia, no advice about (or expected delivery date for) the item was received. Maintenance personnel on HMAS *Success* subsequently made *ad hoc* repairs to ensure the aircraft's operational availability. O'Hara went on to point out that no mail system had been set up for Operation *Lagoon*. The navy ended up making its own single Service arrangements through Buka after 'over 15 bags weighing 300–400 kilos accumulat[ed] at [the] RAAF [Royal Australian Air Force] [base at] Richmond until an unscheduled C-130 [*Hercules*] was finally organised to move this and other stores to Buka'.[41]

The Land Headquarters post operation report pointed out that, 'the overall plan for strategic resupply was not well understood by respective joint logistic planners. ... The role of HQ MC [Movement Control] in strategic resupply was also not well defined.'[42]

Earle had also picked up on the ineffectual role of HQ MC at Logistic Command. He pointed out that 'HQ MC was by-passed occasionally. Strategic lift assets entering or leaving the AO [Area of Operations] should be advised to HQ MC to ensure efficient use of assets for cargo'.[43] The failure of the under-staffed, under-authorised and under-resourced HQ MC clearly demonstrated that the ADF had not applied lessons from the battalion group deployment the year before.[44] The inefficient use of 'assets for cargo' suggested that air resupply was, yet again, not being well managed, and that the navy and the army may not have known when air force aircraft were coming and going from Bougainville.

The failure of strategic level intelligence services to adequately support Operation *Lagoon* was disappointing. Colonel David Buchanan, who had led a

Bougainville Crisis Action Team (BCAT) at HQ ADF during the Operation, pointed out a number of gaps and difficulties in the passage of information.[45] He had formed the BCAT on 6 September 1994. From 7–21 September it operated during office hours, providing intelligence products to the planning process in Canberra, such as a Bougainville contingency planning package and military threat assessments.[46] On 22 September Buchanan and his staff began a regimen of briefing Major General Jim Connolly, Assistant Chief of the Defence Force–Operations (ACOPS), at 4.00 p.m. and Beaumont at 5.00 p.m. each day. According to Lieutenant Colonel Roger Hill, the content of these briefings was not shared with operational decision-makers at Land Headquarters or with Abigail's headquarters on HMAS *Tobruk*.[47]

Operation *Lagoon* posed particular problems for the ADF intelligence community. There were no independent and secure communications between HQ ADF and Abigail's headquarters offshore at Arawa. Consequently, documents containing strategic assessments would have to depend on the command communications system for transmission. Buchanan commented that information collected by the combined force, once it was deployed from Townsville,

> was almost nonexistent outside the overloaded command chain communications link. In the worst case, information from Bougainville was 12 hrs old and filtered twice before it got to the BCAT. Significant information passed [by the BCAT] to CFC [Combined Force Command] on [HMAS] *Tobruk* but did not make its way to INTSUMs and SITREPs [Intelligence Summaries and Situation Reports].[48]

With hindsight, the SPPKF was deployed into a situation where the intentions of the PNG Government and PNGDF force elements in Bougainville were different. Australian diplomats and DIO should have known this and advised Abigail of the risks involved. In the end, it was not the intelligence system but two army intelligence personnel in Arawa who informed Abigail and his staff of the dangers posed by the PNGDF.[49]

In summary, ADF planning processes at the strategic and operational levels were too secret and too slow, and there were deficiencies in deployable logistic support as well as communications technology for force projection. Operation *Lagoon* could have been a strategic tipping-point for Australia in the South Pacific if the PNGDF ambush had succeeded or if Fijian troops protecting secessionist delegates had been involved in a fire-fight with PNGDF forces. Senior ADF commanders preferred to record Operation *Lagoon* as a success. This assessment seemed to obviate a closer examination of its lessons. A review of command, control and communications, intelligence gathering and evaluation and joint logistic support arrangements for ADF operations might have been the result of deeper analysis. Tactical-level reports had been frank. Higher-command reports were less so. Operation *Lagoon* also demonstrated that Australian Prime

Ministers and members of Cabinet will override professional military judgement and take risks to achieve political outcomes—and they will expect the ADF to do likewise.

ENDNOTES

[1] Classified sources, 94 26303, Defence Archives, Queanbeyan.

[2] Major Chidgey concluded that, 'The Force has had insufficient time to assimilate the training and other aspects of the concentration'. He went on to assess that the SPPKF was ill-prepared for its role and lacked the internal cohesion for contingents to work together effectively. Major Colin Chidgey, 'RHC Post Activity Report—Op Lagoon', RHC 611-1-23. Included in Land Headquarters, 'Post Operation Support for Operation *Lagoon*'. Copy held by author.

[3] The term 'bulk out' is used to describe a situation when the volume of cargo cannot fit into the available storage space.

[4] Commodore Jim S. O'Hara, RAN in interview with author, 13 November 1996

[5] Major David L. Morrison in interview with author, 24 October 1997; and Lieutenant Colonel Ian K. Hughes in interview with author, 23 October 1997.

[6] Colonel Sevenaca Draunidalo established his Fijian Ground Force headquarters at Arawa with the Ni Vanuatu contingent providing close protection and a quick reaction force. The Fijians established seven checkpoints around the conference site, with two checkpoints on the main road into town.

[7] N.P. Middleton, 'Post Operation Report—Operation Lagoon', CM 4594, 2 December 1994, p. 3, 94-26834, Defence Archives, Queanbeyan.

[8] Major David Belham, 'Operation Lagoon—Post Operation Report—Communications Aspects', May 1995, p. 2, 94 26303, NAA, Sydney. Belham was Acting Deputy Director Communication Office, Joint Communications and Electronics Branch, HQ ADF.

[9] Belham, 'Operation Lagoon—Post Operation Report—Communications Aspects', May 1995, p. 2, 94 26303, NAA, Sydney.

[10] Warrant Officer RS K.J. Slavin, Op Lagoon—Quickrep, Minute to Chief of Staff, 24 October 1994. Copy held by author.

[11] Land Headquarters, 'OP Lagoon—Post Operation Initial Report', LHQ SIC E3J/I4S, OPS/PLANS 30618/94, 270609Z OCT94, p. 6, K98 18173, NAA, Sydney.

[12] Major William G. Teece, 'Operation Lagoon—Communications Post Operation Report (POR)', 28 October 1994, p. 3, 103 Signal Squadron, 94 26303, Defence Archives, Queanbeyan.

[13] Teece, 'Operation Lagoon—Communications Post Operation Report (POR)', 28 October 1994, p. 2. See also Land Headquarters, 'OP Lagoon—Post Operation Initial Report', p. 6.

[14] Teece, 'Operation Lagoon—Communications Post Operation Report (POR)', 28 October 1994, p. 3.

[15] The communication difficulties during Operation *Lagoon* prompted Arnison to commission a Joint Operations Room at Land Headquarters that was capable of worldwide communications and supported by secure automated command, control and intelligence systems. Staff at Land Headquarters told the author that Operation *Lagoon* exposed several shortfalls in the capabilities of Land Headquarters to command offshore operations. These were overcome under Arnison's personal direction.

[16] Classified sources, 94 26303, Defence Archives, Queanbeyan.

[17] Colonel Feto Tupou, 'BPC [Bougainville Peace Conference] Minutes of meeting held on 9 October 1994'. Copy held by author.

[18] O'Hara, 'POR—Maritime Aspects', p. 6.

[19] Brigadier Peter J. Abigail in interview with author, 18 March 1997. Also classified sources.

[20] Lieutenant Colonel Steve H. Ayling, 'Brief to CDF', HQ ADF Joint Communications and Electronics Branch, 10 October 1994, 94 26303, Defence Archives, Queanbeyan.

[21] Lieutenant Colonel David J. Hurley in interview with author, 3 March 1998.

[22] Bob Breen, *Giving Peace a Chance, Operation Lagoon, Bougainville 1994: A Case Study of Military Action and Diplomacy*, Canberra Papers on Strategy and Defence, no. 412, Strategic and Defence Studies Centre, The Australian National University, Canberra, 2001, pp. 73–76.

[23] Papua New Guinea Government, 'BRA has let Bougainvilleans down says PM', 14 October 1994, 94 26303, Defence Archives, Queanbeyan.

[24] Papua New Guinea Government 'Commitment for Peace Agreement', 18 October 1994, Copy on 94 26303, Defence Archives, Queanbeyan. This agreement was signed by a number of representatives from village councils, church groups, women's groups and local BRA commanders.

[25] Land Headquarters began meaningful planning for Operation *Lagoon* in Sydney on 9 September 1994. Four weeks later, an *ad hoc* combined force, comprised of over 650 ADF personnel supporting nearly 400 South Pacific troops, were present at a peace conference in Bougainville during the period 10–14 October 1994. The combined force was clear of PNG territory by 22 October. The operation involved specific force preparation, deployment, command, sustainment, protection and redeployment of a combined force over long distance and employment in an uncertain threat environment.

[26] Though New Zealand is a close and traditional ally, the New Zealand Defence Force does not bring significant assets or know-how.

[27] The priorities were: command, control and communications; intelligence collection and evaluation; maritime surveillance; maritime patrol and response; air defence; protection of shipping, offshore territories and resources; and protection of important civil and military assets and infrastructure.

[28] Bob Breen, *A Little Bit of Hope, Australian Force—Somalia*, Allen and Unwin, Sydney, 1998, chapter 2.

[29] Land Headquarters, 'OP Lagoon—Post Operation Initial Report', LHQ SIC E3J/I4S, OPS/PLANS 30618/94, 270609Z OCT94, 94-18173, Defence Archives, Queanbeyan.

[30] COSC,' Operation Lagoon—Post Operation Report', Agendum No 5/95, 4 April 1995, p. 1, Defence Archives, Queanbeyan.

[31] General John S. Baker in interview with author, 30 August 2005.

[32] Some overlooked aspects were ROE for navy vessels and their companies, and times to issue cryptographic equipment. O'Hara, 'POR Maritime Aspects', p. 7. Some examples were joint communications procedures, joint intelligence arrangements, mail and resupply. For communications, Land Headquarters did not nominate Officer Commanding 103 Signals Squadron as the combined force chief communications officer until 5 October 1994. As a consequence, no one synchronised instructions or the distribution of codes and equipment. With four weeks to plan, this aspect of the operation was cobbled together in four days. Major William G. Teece, 'Operation Lagoon Communications Post Operation Report (POR)', 103 Signals Squadron, Townsville, 28 October 1994, 94 26834, Defence Archives, Queanbeyan. For mail and resupply, the lessons of Operation *Solace* about HQ Movement Control were identified again. One navy report complained of 'significant time delays regarding supply of urgently required stores'. There was also confusion between navy and army about mail services. Commander Australian Navy Supply, 'OP Lagoon—Strategic Movement of Mail/Stores', COMAUSNAVSUPT, SIC E3J/I4S/QGK, 110420ZOCT94. Copy held by author. Most of the pressure was put on Commander 3rd Brigade and his staff who had to develop concepts and orders and organise the preparation of the combined force before deployment.

[33] By the end of September 1994, HQ ADF had issued seven amplifications of the original operations instruction.

[34] M. Chin, J. Clothier, R. Davis, B. Noakes and J. O'Neill, 'Operations Lagoon and Carmine: A Post Operations Report', Information Technology Division Electronics and Surveillance Research Laboratory, Defence Science and Technology Organisation, 1995, 94 26303, Defence Archives, Queanbeyan.

[35] Earle, 'POR—Operation Lagoon—Quick Rep', p. 4.

[36] Abigail in interview with author, 18 March 1997.

[37] Abigail in interview with author, 18 March 1997.

[38] Bougainville Interim Government, Statement General Sam Kauona, Bougainville Negotiation Team for peace on Bougainville and Papua New Guinea, media release, undated. Copy held by author.

[39] Bougainville Interim Government, Statement General Sam Kauona, Bougainville Negotiation Team for peace on Bougainville and Papua New Guinea, media release, undated. Copy held by author.

[40] Breen, *A Little Bit of Hope, Australian Force—Somalia*, Chapter 6: Commanding, Resupplying and Getting Back.

[41] O'Hara, 'POR Maritime Aspects', p. 6.

[42] Land Headquarters, 'Post Operation Report for Operation Lagoon', pp. 31-32.

[43] Earle, 'POR—Operation Lagoon—Quick Rep', p. 2.

[44] Breen, *A Little Bit of Hope, Australian Force—Somalia*, pp. 58, 226, 250, 266 and 363.

[45] Colonel David J. Buchanan, 'Strat Int Spt to Op *Lagoon*—POR', 8 December 1994, 98 18173, Defence Archives, Queanbeyan.

[46] See Defence Intelligence Organisation, 'Bougainville: Situation Update', 9 September 1994, K94-01400, NAA, Sydney; and Defence Intelligence Organisation, 'Military Threat Assessment—Bougainville (Threats to ADF personnel visiting), 14 September 1994, 98-18173, Defence Archives, Queanbeyan.

[47] Lieutenant Colonel Roger A. Hill in interview with author, 31 October 1997.

[48] Buchanan, 'Strat Int Spt to Op Lagoon', p. 3

[49] The author interviewed Australian intelligence personnel involved in discovering the PNGDF ambush, the presence of PNGDF Intelligence personnel and the non-compliance of local PNGDF commanders to the Cease Fire Agreement.

Chapter 8
Search for Joint Command and Control

In the late 1980s General Peter Gration and then Brigadier John Baker had both shared a vision of a new command appointment and a new joint headquarters that would command Australian Defence Force (ADF) operations.[1] This commander and his headquarters would take over after the Chief of the Defence Force (CDF) and his staff had translated government guidance into planning directives. The first moves began in March 1988 when Defence Minister Kim Beazley approved the establishment of Northern Command (NORCOM) with its headquarters in Darwin. The new command was subordinate to the Land Commander in Sydney. Senior maritime and air force officers in the Northern Territory supported Commander NORCOM (COMNORCOM) as component commanders. His role was to plan and conduct surveillance operations with assigned forces across northern Australia and the northern approaches to the mainland—Australia's geographical frontline.[2] Accordingly, COMNORCOM, a one-star appointment, would coordinate surveillance and then orchestrate initial responses to incursions by hostile forces awaiting arrival of a senior joint commander, his headquarters and follow-on forces—a national projection of military force from the south and east to the northwest.

By 1996, as the new CDF, Baker was determined to complete the reorganisation of ADF command and control arrangements, including synchronising joint intelligence, logistics and movements in support of operations.[3] Co-location of existing environmental headquarters would be insufficient to achieve unity of command.[4] He wanted a new co-located joint force headquarters separated geographically from Canberra.[5] In March 1996, he directed the Maritime Commander, Rear Admiral Chris Oxenbould, to also act as Commander Australian Theatre (Interim) and to raise Headquarters Australian Theatre (HQ AST) at Potts Point in Sydney. He also directed Oxenbould to raise the Australian Theatre Joint Intelligence Centre (ASTJIC) and gave him command of 1 Joint Movements Group (1 JMOVGP).[6]

The raising of HQ AST involved a number of concurrent processes. The first process was the preparation and distribution of a series of papers seeking consensus from the environmental commanders and the Chiefs of Staff Committee (COSC) on the form and functions of what would become known as the theatre level of command. The second was a build-up of staff numbers for HQ AST from the three Services in a refurbished building adjacent to Maritime Headquarters at Potts Point in Sydney. The third was the planning and conduct of the *Crocodile* series of exercises (akin to the *Kangaroo* series of exercises during the 1970s and

1980s) to test these evolving joint command arrangements. The fourth was a search for a site to co-locate environmental and component commanders and sufficient staff to plan and conduct campaigns, operations and prescribed activities.

For the purposes of this monograph, the establishment of HQ AST is only described from the perspective of its impact on Australian military force projection; that is, 'Did it enhance or detract?' and, more specifically, what was the impact of HQ AST on the next regional force projection to Bougainville in 1997? The COMAST and his headquarters faced challenges that obligated astute anticipation, efficient planning and dissemination of guidance, orders and instructions, as well as timely reconnaissance and deployment. The trend since Operation *Morris Dance* had been for the government and the strategic level of command in Canberra to insist on secrecy and to forbid contingency planning at lower levels of command until a few weeks before deployment. Consequently, there was less time for preparation and reconnaissance. Intelligence support also needed attention. Joint logistic support and the air force air resupply chain—major risk factors of earlier operations in the 1990s—needed to be more responsive to deployed forces.[7] Would COMAST and HQ AST mitigate or increase risk?

There was a contest of ideas in 1996. Oxenbould, assisted by Colonel Greg McDowall, developed papers describing the structure of HQ AST and sought to define responsibilities, roles and tasks, as well as relationships, between nine two-star officers and their headquarters as well as COMNORCOM in Darwin and commander of the Deployable Joint Force Headquarters (COMD DJFHQ) in Brisbane, who would be involved in ADF operations operationally or logistically. Oxenbould and McDowall proposed two options in their first paper in May 1996.[8] The first was for COMAST and HQ AST to coordinate the efforts of each component in a collegial way, and for environmental commanders to be responsible for assigned operations 'in their own right'.[9] The second was for each component to be responsible for assigned operations on behalf of COMAST as his environmental deputy commanders.[10] The two options represented similar functional models, but very different staff relationships. The collegial approach suited peacetime and did not change relationships or staff focus on service training and sustainment responsibilities. The integrated option offered 'greater unity of command in war' and would change the staff focus to campaigns and operations as well as peacetime training and sustainment.[11]

Oxenbould distributed a draft organisation for HQ AST to the environmental commanders on 18 December 1996 in preparation for submission to COSC on 26 February 1997.[12] He sought comment by 27 January. This draft described the organisation for HQ AST that reflected Option 1, confirming that, for the time being, joint command and control at the operational level would depend on cooperative rather than command relationships—an evolutionary not revolutionary approach.[13] While COMAST commanded the environmental commanders for operations on paper, his chief of staff only coordinated staff effort from each component through his small joint administrative, planning, intelligence and operations cells and a modest joint command centre.

The challenge for the Joint Administrative Cell at HQ AST, under these cooperative arrangements, was substantial. An officer of colonel equivalent rank was responsible for developing policy and directing planning for joint logistic support to operations, that also included 'drawing extensively' on 1 JMOVGP for movements and each environmental headquarters for personnel administration.[14] This officer and a handful of staff would also be expected to 'direct and control, within the authority delegated by the joint commander, logistic, personnel, health and other administrative support for the joint campaign and coordinate component and subordinate administrative support', and movements.[15] Thus, he or she would interact with seasoned chiefs of staff and equivalent ranks on the staffs of three component commanders in Sydney, three Service headquarters in Canberra and three headquarters of each of the logistic commanders of each Service as well as NORCOM and DJFHQ.

The challenges for the officer of colonel equivalent rank commanding ASTJIC were also substantial. He or she had to prepare joint intelligence estimates and plans, and coordinate the collection, processing and dissemination of intelligence for the planning and conduct of joint campaigns as well as higher-level intelligence support for operations. This officer and a small staff would be interacting with 15 national and three international agencies as well as intelligence staffs at three environmental headquarters and HQ Special Forces, NORCOM and DJFHQ.[16]

More broadly, the Services favoured a 'top down' approach to finding staff for this headquarters that would see HQ AST assuming responsibilities and taking staff from Baker's newly-reorganised Australian Defence Headquarters (ADHQ) rather than taking a 'bottom up' approach that focused on HQ AST assuming responsibilities from the environmental headquarters and taking staff from them.[17] It was on this principle that a contest of ideas ensued that appeared to be based on each Service chief and environmental commander wanting someone else to assign staff positions to HQ AST. Baker knew of these sensitivities.[18] He had already directed Oxenbould to produce a paper that devolved control of ADF operations from ADHQ to HQ AST, which would involve no net increase in staff but would transfer 30 per cent of staff positions from ADHQ to HQ AST.[19] This approach added Air Vice Marshal Brian Weston, his senior operations officer, to the debate to protect staff numbers.

Referring to CDF guidance, Oxenbould argued that ADHQ would 'direct' operations and HQ AST would 'control' them.[20] He recommended transferring a number of staff from ADHQ to HQ AST based on his understanding of what this meant. He envisaged COMAST establishing a strong relationship with the US Commander in Chief of Pacific Command (CINCPAC), located in Hawaii. In his reply to Oxenbould, Weston disagreed with Oxenbould's interpretation of Baker's guidance and proposed minimal staff transfers and retention of the relationship between the CDF and ADHQ, and CINCPAC and Headquarters Pacific Command (PACOM), in Hawaii.[21] He opined that COMAST and HQ AST would not develop political/military relationships with allies in the Australian theatre in general, or become involved in the US–Australian bilateral military relationship in particular.[22] Weston argued that COMAST was a theatre/operational commander, not a theatre/strategic commander.[23]

Oxenbould wrote back to Weston on 21 November 1996, as his tenure as both Maritime Commander and COMAST drew to an end, complaining that he could not believe that the 'CDF would accept such an expensive proposal in duplication of effort, and such a diminished role for HQ AST in the planning and conduct of campaigns'.[24]

Oxenbould's counter-arguments to Weston reveal several dilemmas. He pointed out that CINCPAC was a theatre/strategic commander who had strategic, operational and tactical level responsibilities, but that US armed forces doctrine did not recognise a theatre/strategic level of war. Consequently, Oxenbould argued that CINCPAC and his staff should deal with the CDF and ADHQ for strategic matters and COMAST and HQ AST for theatre matters, 'just as the CDF deals with both CINCPAC and the Pentagon'.[25] Weston's argument was that the US National Command Authority (NCA), comprising the President, the Secretary of Defense and the Chairman of the Joint Chiefs of Staff, commanded each geographic Commander in Chief (CINC). Therefore, CINCPAC was responsible for both shaping the political and military environment of US national interests in the Pacific area and interacting with regional allies for operations. He was also responsible to the NCA for planning and conducting campaigns and operations in his own right. Thus, CINCPAC and his staff dealt with the CDF and ACOPS satisfactorily at the strategic level, and he and his component commanders and staff also dealt harmoniously at operational and tactical levels with Australian forces from the three Services and Special Forces. The question unanswered by Weston was, 'Why did CINCPAC need to deal with COMAST at all, except to recognise him as a standing joint force commander?'

Baker appeared to be mirroring the US CINC system by creating COMAST, but then not allowing COMAST the full powers of a US CINC. As a superpower with global concerns, the United States created several permanent theatre/strategic commanders, but there was no separation of strategic and theatre levels of command within an American theatre. Why then did a middle power like Australia need to add a theatre level of command within its one Australian theatre? In effect, Baker wanted to create an Australian CINC, but then not devolve responsibilities for him to be an Australian equivalent to CINCPAC. A pertinent question was, 'Why did Australia need both a CDF and a separate CINC equivalent?' It may have been simpler to have a CDF and a chief of joint operations within ADHQ reporting to him.

Putting aside these unanswered questions, the more important issue for the ADF was how to synchronise nine two-star officers and their headquarters, as well as a regional commander in Darwin (COMNORCOM) and the commander of a deployable headquarters in Brisbane (COMD DJFHQ) to execute the functions of force projection effectively and efficiently. A permanent joint force headquarters was required. Arguably, if the US CINC model was applied and Weston's arguments supported, the CDF and ADHQ already constituted a CINC for the Australian theatre and only needed to incorporate environmental component commanders and their staff to operate like a CINC. Though COMAST was intended to be an Australian equivalent of a US CINC, he was not given authority over the environmental commanders and their staffs or over the Service logistic commanders to synchronise Australia's military force projection. For his part, Major General Des Mueller, the first Commander Support Command–Australia (COMSPTAS), was given command of each Service logistic support commander, but depended on cooperative arrangements between his staff groups and component headquarters to get things done.[26] The question was whether these arrangements gave sufficient control to synchronise logistics for ADF operations.

Oxenbould also used another argument that sounded fine in theory, but was unlikely to work based on recent operational experience. He wrote:

> In reality, the transition from strategic to operational planning must be a gradual one rather than a clean break, but it is essential that the operational level interaction be established early and that it develops primacy as planning proceeds and the focus moves from strategic to operational decision making.[27]

Here was another dilemma. Since Operation *Morris Dance*, the strategic level of command had never involved subordinate headquarters in early contingency planning. There had been no time for a gradual transition from strategic to operational planning processes for Operation *Lagoon*. Planning processes had to be fast and concurrent—not gradual and sequential. Governments were not giving the ADF time to plan down through each level of command under hierarchical and sequential arrangements because of a political and diplomatic need for secrecy. Australian force projection only worked well when there was plenty of preparation time.

There was also another dilemma. The strategic level was unlikely to delegate decision-making to lower levels of command. International and national media scrutiny and political sensitivity to exposure of tactical errors and incidents to a worldwide audience meant that the strategic level on behalf of political leaders remained intimately interested in both operational level and tactical level decision-making and outcomes. Politicians were unlikely to wait patiently for the military chain of command to process information from the tactical level through to the strategic level via an operational level of command when the Australian public was receiving instantaneous information via television. Nor were they likely to leave it to the military chain of command to contemplate problems through several layers of command and to come up with courses of action, when the next newspaper or television deadline obligated the Australian Government to respond to a tactical incident within hours.

Weston replied to Oxenbould on 18 December 1996, the same day that Oxenbould distributed his pre-Christmas paper on the organisation and tasks of HQ AST.[28] Weston chose not to address substantive issues, but to emphasise an evolutionary approach. He pointed out that HQ AST would interact with allies in the Pacific theatre by managing the combined exercise program and other activities.[29] He also joined Oxenbould in the view that, when the government decided to take military action, strategic and operational decision-making would be sequential and would devolve naturally from the strategic level to the operational level of command, giving COMAST freedom to plan and conduct campaigns and operations.[30] Neither recognised that recent operational experience and political insistence on secrecy, as well as the imperative for rapid politico–strategic responses to tactical level incidents, rendered this orderly model of contingency planning, force preparation and devolved decision-making obsolete.

From 31 January 1997, the first COMAST, Major General Jim Connolly, though he was of the same rank, commanded the environmental commanders for operations. His staff operated with staffs at Maritime, Land and Air Headquarters on a collegial basis for the planning and conduct of campaigns and operations. On 14 July 1997, he submitted an agendum paper to COSC, 'The Permanent Form and Function of HQ AST'.[31] Connolly noted that on 26 February COSC had prescribed a 30 per cent cut in the staff numbers proposed by Oxenbould in his pre-Christmas paper. He also noted that on 1 May 1997 the Vice Chief of the Defence Force (VCDF), Vice Admiral Chris Barrie, had imposed an overall ceiling of 800 staff on HQ AST, DJFHQ and NORCOM, and that HQ AST should be 'structured for war but adapted for peace', in accordance with the Government's Defence Reform Program.[32]

Connolly was not tempted by either the cut in staff numbers or the invitation to structure for war to propose a more integrated model for HQ AST. His paper confirmed that cooperative relations would apply between his staff branches and component staffs, and that ASTJIC, Joint Administrative Branch and 1 JMOVGP would coordinate intelligence, logistic support and movements for joint operations respectively.[33] While Connolly anticipated that the forthcoming *Crocodile* series of exercises would validate these arrangements, real-time events were soon to thoroughly test the form and function of his headquarters.

ENDNOTES

[1] General Peter C. Gration in interview with author, 19 August 2005; General John S. Baker in interview with author, 30 August 2005; and Department of Defence, 'Report on the Study into ADF Command Arrangements', Headquarters Australian Defence Force, Canberra, 1988, (prepared by Brigadier John S. Baker for the Chief of the Defence Force), 623-11-1, HQ AST, Potts Point.

[2] Gration in interview with author, 19 August 2005; and Baker in interview with author, 30 August 2005.

[3] This process began in February 1995 when a small planning staff distributed draft statements of the mission and responsibilities of COMAST to Baker and environmental commanders. HQ AST, 10/1/5, 16 February 1995, HQ AST, Potts Point. In December 1995, Baker distributed instructions specifying his requirements for a single joint operational level commander and a permanent operational level joint headquarters. He also specified that HQ AST would include joint intelligence, logistics and movements staff. General John S. Baker, 'CDF Directive 582/95', 22 December 1995, pp. 1-2, 94 4323, HQ AST, Potts Point.

[4] Baker, CDF Directive 582/95, p. 1.

[5] Baker in interview with author, 30 August 2005.

[6] General John S. Baker, 'CDF Directive 13/96', 5 March 1996, 94 4323, HQ AST, Potts Point.

[7] See Bob Breen, *A Little Bit of Hope, Australian Force—Somalia*, Allen and Unwin, Sydney, 1998, Chapter 6; and Bob Breen, *Giving Peace a Chance, Operation Lagoon, Bougainville 1994: A Case Study of Military Action and Diplomacy*, Canberra Papers on Strategy and Defence, no. 412, Strategic and Defence Studies Centre, The Australian National University, Canberra, 2001, p. 82 and pp. 86–87.

[8] Rear Admiral Chris J. Oxenbould, 'Structure of Headquarters Australian Theatre', HQ AST 31/96, 623-11-1, 20 May 1996, HQ AST, Potts Point.

[9] Oxenbould, 'Structure of Headquarters Australian Theatre', HQ AST 31/96, 623-11-1, 20 May 1996, HQ AST, Potts Point, p. 8.

[10] Oxenbould, 'Structure of Headquarters Australian Theatre', HQ AST 31/96, 623-11-1, 20 May 1996, HQ AST, Potts Point, p. 8.

[11] Oxenbould, 'Structure of Headquarters Australian Theatre', HQ AST 31/96, 623-11-1, 20 May 1996, HQ AST, Potts Point, p. 12.

[12] Rear Admiral Chris J. Oxenbould, 'ADF Command Arrangements Organisation of Headquarters Australian Theatre', HQ AST 23/96, 18 December 1996, 623-11-1, HQ AST, Potts Point.

[13] Rear Admiral Chris J. Oxenbould, 'Organisation of Headquarters Australian Theatre', draft dated January 1997, Annexes A and B, 623-11-1, HQ AST, Potts Point.

[14] Oxenbould, 'Organisation of Headquarters Australian Theatre', draft dated January 1997, p. 11.

[15] Oxenbould, 'Organisation of Headquarters Australian Theatre', draft dated January 1997, Annex G, p. 2.

[16] These agencies were the Defence Intelligence Organisation (DIO), the Defence Signals Directorate (DSD), the Defence Security Branch (DSB), six Defence Centres and six regional counterintelligence sections in Australia. There were also Defence staffs in Indonesia and Papua New Guinea, and intelligence staff at US HQ PACOM in Hawaii.

[17] Director Force Structure Planning, 'Brief for VCDF (through ACPSG) Tri-Service Team Review—Proposed Interim HQ AST Organisational Structure', ADHQ, 18 October 1996, Copy less attachments held by author. This brief summarised the concerns of the three Services contained in 'Tri-Service Team Report—Proposed Interim HQ AST Organisational Structure', unreferenced and undated.

[18] Baker in interview with author, 30 August 2005.

[19] Rear Admiral Chris J. Oxenbould, 'Devolution of Tasks to HQ AST', HQ AST 167/96, 15 October 1996, 623-11-1, HQ AST, Potts Point.

[20] The guidance Oxenbould referred to was, General John S. Baker, 'CDF Directive 13/1996', 5 March 1996, 623-11-1, HQ AST, Potts Point. Rear Admiral Chris J. Oxenbould, 'Devolution of Tasks from HQADF Operations Division to HQ AST', 11 October 1996, p. 1, 623-11-1, HQ AST, Potts Point.

[21] Air Vice Marshal Brian G. Weston, 'Devolution of Tasks to HQ AST', ACOPS BR2573/96, 96 4957, 29 October 1996, pp. 1–2, Copy on HQ AST 623-11-1, HQ AST, Potts Point.

[22] Weston, 'Devolution of Tasks to HQ AST', ACOPS BR2573/96, 96 4957, 29 October 1996, p. 3 and Annex B.

[23] Weston, 'Devolution of Tasks to HQ AST', ACOPS BR2573/96, 96 4957, 29 October 1996, Annex B, p. 4.

[24] Rear Admiral Chris J. Oxenbould, 'Devolution of Tasks to HQ AST', HQ AST 204/96, p. 1, 21 November 1996, 623-11-1, HQ AST, Potts Point.

[25] Oxenbould, 'Devolution of Tasks to HQ AST', HQ AST 204/96, p. 2.

[26] David Horner, *Making the Australian Defence Force*, The Australian Centenary History of Defence, Volume V, Oxford University Press, Melbourne, 2001, pp. 268–74.

[27] Horner, *Making the Australian Defence Force*, pp. 268–74.

[28] Air Vice Marshal Brian G. Weston, 'Devolution of Tasks to HQ AST', ACOPS BC 2842/96, 18 December 1996, 96 4957, HQ AST, Potts Point.

[29] Weston, 'Devolution of Tasks to HQ AST', ACOPS BC 2842/96, 18 December 1996, 96 4957, HQ AST, Potts Point, pp. 2–3.

[30] Weston, 'Devolution of Tasks to HQ AST', ACOPS BC 2842/96, 18 December 1996, 96 4957, HQ AST, Potts Point, p. 2.

[31] Major General Jim M. Connolly, 'The Permanent Form and Function of HQ AST', HQ AST 430/97, 14 July 1997, 623-11-1, HQ AST, Potts Point.

[32] Connolly, 'The Permanent Form and Function of HQ AST', HQ AST 430/97, 14 July 1997, 623-11-1, HQ AST, Potts Point, pp. 1–2.

[33] Connolly, 'The Permanent Form and Function of HQ AST', HQ AST 430/97, 14 July 1997, 623-11-1, HQ AST, Potts Point, Annexes C and G, and p. 10.

Chapter 9

Lead Up to Operation *Bel Isi*

On 17 March 1997, Brigadier General Jerry Singarok, Commander of the Papua New Guinea Defence Force (PNGDF), revealed publicly that the Prime Minister of Papua New Guinea (PNG), Sir Julius Chan, and several members of his Cabinet had arranged for contractors from Sandline International to establish and train a task force that would deploy to Bougainville to kill or capture members of the secessionist leadership group and retake the Panguna copper mine near Arawa. Singarok mounted and conducted Operation *Rousim Quik* to deport members of the Sandline training cadre and to deter incoming aircraft carrying military hardware for the operation.[1] These events constituted a strategic surprise for Australia as well as an intelligence failure.[2]

The Chan Government cancelled the Sandline contract after Singarok's disclosures. In subsequent elections, Chan lost his seat, and his coalition lost power. Prime Minister Bill Skate formed a new coalition, promising a renewal of negotiations in the hope of ending the Bougainville Crisis, rather than pursuing a military solution. The New Zealand Foreign Minister, Don McKinnon, seized this opportunity to contact Skate and offer mediation. In late March 1997, the New Zealand Chief of the Defence Force (CDF), Lieutenant General Alan Birks, summoned his Assistant Chief of the Defence Force—Operations (ACOPS), Brigadier Roger Mortlock, to a meeting with McKinnon and his senior negotiator, John Hayes, Head South Pacific Branch, New Zealand Ministry of Foreign Affairs and Trade. They told Mortlock that New Zealand was looking to broker dialogue between the PNG Government and secessionist leaders in Bougainville. Initially, the New Zealand Defence Force (NZDF) would transport Bougainvillean delegates to and from Bougainville and host talks among the Bougainvillean factions at a military camp in New Zealand.[3]

On 2 July 1997, McKinnon announced that talks between Bougainvillean representatives would be convened on the following weekend at the army camp at Burnham. From Hong Kong, the Australian Foreign Minister Alexander Downer supported the New Zealand initiative as 'a useful development'. He confirmed that Australian Prime Minister John Howard and New Zealand Prime Minister Jim Bolger had been discussing PNG affairs. In short, Australia and New Zealand would be working together.[4] Like Operation *Lagoon*, Australia's Foreign Minister was giving Defence explicit strategic warning of Australian diplomatic reengagement with finding a solution to the Bougainville Crisis and a possibility of something like an Operation '*Lagoon II*'.

The outcome of the talks at Burnham in July was the Burnham Declaration. All Bougainvillean factions agreed to invite the PNG Government to discuss conditions for a truce as the first step towards declaring a ceasefire. The declaration also foreshadowed the use of 'a neutral Peace Keeping Force' on Bougainville to monitor compliance with the truce and ensure that there were no breaches of any agreements made by the PNG Government and Bougainvillean factions.[5]

The successes of the Burnham talks, the safe return of Bougainvillean delegates, and the release of five PNGDF prisoners by the Bougainville Revolutionary Army (BRA) as an act of goodwill, demonstrated that cooperation between New Zealand diplomats and the NZDF was working well.[6] Diplomatic cooperation between Australia and New Zealand was also harmonious. Downer and McKinnon met in New Zealand on 22 August 1997, and the following day released a joint statement emphasising that Australia and New Zealand were united in their desire to assist the new Skate Government to solve the Bougainville Crisis. Downer then flew to Port Moresby to meet with Skate on 25 August, a day before McKinnon was scheduled to meet Skate and then accompany him to Bougainville. The mission of both ministers was to bolster Skate's commitment to a negotiated settlement and to pledge Australian and New Zealand support to assist the peace process and reconstruction in Bougainville.[7]

Use of Warning Time

Downer was also preparing the Australian public for the involvement of the Australian Defence Force (ADF) in a neutral peacekeeping force on Bougainville in similar ways to how his predecessor had prepared the Australian public for ADF involvement in Operation *Lagoon* in 1994. The day before Downer and McKinnon released their joint statement, Lindsay Murdoch, the International Affairs correspondent with the *Age*, wrote an 'exclusive' article about ADF contingency plans for providing logistic support to a regional peacekeeping force on Bougainville, once the PNG Government and Bougainvillean leaders agreed to a truce. Quoting a spokesperson for the Department of Foreign Affairs and Trade (DFAT), Murdoch stated that Australia would be prepared to assist with a peacekeeping force if 'there was a genuine peace to keep'.[8] Australia's role would be to provide transport, communications, and medical services, rather than armed troops that might raise suspicion and hostility among Bougainvillean secessionist leaders, who were still angry about ADF assistance to the PNGDF. A few days after Murdoch's article, an article in the *Weekend Australian* predicted that an Australian and New Zealand Army Corps (ANZAC) peacekeeping force would serve in Bougainville by the end of the year.[9]

By 26 August 1997, Skate had announced his Cabinet's endorsement of the Burnham Declaration as a basis for negotiation for a round of talks between the

PNG Government and Bougainvillean representatives. For his part, Downer pledged over A$100 million in additional aid to Bougainville over five years, but demurred when asked about Australia sending troops to the island. He affirmed Australian support for New Zealand efforts, suggesting that the ADF would provide only logistic support to a New Zealand-led regional peacekeeping force. In the shorter term, he said that Australian service aircraft would transport Bougainvillean delegates to and from Honiara for the next round of talks in Burnham.[10] On 30 September and 1 October 1997, Australian air force aircraft picked up delegates from locations in PNG and the Solomon Islands for another round of talks at Burnham.[11] Downer and his Cabinet colleague, Ian McLachlan, the Minister for Defence, had combined well to underwrite the New Zealand efforts by transporting a broad representation of delegates from both the PNG Government and PNGDF, as well as from Bougainville, to Burnham.

On 10 October 1997, all parties represented at Burnham signed the Burnham Truce Agreement.[12] It contained a timetable for renewal of a new peace process. There was a clause calling for the PNG Government to invite in a neutral peacekeeping force to monitor the truce.[13] The signing of the Burnham Truce Agreement did not trigger engagement with the NZDF and the ADF on arrangements for participation in a regional truce monitoring group. Major General Frank Hickling, Land Commander—Australia, authorised contingency planning at his headquarters.[14]

Combined Planning and Reconnaissance

Lieutenant General John Sanderson, the Chief of the Army, called Colonel David Hurley into his office on 20 October 1997 to advise him to be prepared to accompany Mortlock and a small team of diplomats and military officers to PNG and Bougainville later in the month.[15] Presumably, Sanderson had anticipated deployment of Australian army personnel to Bougainville and had selected Hurley because he had been an adviser to the PNG Government for Operation *Lagoon*.

The next day, Mortlock and his chief of staff for the coming operation, Lieutenant Colonel Richard Cassidy, met with New Zealand diplomats in Wellington.[16] They assessed that there was uneven support for a New Zealand-led regional monitoring operation in Bougainville among senior Australian Defence officers and officials in Canberra. The New Zealand diplomats concluded, however, that the expectations generated by the Burnham Truce and the obvious willingness of Howard and Downer to support New Zealand initiatives would overcome reservations in the Australian Department of Defence.[17]

After meetings in Canberra, Mortlock led a Resource Group, comprised of Australian and New Zealand diplomats and military officers, to PNG to assess expectations for a truce monitoring group.[18] On 28 October, Major General Jim Connolly warned his component commanders and their staffs not to conduct any planning because it was premature to develop options for ADF involvement in Bougainville before the receipt of strategic guidance from Canberra.[19] Coincidentally, on the same day, Lieutenant Colonel Ashley Gunder, Hickling's senior plans officer, issued a draft concept for operations[20] and force structure for a truce monitoring group supported by a 170-strong logistic support team to staff at Land Headquarters and Headquarters Logistic Support Force (HQ LSF), seeking their input.[21]

Staff at Australian Defence Headquarters (ADHQ), Headquarters Australian Theatre (HQ AST), the environmental headquarters (Maritime, Land, and Air), and Deployable Joint Force Headquarters (DJFHQ) had been following developments in Bougainville with great interest in the media. More particularly, they monitored the progress of the Resource Group through Hurley's daily reports that were distributed concurrently to each level of command. They waited impatiently for guidance and authority to take action. Colonel John Culleton, Colonel (Operations) at Land Headquarters, directed his staff to send out a situation report on Bougainville on 3 November 1997. This report was a thinly-disguised warning order. Culleton had assessed that it was easier to apologise than to ask permission.[22] It alerted DJFHQ and LSF that ADF logistic elements would most likely be deployed to Bougainville soon. Connolly sharply criticised Culleton for 'jumping the gun' through his Chief of Staff, Air Commodore Angus Houston.[23] The Strategic Watch Group met on 4 November and Land Headquarters staff acquired a copy of a warning order drafted by General John Baker's staff later that evening.[24] Baker issued his warning order later that night, while Connolly issued his own warning order the following day (5 November 1997), which included ordering the immediate deployment of planning and liaison officers to New Zealand—a rush was on. Baker's warning order foreshadowed ADF involvement in Bougainville, but it provided no guidance on the nature of ADF support or deployment timings. Despite this warning, Connolly continued to put contingency planning on hold for a truce monitoring group until further clarification arrived from Canberra.[25]

On 6 November 1997, the Resource Group recommended that a peacekeeping organisation, called the Truce Monitoring Group (TMG), be established, comprising 85 monitors and 65 support troops not including helicopter support.[26] It was a very optimistic assessment of the number of support troops that would be required. Military staffs in Canberra and Sydney now waited expectantly for the outcomes of discussions between Baker and Birks. By this time, Hickling's staff had assessed that a 170-strong logistic and communications support force, including a headquarters supplemented by intelligence capabilities, would be required to support about 85 monitors deployed in four teams around Bougainville, and that HMAS *Tobruk* was needed.[27]

Planning and Deployment

It was now up to Baker and Birks to issue strategic guidance for planning, preparation and despatch of troops for what was to become known as Operation *Bel Isi*. Lieutenant Colonel David Bell, a senior logistic officer from HQ AST, and Majors Gary Watman and Roger Holmes, from Culleton's planning staff, left for New Zealand on 6 November 1997. Culleton soon knew through informal channels opened with DFAT that Howard had told McLachlan and Downer that, when the New Zealanders deployed to Bougainville, it was diplomatically and politically essential that ADF personnel deploy with them.[28] After Watman arrived in New Zealand on 6 November, he informed Culleton that the NZDF was planning to send a reconnaissance group to Buka on or about 17 November and an advance party and main body of troops would depart for Bougainville by the end of November. Based on these timings, Hickling and his staff had about three weeks to assemble, prepare and dispatch a support force comprised of headquarters and logistic support personnel as well as their vehicles, equipment and stocks to Bougainville.

On Thursday 6 November 1997, Connolly's staff considered the Resource Group Report and a brief prepared by DFAT officials in Canberra advising the Government of possible options for supporting the TMG.[29] The question was: 'What type of organisation would be required to support 85 monitors from New Zealand, Fiji and possibly Vanuatu, dispersed in four or more team sites around Bougainville?' Authors of the brief recommended that the Australian Government opt for 85 monitors supported by 65 troops as had been recommended by the Resources Group. They preferred the figure of 150 personnel, but recognised that 'the group is limited in logistic support capability'.[30] A TMG of '220 plus' personnel was discussed in the brief as more logistically viable, but dismissed because the ADF was about to support drought relief operations in PNG [Operation *Sierra*] as well as the TMG.[31] For their parts, Baker and Connolly wanted the NZDF to assume as much logistic support responsibility in Bougainville as possible and to limit ADF support to delivering stocks to a port and an airfield.[32] The New Zealanders would be responsible for distribution of stocks from these two points of entry and providing tactical air and ground transport, as well as communications, medical, repair, maintenance and engineering support.[33]

By Friday 7 November, the ADF and the NZDF, in consultation with their respective foreign affairs departments, had agreed to some key appointments. Mortlock would command the TMG with an Australian colonel as his Chief of Staff. Hickling offered Colonel Steve Joske, his Colonel (Artillery), to fill this appointment. He also recommended Lieutenant Colonel Paul Rogers, Commander, 9 Force Support Battalion, based in Randwick, Sydney, to command an ANZAC logistic support team. This composite unit would provide a range of logistic services to HQ TMG and monitoring teams.[34]

Over the weekend 8 and 9 November 1997, staff in Canberra, Sydney, Auckland and Wellington developed those documents that would decide the structure and set the direction for the TMG. On 9 November, at a theatre commanders' meeting convened by Connolly, there was some robust discussion about the timings for deploying reconnaissance groups, advance parties and the main body of ADF personnel and equipment to Bougainville. Hickling, who knew the New Zealand timetable, wanted as much warning and authority as possible so that he and his staff could give subordinate headquarters and troops time to prepare. After several specific questions, Connolly promised Hickling that there would be over two weeks warning and preparation time before assigned units would begin a period of specific force preparation. This subsequent preparation period would comprise three days for personnel to prepare in their units and a 14-day training period in Sydney before deployment. Connolly appeared to be unaware of the New Zealand timetable or had chosen to ignore it.[35] He appeared to have missed the point in the DFAT advice to the Australian Government of 6 November that the TMG could be assembled in two weeks and that New Zealand was

> willing to put [its] own people (including support personnel) into Bougainville as soon as practicable after 14 November. Notwithstanding ADF planning constraints, if we are to have any influence Australia must not be seen to [be] lagging behind New Zealand support for the TMG.[36]

As ADF planning began over the weekend of 8 and 9 November, differences of opinion emerged over the ADF deployment timetable and whether 65 logistic personnel were sufficient to support 85 monitors in four dispersed locations. Hickling was convinced that the New Zealand deployment timetable would apply because the New Zealanders were in command and it was the Australian Government's intention to support their efforts.[37] Connolly's staff assessed that, as the ADF was providing the strategic lift and most logistic and higher level communications support, Connolly's timetable would apply.[38]

Birks issued a planning directive to a Joint Operational Commanders Group on Monday 10 November to prepare a plan for a NZ-led TMG for what was then called Operation *Polygon* by Friday 14 November 1997.[39] Birks' timetable for reconnaissance and deployment of force elements was ambitious. He wanted the composition of a reconnaissance party to accompany the plan on 14 November.[40] He envisaged the NZ Cabinet giving approval for his planning directive on 11 November and authorising deployment of a reconnaissance group on

18 November with the concurrence of the PNG Government. An advance party would arrive in Bougainville six days later on 24 November and the main body of personnel and *matériel* would arrive by sea a week later, on or about 2 December 1997. Presumably, Birks anticipated the ADF conforming to these timings.

Connolly's staff released a second warning order on 11 November that conformed to Birks' deployment timings.[41] The mission was, 'to co-ordinate the provision of selected ADF administrative elements in support to the [TMG] in order to promote conditions for success of truce monitoring operations in Bougainville'.[42] He tasked Hickling to prepare an ADF reconnaissance group for movement to Bougainville in five days time, an advance party to move in 17 days time on 28 November by air, and the main body of troops to leave by sea on HMAS *Tobruk* in 19 days time on 30 November, with an arrival planned for 6 December in Loloho, the port near Arawa. Connolly's intention at this time was to command ADF participation himself until he was ready to delegate responsibilities to either Hickling or the commander of the joint deployable headquarters in Brisbane, Major General Tim Ford. Within minutes of receiving Connolly's warning order, Hickling's staff released a warning order to concentrate, train and administer a reconnaissance group in Sydney.

Guidance from Birks and Connolly, on 10 and 11 November respectively, triggered urgent NZDF and ADF planning for Operation *Bel Isi*.[43] After months of warning, the ADF and NZDF were about to begin combined planning for the deployment of a TMG that had to be on its way to Bougainville in less than three weeks. The only land force elements on this notice to move were members of 3rd Brigade in Townsville. However logistic personnel earmarked for deployment would be coming from Rogers' 9 Force Support Battalion (FSB), which was on several months notice to move. Given the agreed timetable for deployment, individuals and units looked like receiving very little time to prepare at home locations before concentration in Sydney. Rogers' troops may not have been on the right notice to move, but they were in the right place to move from.

Despite the receipt of a warning order on 11 November to prepare a reconnaissance group by 18 November, Hickling was concerned that higher-level planning processes were already falling behind the political and diplomatic timetable, and that pre-deployment preparation would be rushed. While he and his staff could dispatch a reconnaissance group quickly, there was an urgent need to identify, concentrate and prepare both an advance party and the main body of troops with their vehicles, equipment and stocks. It would be embarrassing if the New Zealanders and regional monitors arrived in Bougainville and the ADF did not have logistic arrangements in place to support them. Connolly's assurances to Hickling on 9 November were now redundant. Birks' timetable meant that an ADF reconnaissance group would have less than six days to concentrate in Sydney and conduct pre-deployment preparations. An advance party would also have less than a week after that to prepare, unless Hickling received authority to issue a warning order soon that specified the composition and pre-deployment timetable for an advance party and the bulk of the force.

The problem was a disagreement in New Zealand among ADF and NZDF planning staffs on the composition of the TMG.[44] By 13–14 November 1997, planning for Operation *Bel Isi* split into two processes. At the strategic and operational levels of command in Canberra, Sydney and Wellington, staff debated concepts for operations and discussed two proposals for the structure of the TMG. Concurrently, they prepared briefs for senior ADF officers and Defence officials who were concerned about aspects of Operation *Bel Isi*—especially force protection now that the New Zealanders had decided to go unarmed. The tactical levels of command in New Zealand and Australia were seized by Birks' deployment timetable and began issuing warnings informally in anticipation of the results of higher level negotiations.

With strategic negotiations bogged down, Hickling's staff took risks and warned units informally based on the contingency of a 260-strong TMG: 175 Australian and New Zealand logistic and communications personnel supporting 85 monitors. Cassidy at the army camp at Linton, New Zealand, also issued warning orders for a 260-strong TMG, with contingencies for it to deploy to Bougainville with or without ADF support.[45] While the strategic level of command continued developing a combined concept for operations and negotiating numbers, the lower levels of command in Australia and New Zealand began a race to prepare, pack, load and go.

Specific Force Preparation

On the evening of Friday 14 November, an ADF reconnaissance group under the command of Colonel Steve Joske, who had only received notice of his appointment as Mortlock's Chief of Staff 48 hours earlier, assembled in Randwick and began two days of training and administration. Across the Tasman Sea in New Zealand, Cassidy had set up HQ TMG in a Territorial Army depot at Linton, and was also concentrating and preparing a reconnaissance group.[46] He was in contact with Watman, a liaison officer from Land Headquarters, and Watman was in contact with Culleton, who had returned from negotiations in New Zealand. Joske and his team packed for a 90-day deployment, despite being briefed by HQ AST staff that the reconnaissance would last for six days and the team would return to brief preparing troops. Joske received advice from Hickling's staff that his team would be obliged to continue liaison after arrival in Bougainville rather than return to Australia to inform specific force preparation.[47]

While reconnaissance groups assembled in Randwick and Linton, negotiations continued at the higher levels in Canberra and Wellington. Hickling's staff hoped that a 260-strong TMG would be endorsed, because they had taken the risk of warning out troops based on that structure and advising them of New Zealand intentions. Time was of the essence, because it would be necessary for these units and individuals to top up with stocks and pack, and then concentrate in Sydney and embark in less than two weeks.

On Monday 17 November 1997, Downer and McLachlan issued a joint statement advising the Australian Government's acceptance of an invitation from the PNG Government to participate in the TMG and the deployment of 'a small joint Australian and New Zealand advance party … in the very near future'.[48] The next day, Joske's reconnaissance group flew to Townsville. After they lifted off, Connolly assumed command from Hickling. Baker's intention was to have Joske meet up with the New Zealand reconnaissance group in Townsville, fly to Port Moresby for a briefing from the PNG Government, and then fly to Buka from Port Moresby. Staff at HQ AST told Joske and his deputy, Paul Rogers, that they would be in Townsville for at least 48 hours, awaiting the arrival of the New Zealanders before leaving on or about 21 November.[49]

At about 7.00 p.m. on 18 November 1997, Watman advised staff at Land Headquarters that the New Zealand reconnaissance party was going to fly out at midnight (New Zealand-time) to Buka. There was no intention to rendezvous with Joske's group in Townsville. After receiving a telephone call from Connolly's staff at 10.30 p.m., Joske flew out to Buka the following morning.[50] The New Zealanders were maintaining their schedule for deployment to Bougainville, while the ADF was still catching up.

As the NZDF and ADF reconnaissance groups flew to Buka on 19 November, Hickling's staff issued the next warning order for the concentration and preparation of an advance party. At the same time, ADF and NZDF staff in Wellington and Auckland continued to refine a combined concept for operations for Operation *Bel Isi*. Realising that the New Zealand timetable was being executed despite delays in confirming a concept for operations and structure for the TMG, Hickling's staff went ahead with training and administrations for a 260-strong force.

Deployment

The New Zealand reconnaissance party arrived at Buka on 20 November 1997. An enthusiastic crowd of Bougainvilleans gave Colonel Clive Lilley and his team a warm welcome. Joske's group arrived soon after and they joined a nearby reception function guided by the New Zealand defence attaché, Wing Commander Athol Forrest. Lilley's priority was to move his engineer troop commander and group of engineers across the Buka Passage, a body of water separating the northern and southern islands of Bougainville, and then to drive south. His objectives were to report back on the viability of the route to Arawa and then to proceed to Arawa so as to begin negotiations and preparations for opening the nearby port at Loloho and the airfield at Kieta.[51] Initially, Joske thought that Lilley was moving too quickly. The group could afford to wait until the next day to settle in and issue comprehensive orders before crossing the Buka Passage and heading south. Lilley pointed out that he had issued his orders in New Zealand before departure. Joske could decide to accompany his engineers down the road or be left behind. Joske and his group joined the New Zealanders and crossed the Buka Passage later that afternoon.[52] For his part, Forrest hired a helicopter for Lilley, who flew out for Arawa late that afternoon to begin negotiations with the BRA and local authorities for accommodation and facilities for the TMG. Diplomatically and militarily, the ADF appeared to be flatfooted.

The NZDF and the ADF had differing views on what this phase of Operation *Bel Isi* was supposed to achieve. Connolly and his staff had a traditional sequential view of reconnaissance. Joske and his group would return to Australia and report back before the advance party and the main body of troops departed. The New Zealanders envisaged their reconnaissance group, acting more like an advance party, reporting back *en route* and opening up a forward headquarters at Arawa, the port at Loloho and the Kieta airfield in preparation for the imminent arrival of ships and aircraft carrying troops and *matériel*. Lilley's group also engaged and reassured Bougainvillean leaders and the populace about the TMG mission. Australian planners had not anticipated this political task. Joske had neither linguistic nor public relations support, while Lilley had several interpreters in his team. With hindsight, neither the NZDF nor the ADF had fully anticipated the political requirements. The arrival of the first elements of the TMG was significant, but could not be exploited because Lilley had to fly south as soon as possible to prepare the way for the remainder of the TMG. During their journey south, that began from the other side of the Buka Passage early on 20 November, Joske had to disappoint most villages on the way that had organised welcoming ceremonies for them—a culturally clumsy start for the TMG.[53]

The 170-kilometre journey south to Arawa took 11 hours because of the need to cross several rivers and damaged bridges, and to collect engineer information along the way.[54] For Connolly and his staff at HQ AST, this was an anxious period. They were unable to communicate with Joske and his group, who had taken their satellite communications with them on the drive south. This Inmarsat equipment, the same type that had been fitted to HMAS *Tobruk* for Operation *Lagoon*, could not operate from moving vehicles. Lilley left a rear link signals detachment at Buka to communicate with HQ TMG in New Zealand and to maintain tactical-level communications with his group during the potentially dangerous journey south. Much to his reported chagrin, Connolly and his staff had to use this New Zealand link to ascertain movements and progress.[55]

In the following days, Rogers spent a frustrating time trying to obtain information from HQ AST on the composition of the TMG and what stocks and equipment were about to be loaded on HMAS *Tobruk*. He needed to know how much accommodation and working space was required at Loloho, and whether there were sufficient tents, camp stores and other items being loaded on HMAS *Tobruk* to satisfy requirements. Rogers was not receiving any information from logistic planners at HQ LSF (in both Randwick and Land Headquarters), who were responsible for loading HMAS *Tobruk*. He commented in his diary that there appeared to be no combined planning with the New Zealanders, ineffective coordination of logistic preparations at HQ AST and no understanding among HQ AST staff of the need for him to influence what was being loaded. He wondered why he was on a reconnaissance if his information was not being used to inform logistic preparations. He knew what conditions were like on the ground and what resources would be needed to clean up Loloho port and get logistics operating efficiently.[56] For their parts, Connolly and his staff were not responsible for force preparation. They may have been seized by the fate of Joske and his reconnaissance group in Bougainville and less interested in the fate of *matériel* being assembled on wharves and loaded at Woolloomooloo—the navy's fleet base on Sydney Harbour.

Rogers' other observation at the time was that Connolly's staff were micro-managing and minimising the numbers of army personnel. However, there was no similar examination of maritime or aircrew numbers. The navy and the air force could decide on the numbers needed to support an operation but the 'army was given a number and told to get on with it'.[57] Rogers wondered why higher levels of command caused so much disruption and disappointment among army personnel who had trained together and wanted to deploy together on operations. Staff officers had directed him to downsize his logistic support elements at short notice and form *ad hoc* organisations that had neither trained nor worked together. None of these decisions were made with the benefit of reconnaissance. Now that he needed more personnel to clean up the wharf area at Loloho and help set up logistic support facilities and accommodation areas, staff advised him no further personnel were available, even on a temporary basis. The figures for the TMG appeared to have been decided on or rounded off by senior officers and their staffs without the benefit of an analysis of the roles and tasks of HQ TMG and Rogers' logistic support team, or reconnaissance.[58]

Connolly's staff issued an operation order for Operation *Bel Isi* just after midnight on 20 November 1997. This was the first formal guidance since 11 November. It gave five days warning for the dispatch of an advance party and nine days for a main body of troops. Staff at Land Headquarters had warned

Colonel Jeff Wilkinson, Commander LSF, and his staff earlier in November about the forthcoming deployment. Soon after receiving the operation order from HQ AST, Hickling's staff nominated HQ LSF as the mounting headquarters for Operation *Bel Isi*. Aside from assembling, training and administering personnel using his Deployed Forces Support Unit, Wilkinson's major challenge was to concentrate stocks, vehicles and equipment at Woolloomooloo and load HMAS *Tobruk*. He and his staff had to meet these practical challenges in less than 10 days. On 23 November, an advance party arrived in Randwick for three days pre-deployment training and administration. On the afternoon of 26 November, after the advance party flew out to Bougainville from Richmond, the main body of troops arrived. Concurrently, Wilkinson's staff organised the concentration of heavy engineering equipment, a number of Land Cruisers, Land Rovers and heavy vehicles as well as tonnes of equipment and stocks at Woolloomooloo.

Birks and Connolly signed a combined operation plan on 27 November—too late to influence specific force preparation or deployment. HMAS *Tobruk* sailed on 29 November 1997.[59] They foreshadowed that the TMG would transition into another organisation after Leaders' Talks were to be held on or about 31 January 1998. The PNG Government and representatives from Australia, New Zealand, Fiji and Vanuatu signed an agreement for their contribution to the TMG on 5 December 1997. By that time, advance parties of the TMG had arrived in Bougainville, and the main bodies of troops were either in the air or at sea heading for Bougainville.[60]

Once again, the ADF appeared to have effectively and efficiently planned, prepared and deployed force elements on time and in good order at short notice. The timely sequence of events beginning after the joint statement by Downer and McLachlan on 17 November justified this perception of Australian military force projection. Within 48 hours, a reconnaissance group left Australia. An advance party flew out on 24 November, and the main body on 30 November 1997. Based on these outcomes, Operation *Bel Isi* was an example of a synchronised diplomatic and military effort that confirmed extant arrangements and justified the introduction of COMAST and HQ AST into the ADF chain of command for operations. In reality, the New Zealanders had shown the way and unknowingly driven the ADF decision cycle. Formal processes for Australian military force projection had been too slow. It had been *ad hoc* arrangements between internal coalitions of willing staff at the tactical level within the ADF and NZDF, as well as the PNG Section at DFAT that had delivered these impressive results.

Problems with Force Command

There were problems with ADF arrangements for commanding its participation in Operation *Bel Isi* from the beginning. There was no gradual devolution of command and control and decision-making from the strategic level to the operational level. At the strategic level, Baker delved into the tactical employment of ADF personnel by not allowing Australian military personnel to move outside the Arawa–Loloho–Kieta area, or for female Australian Public Service (APS) truce monitors to deploy to monitoring team sites until security had been assessed to his satisfaction.[61] At the operational level, Connolly commanded an accompanying force protection operation that restricted the employment of HMAS *Success* and its *Sea King* helicopter that were positioned in support of TMG operations in Arawa Bay.[62] Hickling was left to command the military mechanics of Operation *Bel Isi* as the nominated lead joint commander, under the watchful eyes of Baker and Connolly. Like his predecessor, Major General Murray Blake, the lead joint commander of the battalion group deployment to Somalia in 1993, Hickling had no control over maritime or air force assets. HMAS *Tobruk* sailed immediately after unloading, and the air force refused to support Operation *Bel Isi* with a weekly courier flight from Townsville.[63] For his part, Mortlock resented Australian micro-management. He interpreted Baker's restrictions on his employment of Australian personnel and use of assets located in his area of operations as a lack of trust as well as confidence in his competence and judgment.[64]

Joske reported to both Connolly and Hickling. Staff from both HQ AST and Land Headquarters contacted him wanting to discuss issues. He had to keep staff from both headquarters aware of the content of his conversations with staff from the other headquarters. There was much duplication of effort and reporting. The origin of this arrangement, according to Connolly's staff, was Connolly's desire to retain control of the political and military dimension of ADF involvement in Operation *Bel Isi* and also to personally direct any responses to emergencies that might threaten Australian lives.[65] Joske wrote at the time, 'I predict that before long there will be a turf battle'.[66]

The NZDF arrangements for Operation *Bel Isi*, like Canadian arrangements for their contingent in Somalia in 1993, were more cohesive and cooperative. The crews of the New Zealand ships HMNZS *Canterbury* and HMNZS *Endeavour* and their embarked helicopters became active participants in the clean up and establishment of the logistic support team at Loloho, as well as monitoring team sites at Buin and Tonu in southern Bougainville in early December 1997.

Arguably, split Australian command and control arrangements increased risk. In a complex emergency, such as an armed attack by Bougainvillean hardliners opposed to the peace process that resulted in TMG casualties, both Connolly's and Hickling's staff would become involved simultaneously, while staff from Maritime and Air headquarters would also become involved in tasking ships and aircraft. The ADF appeared to still have some way to go in synchronising joint command and coordinating assigned navy, army and air force assets.

ENDNOTES

[1] See Mary Louise O'Callaghan, *Enemies Within*, Double Day Australia, Sydney, 1999; and Sean Dorney, *The Sandline Affair*, Allen and Unwin, Sydney, 1998, for detailed accounts of the circumstances and outcomes of what became known as the Sandline Affair.

[2] Mary-Louise O'Callaghan, 'Hidden Agenda', *Australian Magazine*, 14–15 August 1999, pp. 28–33.

[3] Brigadier Roger C. Mortlock in interview with author, 27 October 1998.

[4] New Zealand Press Association, Australian Foreign Press and Australian Associated Press correspondents, 'NZ talks aim at ending Bougainville crisis', *The Australian*, 3 July 1997.

[5] 'The Burnham Declaration, By Bougainville Leaders on the Re-establishment of a Process for Lasting Peace and Justice on Bougainville', 5–18 July 1997, paragraphs 4–5. Copy held by author. Text included as Appendix A in (eds) Monica Wehner and Donald Denoon, *Without a gun: Australians' experiences monitoring peace in Bougainville, 1997–2001*, Pandanus Books, Research School of Pacific and Asian Studies, The Australian National University, Canberra, 2001.

[6] David Barber, 'Bougainville rebels free five soldiers in goodwill gesture', *Sydney Morning Herald*, 23 July 1997.

[7] Correspondent in Wellington, 'Anzac force on cards for Bougainville', *Weekend Australian*, 23–24 August 1997.

[8] Lindsay Murdoch, 'Troops may join PNG mission', *Age*, 21 August 1997.

[9] A correspondent in Wellington, 'ANZAC Force on Cards for Bougainville', *Weekend Australian*, 24 August 1997.

[10] Geoffrey Barker, '$100m in extra PNG aid but troops not on the agenda', *Australian Financial Review*, 26 August 1997; and Craig Skehan, '$100m to rebuild war-torn island', *Sydney Morning Herald*, 26 August 1997.

[11] Lindsay Murdoch, 'Australia flies rebels from Bougainville', *Age*, 30 September 1997.

[12] Copy held by author. Text included as Appendix B in Wehner and Denoon, *Without a gun: Australians' experiences monitoring peace in Bougainville, 1997–2001*.

[13] See David Barber and Craig Skehan, 'PNG pact with rebels', *Sydney Morning Herald*, 11 October 1997; and Jane Dunbar, 'Bougainville truce creates climate for lasting peace treaty', *Weekend Australian*, 11–12 October 1997.

[14] The author was working full time at Land Headquarters during this period and attended all the meetings of Hickling's Bougainville Watch Group. The first meeting was on 26 September 1997. Hickling recognised the high probability of ADF force elements deploying to Bougainville in November after the signing of the Burnham Truce Agreement. He authorised contingency planning and other preparations, such as updating maps, identifying availability of logistic force elements and gathering intelligence. On 3 November 1997, the author briefed him on lessons from Operation *Solace* and Operation *Lagoon*.

[15] Lieutenant Colonel David J. Hurley in interview with author, 3 March 1998.

[16] Lieutenant Colonel Richard P. Cassidy in interview with author, 8 February 1998. Cassidy was Mortlock's senior NZDF staff officer and chief negotiator for Operation *Bel Isi*.

[17] Cassidy in interview with author, 8 February 1998.

[18] Resources Team comprised Brigadier Roger C. Mortlock, John Hayes, New Zealand Ministry of Foreign Affairs and Trade, David Irvine, Australian Ambassador to PNG, Greg L. Moriarty, PNG Section, DFAT, Colonel David J. Hurley, Lieutenant Colonel Richard P. Cassidy, Nigel Moore, New Zealand Embassy, PNG.

[19] Author's note in his personal diary on 28 October 1997.

[20] **concept for operations**: A verbal or graphic statement, in broad outline, of a commander's assumptions or intent in regard to an operation or series of operations. The **concept of operations** frequently is embodied in campaign plans and operation plans; in the latter case, particularly when the plans cover a series of connected operations to be carried out simultaneously or in succession. The concept is designed to give an overall picture of the operation. It is included primarily for additional clarity of purpose. Also called 'commander's concept' or CONOPS (DOD).

21 Lieutenant Colonel Ashley L. Gunder, 'CONOPS—Truce Monitoring Group (Bougainville)', email, 28 October 1997. Copy held by author.

22 Author's note in personal diary, 3 November 1997.

23 Author's note in personal diary, 3 November 1997. Colonel John J. Culleton in discussions with the author during this period. In early November 1997, the author attended all the meetings related to the deployment to Bougainville convened in Land Headquarter.

24 Note in author's diary, 4 November 1997.

25 Note in author's diary, 4 November 1997.

26 Resource Group Report on a Proposed Truce Monitoring Group for Bougainville, undated, but covered by a facsimile sheet signed by Hurley on 6 November 1997. Copy held by author.

27 Gunder in discussions with author in early November 1997. Gunder was Staff Officer Grade 1 (Joint Plans) at Land Headquarters. He chaired the Bougainville Watch Group and coordinated contingency planning. He had been receiving copies of Hurley's daily progress reports from the Resource Group.

28 Discussions between the author and DFAT officials in November 1997.

29 Department of Foreign Affairs and Trade, 'Bougainville—Australian Involvement in a Truce Monitoring Group', Brief prepared by DFAT for the Ministers for Foreign Affairs and Trade, and Defence, 6 November 1997. A copy was distributed informally to all levels of ADF command. The author received a copy on 7 November 1997. Copy held by the author.

30 Department of Foreign Affairs and Trade, 'Bougainville—Australian Involvement in a Truce Monitoring Group', p. 2.

31 Department of Foreign Affairs and Trade, 'Bougainville—Australian Involvement in a Truce Monitoring Group', p. 3.

32 General John S. Baker in interview with author, 30 August 2005.

33 Colonel John J. Culleton to author at the time. Culleton attended most of Major General Jim Connolly's briefings and staff planning meeting at HQ AST in early November. Baker confirmed that it was Australian Prime Minister John Howard's intent for ADF elements to accompany NZDF elements into Bougainville (General John S. Baker in interview with author, 30 August 2005.)

34 Notes in author's personal diary, 7 November 1997.

35 Hickling passed on this information to Culleton on Monday 10 November 1997.

36 Department of Foreign Affairs and Trade, 'Bougainville—Australian involvement in a Truce Monitoring Group', p. 4.

37 Hickling briefed his staff to this effect on Monday 10 November 1997. Notes in author's diary, 10 November 1997.

38 Interview and discussions, Culleton.

39 Lieutenant General Alan L. Birks, 'Planning Directive by the Chief of the Defence Force to Brigadier J.A. Dennistoun-Wood, Chairman, Joint Operational Commanders Group (JOCG) for Operation POLYGON, Bougainville Truce Monitoring Group', CDF Directive 13/97, 10 November 1997, HQ NZDF 03130/PNG/1. Copy held by author.

40 Birks, 'Planning Directive by the Chief of the Defence Force to Brigadier J.A. Dennistoun-Wood, Chairman, Joint Operational Commanders Group (JOCG) for Operation POLYGON, Bougainville Truce Monitoring Group', CDF Directive 13/97, 10 November 1997, HQ NZDF 03130/PNG/1, p. 5.

41 COMAST 'Warning Order for OP Terrier', COMAST 9/97, 11 November 1997. Copy held by author.

42 COMAST 'Warning Order for OP Terrier', COMAST 9/97, 11 November 1997. Copy held by author.

43 Originally the NZDF named the operation to support the TMG *Polygon* and ADHQ named ADF participation as *Terrier*.

44 Culleton in telephone discussion with author, 14 November 1997. Notes in author's diary, 14 November 1997. Culleton was in New Zealand with ADF negotiators.

45 Cassidy in interview with author, 8 February 1998

46 Hickling informed Joske on Thursday 13 November after breaking a deadlock, on whether he or Major General Tim Ford, COMD DJFHQ, would be the lead joint commander for Operation *Bel Isi*, by having Lieutenant General John Sanderson intervene with Baker personally to press Connolly to make an appointment so orders and instructions could be issued.

47 Lieutenant Colonel Paul M. Rogers, Personal diary entry, 15–16 November 1997. Copy held by author.

48 Australian Government, 'Joint Statement The Minister for Foreign Affairs, Hon Alexander Downer and the Minister for Defence Hon Ian McLachlan, Australian Participation in the Bougainville Truce Monitoring Group', FA 140, 17 November 1997. Copy held by author.

49 Lieutenant Colonel Paul M. Rogers in mobile telephone discussion with author, 18 November 1997.

50 Colonel Steve K. Joske, Commander's Diary entry, 19 November 1997. Copy held by author.

51 Colonel Clive W. Lilley, Interview with author, 25 October 1998.

52 Colonel Steve K. Joske, Commander's diary entry, 20 November 1998. Copy held by author.

53 Diary entry, Rogers, 20 November 1997.

54 Diary entry, Rogers, 20 November 1997.

55 Major John G. Howard in interview with author, 10 February 1998. Howard, a NZDF Special Forces officer, was a member of Lilley's reconnaissance party and then operations officer for Monitoring Team Buin.

56 Diary entry, Rogers, 24 November 1998.

57 Diary entry, Rogers, 27 November 1998.

58 The author monitored issues related to numbers for Operation *Bel Isi* soon after the Resources Group submitted their report on 6 November, nominating a 150-person structure. There was no logistician in the group to point out that this was unworkable. Subsequently, after exhaustive analysis, the bare minimum was assessed by staff in both New Zealand and Australia as 264 personnel. The final cap figure issued by HQAST was 250, suggesting that the 264 figure had been arbitrarily rounded off.

59 Major General Alan L. Birks and Major General Jim M. Connolly, 'Combined AS/NZ Operational Plan Operation BEL ISI', HQNZDF 03130/PNG/1, 27 November 1997. Copy held by author.

60 'Agreement between PNG, Australia, Fiji, New Zealand and Vanuatu Concerning the Neutral Truce Monitoring Group for Bougainville', signed in Port Moresby, 5 December 1997. Copy held by author.

61 Brigadier Roger C. Mortlock in interview with author, 27 October 1998.

62 Classified sources.

63 Interview with Rogers; and Letter from Hickling.

64 Mortlock in interview with author, 27 October 1998.

65 Discussions with Culleton.

66 Commander's diary entry, Joske, 13 December 1997.

Chapter 10
Challenges during the first 12 months

Unlike Operations *Morris Dance* and *Lagoon*, Operation *Bel Isi* would turn out to be a longer-term operation. Its duration would exceed the four and a half month tour of the 1000-strong joint force deployed to Somalia in 1993, which had first exposed the Australian Defence Force (ADF)'s weaknesses in logistics and command and control.[1] The challenges faced in the first 12 months of Operation *Bel Isi* illustrated persistent problems with force command and sustainment that had been glimpsed during Operations *Morris Dance* and *Lagoon*. Headquarters Australian Theatre (HQ AST) had not understood the requirements for specific force preparation and deployment. Problems soon emerged with force sustainment.

The momentum of the establishment of the Truce Monitoring Group (TMG) at Loloho increased significantly with the arrival of HMAS *Success* and HMAS *Tobruk*, on 5 December 1997.[2] Lieutenant Colonel Paul Rogers was surprised and disappointed to find that HMAS *Tobruk* had been slowed down for several hours doing 'figure 8s' to allow HMAS *Success* to catch up, so that both ships could arrive together. Rogers needed to discharge HMAS *Tobruk* as soon as possible to set up the Logistic Support Team (LST) to support monitoring operations.[3] The New Zealanders had already conducted site reconnaissance and were calling on Rogers to provide the logistic support to set them up. Rogers had anticipated he would have to accommodate no more than 200 personnel in Loloho in line with the numbers cap put on the Headquarters Truce Monitoring Group (HQ TMG) and the LST. Unlike higher headquarters in Australia, the New Zealanders did not seem to be fussed if their numbers exceeded agreed limits. By 8 December 1997, Rogers was accommodating 207 New Zealand Defence Force (NZDF), 145 Australian Defence Force (ADF) personnel, a Fijian liaison officer, and a Ni Vanuatu liaison officer—a total of 354 persons.

Logistic support was one of the contentious issues between the NZDF and the ADF during the lead up to Operation *Bel Isi*. Two separate national logistic systems ended up supporting the TMG. There was no coordination of these supply chains. During the rushed days in November 1997, there were robust discussions at Land Headquarters and the Logistic Support Force (LSF) about the command and control of logistic support for Operation *Bel Isi*, including the provision of weekly air force courier flights and arrangements for mail.[4] Colonel John Culleton and Lieutenant Colonel Murray Slip, a senior logistician at Land Headquarters, offered that problems identified supporting troops in Somalia in 1993 could be overcome by including logistic staff with operations staff at Land

Headquarters and establishing a special 'Operation *Bel Isi* Coordination Cell' at the Defence National Supply and Distribution Centre (DNSDC) to monitor resupply.

Colonel Jeff Wilkinson sought to be appointed Commander Joint Logistics as a component commander at HQ AST. Wilkinson commanded most of the logistic personnel and assets before their assignment to Operation *Bel Isi*. Unlike Culleton's staff, Wilkinson's formation was involved in the practical challenges of running logistic operations in Australia on a daily basis. Culleton's logistic operations staff did not have habitual relationships with deployed logistic personnel or day-to-day experience of ensuring that items of supply reached customers on time. As a joint logistic commander, Wilkinson envisaged being responsible to Jim Connolly and Frank Hickling for force sustainment of Operation *Bel Isi*. He sought command of Rogers and the LST, as well as influence over DNSDC, 1 JMOVGP and navy and air force assets.[5]

Hickling did not concur with Wilkinson's views, or that results of operational analysis of Operation *Solace* in Somalia and Operation *Lagoon* warranted the appointment of a joint logistic component commander.[6] Hickling took Culleton's advice that the remedial measures which he and Slip had put in place should be given the opportunity to work. He did not press Connolly to appoint a combined and joint logistic commander, who would monitor NZDF logistic support as well as control the ADF supply chain to Bougainville—a chain that would rely on navy and air force assets.

A comparative examination of the Australian and New Zealand force sustainment for Operation *Bel Isi* reveals gaps between intent and outcome. Connolly and Commodore Mark Wardlaw Royal New Zealand Navy (RNZN), Assistant Chief of the Defence Force—Operations (ACOPS) NZDF, signed a combined New Zealand–Australian logistic support instruction for Operation *Bel Isi* on 4 December 1997. Hickling signed his administrative instruction for Operation *Bel Isi* two days later.[7] Wardlaw's and Connolly's instruction contained descriptions of the New Zealand and Australian arrangements for resupply that also specified coordination requirements. On paper, both their combined instruction and Hickling's instruction synchronised force sustainment effectively. There were some differences between NZDF and ADF approaches, but overall the NZDF and ADF resupply chains were viable, if nominated agencies complied with directions given to them.

By coincidence, both NZDF and ADF nominated their corresponding Land Headquarters to set up 24-hour logistic operations cells and to coordinate resupply. Headquarters Land Force Command in Auckland established a TMG Logistic Support Agency.[8] Land Headquarters in Sydney supplemented its operations room with logistic watch keepers, who came from Wilkinson's staff at Headquarters Logistic Support Force (HQ LSF) in Randwick. Both instructions made their equivalent support commanders and joint movements organisations responsible for the provision of supply and movement of personnel and *matériel* to and from Bougainville. The instructions sought 24 hour-a-day responsiveness as well as cross-Tasman coordination of resupply flights. These flights were to occur on a weekly basis, with the Royal New Zealand Air Force (RNZAF) and the Royal Australian Air Force (RAAF) providing flights on alternate weeks.[9]

Aside from logistic watch keepers at Land Headquarters, the engine room for the ADF resupply chain was to be a DNSDC Operation *Bel Isi* Coordination Cell, with representation from 1 JMOVGP, 'to ensure all demands from Bougainville are actioned IAW [in accordance with] required timeframes'. Hickling's instruction directed this cell to provide periodic reports to his staff and Major General Des Mueller, Commander Support Command–Australia in Melbourne, on progression of demands with information copies to HQ AST on the volume of demands and any problems that might arise. The instruction by Wardlaw and Connolly directed Mueller to 'ensure all demands placed on the AS [Australian] resupply system for Op Bel Isi are tracked and satisfied within AUSMIMPS [Australian Standard Matériel Issue and Movement Priority System] time frames'. In addition, Mueller was to 'provide details to HQ TMG LST on delivery date/time for all demands placed on the AS [Australian] resupply system for duration of Op Bel Isi'.[10]

The demand chain for resupply was included as Annex B to the combined instruction as a 'flow diagram'. It showed that LST staff at Loloho would send demands for supply to logistic staff at HQ TMG in Arawa, who would send them onto Land Headquarters staff. Presumably logistic watchkeepers would then forward them to DNSDC, who would satisfy demands and arrange with the joint movements group (1 JMOVGP) for consignments to go to Richmond RAAF Base for onward movement to Bougainville, either in RNZAF aircraft transiting through, or on Australian aircraft from Air Lift Group (ALG) based at Richmond. In short, General John Baker delegated theatre command of Operation *Bel Isi* to Connolly, who delegated operational command to Hickling, who directed Mueller, the national distribution centre at Moorebank, 1 JMOVGP and Headquarters Air Command—in an instruction—to make the supply chain to Bougainville work, in conjunction with the RNZAF.

Thus, Hickling and his staff had responsibility for resupply, but depended on the cooperation of enabling supply and movements agencies that they did not command and had no habitual relationship. Would Mueller's staff, Connolly's Joint Administration Branch and his joint movements group, as well as a special Operation *Bel Isi* Cell at DNSDC make the system work better than it had for Operation *Solace* in 1993 and Operation *Lagoon* in 1994? Would assigned logistic staff from Administration Branch, Land Headquarters and watchkeepers from Wilkinson's headquarters, who were supplementing Culleton's operations staff, be sufficient to solve problems as they arose? Discussions over the provision of a weekly air force courier to Bougainville quickly faltered: there would be no courier.[11] Staff from ALG at Richmond advised that once a C-130 *Hercules* load of stores and personnel was ready for onward movement, they would assign an aircraft in accordance with extant priorities.

By January 1998, the consequences of rushed logistic planning and capping numbers without analysing services to be provided were now being felt. Resupply arrangements had also begun to fail.[12] There was no coordination of air movements by the NZDF and the ADF into and out of Bougainville.[13] Staff at joint movements groups in Auckland and Sydney had no mechanism to achieve coordination either through a joint logistic commander and his headquarters or through the New Zealand Land Force Headquarters or Land Headquarters in Sydney. The only communication between the two land headquarters across the Tasman Sea was through liaison officers, who reported what they saw but were not employed to remedy coordination problems. Major Neil Smith, the ADF Liaison Officer at Land Force Headquarters in Auckland, wrote:

> In summary, the co-ordination of air movements, and the use of each other's aircraft for the onward movement of personnel and stores had not been well coordinated at this stage of the operation, which means that it could be not described technically as a combined operation, i.e. not one whereby the logistic resources are put under the command of an individual either to move or to resupply.[14]

In effect, Operation *Bel Isi* incorporated two parallel force sustainment operations. According to Rogers, there was no monitoring of the priorities of demands for items of supply. Onward movement of consignments from Australia and New Zealand was decided by order of arrival at air force bases rather than by operational priorities. There were numerous examples of where low-priority items were flown to Bougainville ahead of more critical items.[15] On 23 and 24 January 1998, Rogers sent minutes to Culleton's staff listing those items that had not been delivered on time or, indeed, at all.[16] He recognised that the Christmas period meant that the ADF logistic system would be less responsive; however, the operational tempo in Bougainville did not take a Christmas holiday. He anticipated that delays would mean that vehicles and equipment would continue to be unserviceable for excessive periods of time. He pointed out that his authorised holding of spare parts in Bougainville was limited. As a consequence, the LST had to rely on a 'just in time' responsive resupply system from Australia. Furthermore, all vehicles and specialist equipment items had been kept to a minimum; thus, there were no spare vehicles or major items of equipment to bring on line if others became unserviceable while awaiting spare parts.[17] He wrote: 'The result is that if an item is unserviceable, the LST capability becomes severely limited until parts can be obtained.'[18]

In his minute to Culleton on 23 January 1998, Rogers provided specific examples of critical spare parts not arriving on time. One of the two refrigeration containers broke down on 29 December 1997 and still awaited spare parts before it could be repaired three weeks later. For the time being, HMNZS *Endeavour*, alongside at Loloho, kept perishable food cool. One of two 60 kVA generators had been unserviceable since 14 December awaiting spare parts. If the other generator broke down, there would be no electrical power in Loloho except that provided by New Zealand ships moored alongside. Rogers emphasised that the LST should not have to depend on RNZN goodwill. After the New Zealand ships left on 31 January, the ADF logistic support system for Operation *Bel Isi* would be on its own.[19]

Rogers detected that the Australian air force's air freight system was off-loading consignments for Operation *Bel Isi* and reloading them later. Some items were just not arriving or were being lost somewhere along the air supply chain. From mid-December until mid-February 1998, the number of outstanding demands not satisfied by their requested delivery date grew steadily. Fifty per cent of items, on average, were late; with about half of them being over two weeks late.[20] Rogers was sending logistic reports each week describing the deterioration in resupply, including his highest priorities for remedial action. The ADF logistic system was simply unable to supply spare parts to an offshore operation in a timely manner. Well-meaning staff at Land Headquarters could only pass on Rogers' concerns to Mueller's headquarters in Melbourne. Rogers wrote:

> To put it quite simply, the satisfaction rate is disappointing, and does not reflect what should be expected on an operation. It is apparent that delays are occurring in some instances within the supply system and other instances because consignments were unable to be married up with aircraft in a timely manner. In particular there had been a number of opportunity aircraft flying into Bougainville which have been poorly utilised.
>
> The LST was structured on very light manning on the basis of receiving regular and responsive resupply from Australia. The commitment to provide the latter has changed, and it may be appropriate to reconsider a number of key premises regarding the structure and operation of the LST. If this would occur, we would need to increase the holdings of some critical items in order to ensure greater redundancy [spare capacity] on the ground. Holdings of repair parts would also need to be to be increased in Bougainville with the additional manning required to manage those holdings.[21]

Culleton passed Rogers' concerns through staff channels to distribution staff at the DNSDC and supply staff at HQ Support Command. There is no evidence that anything was done to implement Rogers' recommendations.[22] The air force freight handlers continued to off-load and delay Operation *Bel Isi* consignments *en route*. Distribution staff delivered consignments of stores for Bougainville, either boxed or not, to Richmond Air Base for onward movement on the next available aircraft. They left it to someone else to pack, load and dispatch consignments. Once Operation *Bel Isi* consignments were picked up in accordance with air force priorities, aircraft flying north often stopped off at Amberley Air Base near Brisbane and Townsville Air Base to refuel and take on further consignments. On several occasions, Bougainville consignments were off-loaded to make way for consignments assessed by air force freight movements staff to be of a higher priority. Thus, Bougainville consignments remained at Richmond until they came to the head of the air freight queue, and they began to accumulate in hangers at Amberley and Townsville awaiting onward movement when there was space available on transiting aircraft. There was no automated means to identify when, where or why air force staff off-loaded Operation *Bel Isi* consignments, or when they were likely to be loaded for onward movement again. Bags of mail were in stranded consignments waiting in Sydney or off-loaded at Amberley and Townsville. No one was counting the mail bags into the air force air freight system and verifying their arrival in Bougainville. Intermittent mail diminished the morale of those serving in Bougainville, who were disappointed because their Operation was only a few hours flight time from Townsville.[23]

By mid-February 1998, the ADF resupply system into Bougainville was becoming more unreliable and the NZDF system had virtually stopped. Roger's staff had submitted just over 850 demands for resupply during the previous 10-week period. An average of 56 per cent of demands arrived on time, 28 per cent arrived over two weeks late and a further five per cent arrived over four weeks late. Just over 10 per cent of demands failed to arrive at all. During the same period, his staff submitted 770 demands to the NZDF logistic system under combined logistic support arrangements agreed by the ADF and NZDF. An average of 16 per cent was satisfied on time, with a further 14 per cent arriving over two weeks late. By the end of the period, 68 per cent of demands had not been met at all. After 31 January 1998, the NZ resupply system shut down, leaving 90 per cent of outstanding demands unsatisfied.[24]

It was somewhat ironic that Colonel Wilkinson, who had failed in his quest to be appointed Joint Logistic Commander in December, arrived at Arawa on 15 February 1998 to take over from Colonel Steve Joske as Chief of Staff. He received a personal insight into the problems of resupply. His trunk containing his personal effects was off-loaded without his knowledge or consent in Townsville. Subsequently, it took 10 days for his trunk to reach him in Bougainville.[25] By the time Wilkinson arrived, Rogers had handed over to Major

Kim Faithfull and returned to Australia. Before his departure, Rogers wrote in his final report that air resupply arrangements and lack of spare parts were limiting operational effectiveness.[26]

By the end of February 1998, Hickling was frustrated with the management of re-supply to Bougainville. He directed the acting Commander LSF, Lieutenant Colonel Craig Boyd, to manage demands from the TMG and to monitor and trouble shoot the Operation *Bel Isi* resupply system. The provision of logistic watchkeepers in Culleton's operations room had failed. The Operation *Bel Isi* Coordination Cell at DNSDC was disbanded. Yet again the ADF's national distribution organisation had proved to be base-centric and unresponsive. The ADF's 1 JMOVGP proved to be a booking agency rather than a logistic agency, monitoring the movement and delivery of consignments. The air force air freight system continued to disappoint. Hickling, and his staff had failed to ensure a responsive resupply chain to a deployed force, just as Arnison and his staff had failed to do so for Operation *Lagoon*, and Major General Murray Blake, the Land Commander in 1993, and his staff had failed to do so for Operation *Solace* in Somalia. None of these officers had authority or control over the enabling logistic organisations or transport assets.

In an effort to improve the management of the Operation *Bel Isi* resupply system, Boyd established a 24-hour-a-day logistic operations room, dubbed the Logistic Management Centre, run by captains and warrant officers at HQ LSF. He and his staff performed the functions of processing, monitoring and troubleshooting the supply chain for Operation *Bel Isi*, but were not given any authority over enabling agencies operating the chain or access to Hickling to discuss resupply issues. Operations and logistic staff at Land Headquarters ensured that they would still be conduits to Hickling on issues related to Operation *Bel Isi*.[27] Thus, Boyd had responsibility for the performance of the resupply system, but no authority to report directly to Hickling (who commanded ADF participation in Operation *Bel Isi*) or to influence the air freight system.

In March 1998, staff at the Logistic Management Centre managed to improve the resupply and air movements system substantially by hectoring distribution staff at DNSDC and staff at supply depots. Though there was no automated cargo visibility system in the air force freight system, Boyd's staff monitored the movement of consignments by telephone. He requested that army corporals from Joint Movements Control Offices at Amberley and Townsville search air force aircraft for Operation *Bel Isi* consignments wherever those aircraft might be in the air force system. The dogged approach of these corporals kept Operation *Bel Isi* consignments on aircraft and moved off-loaded consignments back onto transiting aircraft as well as ensuring a regular delivery of mail bags.[28]

For the first time, a group of logisticians led by an experienced logistic commander followed up on every supply demand, and manually tracked every

Operation *Bel Isi* consignment through the air freight system. Boyd and his staff, with the assistance of communications specialists from the army's 145 Signals Squadron, developed software to automate the processing and tracking of demands for items of supply dubbed LNIDS—Logistic National Interim Demand System. For the first time in its history, the ADF had an automated system of following the progress of demands for an offshore operation—from the time they were raised to the time when they were delivered.

The transfer of day-to-day logistic management to HQ LSF proved to be timely. In April 1998, the TMG was about to transition under a new mandate called the Lincoln Agreement to an Australian-led Peace Monitoring Group (PMG). On 4 March, Brigadier Roger Mortlock's replacement, Colonel Jerry Mataparae, distributed a brief on preparing the TMG for a reduced New Zealand presence.[29] He recommended an abrupt reduction of numbers of NZDF personnel from 160 to 30 and return of selected vehicles, stores and equipment to New Zealand. He envisaged achieving the transition by 30 April. He was trying to draw in ADF resources as soon as possible to achieve this transition.

Wilkinson had been aware of the New Zealand policy to minimise support to Operation *Bel Isi* soon after his arrival in mid-February. Indeed, Baker recalled later that the NZDF had been trying to maximise ADF support and minimise their own from the inception of New Zealand diplomatic initiatives to seek a political solution to the Bougainville Crisis.[30] Wilkinson had also become concerned about the serviceability of NZDF vehicles and radio equipment. Unroadworthy vehicles and faulty radio equipment increased the risk of accidents and breakdown in communications during emergencies when patrols were away from base camps. Beginning on 1 March, Wilkinson began sending special situation reports to Hickling describing the deterioration in safety and operational effectiveness caused by vehicle and radio unserviceability. Risk was also accumulating because the NZDF was not replacing those NZDF Special Forces personnel who had completed their tours of duty. In their stead came inexperienced drivers, medics and radio operators.[31] Wilkinson wrote on 5 and 6 March specifying the challenges Mataparae and he faced trying to get sufficient NZDF support.[32] Mataparae and senior officers in New Zealand were at loggerheads over safety issues related to the numbers of helicopters and air hours; the serviceability of vehicles and communications equipment; supply issues, such as spare parts; the replacement of Special Forces personnel; and lack of canteen services. After not receiving reinforcement and satisfactory resupply in the first week of March, the RNZAF advised that the next resupply flight would not arrive before 18 March 1998.

Wilkinson now requested 10 Land Cruisers and Australian drivers with radio communications skills to be dispatched urgently to ensure that team operations could be conducted safely. He also sought support to establish a back-up ADF tactical communications network to guarantee communications in an emergency. He wanted experienced Australian driver/signallers assigned to each monitoring team to ensure that each team had an experienced operator at its base camp 24 hours a day. He assured Hickling that ADF personnel would be safe in monitoring teams now that Bougainvillean moderates had convinced hard-liners that the ADF would have to assume control because the New Zealanders could not be expected to meet the costs of monitoring operations indefinitely.[33]

Connolly directed Hickling not to act upon Wilkinson's requests until further clarification was sought from the NZDF. In Wilkinson's opinion, the achievement of TMG objectives and the safety of monitoring team personnel were now being threatened by New Zealand pride and Australian stubbornness. Nothing was being done about the serviceability of vehicles or radio equipment. Of the 23 NZDF vehicles located with monitoring teams, 12 were off the road; and team commanders were operating most of the remaining vehicles in an unroadworthy condition.[34]

By the second week of March, the situation on the ground in Bougainville with vehicle and radio serviceability was not improving. The promised experienced drivers had not arrived from New Zealand. The NZDF was not improving the supply of spare parts or sending replacement vehicles. On Monday 9 March 1998, David Ritchie, First Assistant Secretary South Pacific, Africa and Middle East Division, at the Australian Department of Foreign Affairs and Trade (DFAT), spoke with Admiral Chris Barrie, the Vice Chief of the Defence Force (VCDF), at an inter-departmental meeting. Ritchie made it clear to him that the situation on the ground in Bougainville was unsafe and endangered Australian Public Service (APS) monitors. He referred to Wilkinson's signals that had been passed to him by Reece Puddicombe, the Australian diplomat serving as the Deputy Commander of the TMG. Ritchie recommended immediate action to clarify the situation on the ground and to determine the way ahead for logistic support.

Barrie reacted to Ritchie's recommendation by contacting Connolly and directing him or Hickling to proceed to Bougainville and take every necessary action. Connolly was reported to have been irritated by this unexpected intervention from Canberra and the release of Wilkinson's correspondence to DFAT.[35] Connolly wrote to Barrie on 12 March suggesting that Wilkinson had been guilty of 'special pleading' outside his chain of command and that he had provided unbalanced reports.[36] Nonetheless, Connolly directed his staff to facilitate the deployment of 10 Land Cruisers and drivers.

Baker appointed Brigadier Bruce Osborn, a senior officer with years of recent experience specialising in intelligence, as the first commander of the new PMG that would be established under the Lincoln Agreement. Connolly signed his directive to Osborn on 29 April 1998, the day before he took command.[37]

Connolly would retain 'theatre' command and delegate 'operational command' to Hickling, including administration and logistic support.[38] Connolly stated that Australia's military strategic intent was 'to conduct peace monitoring group operations in accordance with the Lincoln Agreement, and to that end you are required to ensure that the monitoring and reporting are to remain the main effort'. Connolly directed Osborn

> to manage a phased transition from the current predominantly military operation to a civil commercial undertaking as soon as feasible [and] to co-ordinate the transition to civil and commercial arrangements in a way that focuses combined efforts and does not compromise the impartiality of the PMG, yet still allows effective monitoring of the situation on Bougainville during the time of increasing political and reconstruction activity.[39]

On 5 May 1998, Osborn received a written directive from Hickling detailing his responsibilities and reporting obligations.[40] Though not differing substantially from Connolly's directive, it did formalise that Osborn was serving two masters and had two lines of reporting and communication. Connolly's directive also confirmed that navy vessels and air force aircraft moving in and out of Osborn's area of operations (AO) would remain under operational control of the Maritime and Air commanders. Though titled, 'Combined Force Commander' and 'Joint Task Force Commander' respectively, Connolly and Osborn were neither.

Immediately after arrival, Osborn began sensitive negotiations to ensure that the parties to a ceasefire agreement, signed on HMAS *Tobruk* at Loloho on 30 April 1998, would comply with the conditions of that agreement.[41] Unhelpfully, Francis Ona, self-proclaimed President of an independent Bougainville and hard-line secessionist, delivered public and private threats to the PMG.[42] Osborn presented Connolly with his assessment of the future of the PMG during his initial visit to Bougainville on 27 May 1998.[43] In his opinion, Connolly and Baker were overly focused on extracting the ADF from Bougainville as soon as possible, and handing the task over to DFAT and the Australian Government's overseas aid program, AusAID. In Osborn's view, they did not appear to appreciate the complexity and exhausting nature of negotiations and the fractiousness of armed groups in Bougainville, or that there was an ever-present danger of a return to fighting.[44] Osborn was drawn to his DFAT confidants, who worked closely with him on a daily basis to facilitate progress towards a political solution to the Bougainville Crisis. Since taking command on 1 May 1998, Osborn found that his most important advisor was his Australian chief negotiator, Greg Moriarty, and his most important strategic level confidant was David Ritchie, who attended all of the key negotiations and had an astute understanding of the issues in Bougainville and Papua New Guinea (PNG). Ritchie in Canberra, along with Ambassador David Irvine and his staff in Port Moresby, provided the political 'back stopping' that Osborn sought. Like Osborn, Ritchie assessed that the future of the PMG should be decided by events rather than by a timeline, and that the continued participation of the ADF would be crucial for success.[45] Osborn felt that Operation *Bel Isi* required 'a whole–of-government approach', but that this was not being achieved because Connolly and Baker wanted to withdraw ADF assets.[46]

Though the PMG was evolving into a reasonably capable *ad hoc* regional peacekeeping organisation—one well-supported by an intensively managed supply chain from Australia, as at July 1998 there were still problems with monitoring operations and morale.[47] The internal and external political and cultural dimensions of the PMG's mission were still immature. Much of the internal friction as well as politically and culturally insensitive behaviour were due to poor selection and inadequate pre-deployment training of both Australian and New Zealand personnel.[48] Specific force preparation and rotation were not working effectively. Some Australian and New Zealand personnel remained ignorant of the cultures of the Fijians and Ni Vanuatu, and were also antagonistic to their more relaxed South Pacific colleagues. This attitude also applied to Bougainvilleans. Some Australian and New Zealand patrol commanders had been making political gaffes in their addresses to village gatherings that exposed their ignorance of the origins and nature of the Bougainvillean Crisis and Bougainvillean culture.[49]

Specific force preparation and rotation for the transition from the TMG to the PMG had not been well-designed. Pre-deployment administration and training for the Australian contingents at Randwick was unsatisfactory. Many Australian personnel had to endure late warning for deployment and poor administrative support from their units and higher headquarters.[50] Often they had received either incorrect or insufficient information on what personal equipment and clothing to take to Bougainville. Those assigned to monitoring teams felt that they received insufficient relevant information on the political and cultural dimensions of monitoring operations. Despite being located at Randwick Barracks alongside Rogers, and his men and women who had served in Bougainville with the TMG, no Australians who had served with the TMG were invited to brief the next rotation of personnel during their pre-deployment training on conditions in Bougainville.[51] It appeared that the enabling ADF personnel management agencies and staff at the Deployed Forces Support Unit were unable to properly select and prepare ADF personnel for politically or culturally sensitive regional force projection.

On 29 July 1998, Osborn took the opportunity, during a visit by the newly appointed Land Commander, Major General John Hartley, to air his concerns about a range of issues that he assessed were impeding him in achieving his mission.⁵² One of Osborn's key areas of concern, aside from insufficient 'political backstopping' by his military chain of command and a lack of a 'whole-of-government' approach, was intelligence. He raised his concerns during Hartley's visit, as well as in a letter on 9 August 1998 and in his post-Operation report on 20 October. Frustrated at the lack of improvement in intelligence arrangements over the six months of his time in Bougainville, he was scathing in his assessment of the Defence Intelligence Organisation (DIO), Connolly's Australian Theatre Joint Intelligence Centre (ASTJIC) and the Office of National Assessments (ONA) in Canberra.⁵³ He noted that ASTJIC had provided one substantive assessment of the future of the peace process, and that the last advice from DIO had been in January 1998. He wrote:

> My real concerns at the time [9 August] was that I was basically having to operate in an information vacuum because of very limited collection and processing capabilities in the PMG and that we were seeing virtually no reporting on Bougainville from DIO, ONA and ASTJIC.⁵⁴

He concluded his criticisms by stating: 'I still remain concerned with the continuing low level of intelligence support available to the PMG from outside the theatre.' He pointed out that the PMG had 'regularly articulated its information requirements to the theatre level [ASTJIC], [but that] 'the PMG [never] received any advice from the theatre level as to how or when it would meet the PMG's requirements'.⁵⁵

After apprising Hartley of a range of problems in July 1998, there was a steady improvement in force preparation, rotation and logistics for Operation *Bel Isi*. He wrote, just before his tour of duty ended in October 1998, that, 'the level of support provided by LHQ [Land Headquarters] and the LSF are of the highest order and staffs are to be congratulated on the improvements that have been implemented over recent months'.⁵⁶ He commented that

> the overall coordination and effectiveness of supply will [not] be further improved until a single person is made responsible for overseeing the supply and delivery of all *matériel* to the PMG regardless of the sourcing Service. I believe that this will not be possible until a Joint Logistic Command is established. In the meantime, we welcome LCAUST's [Land Commander—Australia] recent decision to place the LSF in direct support of the PMG and note there has already been a significant improvement in the responsiveness of the LSF as a result.⁵⁷

Osborn's period of command ended on 15 October 1998. Prospects for the peace process were still uncertain, though the initial truce and ceasefire had held for 12 months since the Burnham II talks in October 1997. There was plenty of unfinished business to keep his successor, Brigadier Roger Powell, busy. The election of a Bougainville Reconciliation Government was dependent on agreements on governance for Bougainville that would take some time to conclude and involve an amendment to the PNG Constitution—another lengthy process. If legislation was not enacted to make way for autonomy, Bougainvillean moderates would face significant pressure from hard-line secessionists to withdraw from the peace process. Thus, with issues perilously balanced, Osborn left Bougainville and Powell began his six month tour of duty.

Observations

The first 10 months of Operation *Bel Isi* demonstrated that Baker's introduction of Connolly and his headquarters, as well as Mueller and his headquarters, into the chain of command for ADF operations was not working. Command, control and communications as well as resupply of spare parts had not improved substantially since operations in Somalia in 1993 and Operation *Lagoon* in 1994.[58] Unity of command was not achieved. Theory was not validated in practice. Joske, Wilkinson and Osborn all reported to two commanders simultaneously. Connolly retained what he called 'theatre command' for Operation *Bel Isi*, and 'operational command of reactive force protection operations', while delegating overall operational command to Hickling as a lead joint commander.

Baker's efforts to establish an effective permanent joint force headquarters and to delegate responsibility for synchronisation of the environmental commands and joint logistic support for ADF operations were not achieving success on the ground. Theoretical expectations of cooperation and synergy between the environmental commanders, the Service chiefs and the Service logistic commanders were not met. It might have been different if Connolly had been a three-star officer and been given full command over the environmental commanders, as well as their staffs, rather than having to coax them and have his small joint staff groups merely interact. However, Connolly appeared to be facing deeply-rooted resistance from the three powerful Service tribes to joint command. General Peter Gration, General John Baker and Admiral Alan Beaumont had been unable to exercise effective joint command for recent joint operations, so it was unsurprising that Connolly found it difficult during Operation *Bel Isi*. He was impeded by sharing the same rank as his subordinate commanders, his lack of authority over maritime and air assets for deployment and resupply, and naïve expectations of collegial cooperation between Service commanders and their staffs and his small joint staff groups.

Baker's appointment of Mueller as a joint logistic commander did not result in effective joint force sustainment for Operation *Bel Isi*. Based on Rogers' tactical level reports of faulty resupply, Mueller may have had command over service logistic commanders, but navy and air force transport assets remained outside his influence. Fleet managers from Headquarters Support Command–Australia (HQ SCA), formerly Logistic Command, and distributors and fleet managers from DNSDC, formerly Moorebank Logistic Group, as well as staff at ALG, controlled the ways and means to support Operation *Bel Isi*. The same competing priorities that were extant in 1993 for supporting a battalion group in Somalia applied again in 1998, because the core business of these agencies was providing logistic and movements services to the ADF in Australia, not to offshore land operations. Like Connolly, Mueller faced resistance to joint command and control of logistic resources and maritime and air assets for operations.

Hickling declined to press Connolly to appoint a logistic component commander to coordinate joint logistic support for Operation *Bel Isi*. Aside from the results of his staff's operational analysis of Operations *Morris Dance*, *Solace* and *Lagoon*, he had no precedents to follow. The *Kangaroo* series of exercises in northern Australia did not rehearse joint force sustainment under a joint logistic commander. For the time being, Mueller had responsibility for coordinating joint logistic support for Operation *Bel Isi*. He may not have welcomed the appointment of a joint logistic commander at Connolly's headquarters. In 1993, General Officer Commanding Logistic Command might have been equally resistant to such an appointment in Land Headquarters, because resupply to offshore operations was his responsibility.

From the perspective of the functions of force projection, Operation *Bel Isi* was not all bad news. Hickling, his successor (Hartley) and staff at Land Headquarters maintained habitual links with DFAT for APS peace monitor training. These links doubled as early warning of Australian Government considerations for taking military action. Hartley, like Hickling, wished to avoid being forced into rushed planning and preparation for future offshore operations because he and his senior staff were not included in initial strategic-level contingency planning. Habitual links strengthened between Land Headquarters, the Deployable Joint Force Headquarters (DJFHQ) in Brisbane and 3rd Brigade to ensure that information on possible contingencies was passed quickly in an environment of trust, rather than one characterised by fear of leaks. Staff from Land Headquarters conducted seminars for DJFHQ and 3rd Brigade on lessons from previous short notice deployments, such as Operation *Solace* (to Somalia), Operation *Tamar* (to Rwanda) and Operation *Lagoon* (to Bougainville) that emphasised making good use of warning time that would more often come from the media in general, and Cable News Network (CNN) in particular, rather than the ADF chain of command. Based on the adage that '50 per cent of solving a problem is knowing what it is', commanders and staff learned from these seminars how to anticipate and manage risk factors, such as numbers caps; short notice for preparation; raising *ad hoc* headquarters; and unresponsive logistics, including inefficient air resupply.[59]

One of the major enhancements for force projection derived from Operation *Bel Isi* was in supply chain management. Osborn's post-Operation report testified to his satisfaction. Hartley's decision to place newly-promoted Brigadier Jeff

Wilkinson and his LSF in direct support of Operation *Bel Isi* removed Land Headquarters, a logistic support 'post office', from being accountable for the performance of the supply chain. Hartley did not have the authority to create a joint logistic commander, but he made force sustainment a subordinate command—not a subordinate staff—responsibility. The Logistic Management Centre, backed by the authority and experience of a one-star logistic commander, proved to be more effective in improving the ADF supply chain to a deployed force than the *ad hoc* Operation *Bel Isi* Coordination Cell at DNSDC, which had failed almost immediately in 1998.

The arrangements that Hartley put in place to anticipate short notice force projections, to educate subordinate headquarters and formations, and to improve force sustainment, recognised lessons from the past and trends evident for the future. These arrangements reduced, but did not remove, the element of risk from Australian force projection created by higher-level ADF command and logistic arrangements. The ADF still did not have a military commander-in-chief for operations and a permanent joint force headquarters with the authority and resources to deliver prompt, strong and smart force projection as part of a 'whole-of-government' response to international or regional events. The ADF also lacked a permanent joint logistic commander or headquarters capable of establishing and managing supply chains to deployed forces—whether they were deployed for Australian territorial operations or further afield.

For the time being, the Land Commander and his operations staff, supported by Commander LSF and his headquarters, made the military mechanics of Operation *Bel Isi* work. Concurrently, informal links with DFAT created an early-warning mechanism for force projection as well as establishing an informal inter-departmental conduit for the political and cultural dimensions of force projection into Australia's near region. These *ad hoc* arrangements made Operation *Bel Isi* an exemplar of sustained force projection, but they would only work if the Land Commander was in command. The challenge for Baker, Connolly and Mueller was to learn from Operation *Bel Isi* and put in place arrangements that would make joint command of operations, with accompanying logistic support, work more effectively.

ENDNOTES

[1] See Bob Breen, *A Little Bit of Hope, Australian Force—Somalia*, Allen and Unwin, Sydney, 1998.

[2] Diary entry, Lieutenant Colonel Paul Rogers, 5 December 1997.

[3] Diary entry, Lieutenant Colonel Paul Rogers, 5 December 1997.

[4] The author attended all meetings at Land Headquarters related to these matters and received briefings on outcomes of meetings at HQ AST from Land Headquarters staff.

[5] The author attended a meeting between Colonel Jeff Wilkinson and Major General Frank Hickling on Monday 24 November 1997.

[6] The author attended a meeting between Wilkinson and Hickling on Monday 24 November 1997.

[7] HQ NZDF, 'Combined Australia—New Zealand Logistic Support Plan *Bel Isi* Truce Monitoring Operations on Bougainville', NZDF03130/PNG/1, 4 December 1997. Signed by Commodore Mark J. Wardlaw, RNZN, Assistant Chief of the Defence Force (Operations) and Major General Jim M. Connolly, Commander Australian Theatre. Copy held by the author. Major General Frank J. Hickling, 'Admin Instr 01/97—OP *Bel Isi* 051210LDEC 97', 5 December 1997, K97-01255, NAA, Sydney. Copy held by author.

[8] HQ New Zealand Defence Force, 'Combined Australia—New Zealand Logistic Support Plan', p. 5.

[9] See HQ New Zealand Defence Force, 'Combined Australia—New Zealand Logistic Support Plan', pp. 5 and 7, for New Zealand arrangements; and pp.8 and 9 for Australian arrangements. Hickling, Admin Instr 01/97, pp. 1, 2 and 4 restated ADF arrangements.

[10] HQ New Zealand Defence Force, 'Combined Australia—New Zealand Logistic Support Plan', p. 8.

[11] The author attended these discussions in early December 1997.

[12] Lieutenant Colonel Paul M. Rogers, 'Administration for the Truce Monitoring Group', Annex C to proposed 1 Australian Service Contingent Operation *Bel Isi* Report, p. 1. Forwarded to author on 13 August 1998 with a covering note advising that the annex was intended for inclusion in a Post Operations Report from Australian Service Commander 1, but Colonel Steve Joske did not produce a Post Operations Report.

[13] Rogers, 'Administration for the Truce Monitoring Group', Annex C to proposed 1 Australian Service Contingent Operation *Bel Isi* Report, p. 4, paragraphs 21–23. Also Major Neil Smith, 'Morning Situation Report', 20 January 1998, 'the joint movements group in NZ are not receiving timed information on RAAF flights in and out of theatre. I am not sure whether the problem is at Air Command in Australia or 1 JMOVGP. JMOVNZ would appreciate being informed of flight schedules.' Smith was ADF Liaison Officer at Land Force Headquarters in Auckland. He wrote several reports in January about lack of coordination of resupply flights.

[14] Rogers, 'Administration for the Truce Monitoring Group', Annex C to proposed 1 Australian Service Contingent Operation *Bel Isi* Report, p. 4, paragraphs 21–23. Also Smith, 'Morning Situation Report', 20 January 1998.

[15] Rogers, 'Administration for the Truce Monitoring Group', p. 4.

[16] Lieutenant Colonel Paul M. Rogers, 'Satisfaction of Demands for OP BEL ISI', LST 05/98, HQ TMG 611-1-1, 23 January 1998. Lieutenant Colonel Paul M. Rogers, 'Satisfaction of Demands for OP BEL ISI', LST 06/98, HQ TMG 611-1-1, 24 January 1998. Copies held by author.

[17] The key items requiring spare parts at the time were Land Cruisers and Land Rovers, LCM8 landing craft, generators and refrigerators.

[18] Lieutenant Colonel Paul M. Rogers, 'OP *Bel Isi* LST LOGREP 01/98 for Period ending 30 Jan 98', LST 19/98, 31 January 1998, HQ TMG 611-1-1. Copy held by author.

[19] Rogers, 'Satisfaction of Demands for OP BEL ISI', 23 January 1998.

[20] Lieutenant Colonel Paul M. Rogers, Minutes 5/98 and 6/98 of 23 and 24 January 1998 respectively. Lieutenant Colonel Paul M. Rogers, 'OP BEL ISI LST LOGREP 02/98 for Period Ending 7 February 1998', LST Minute 23/98, 7 February 1998, HQ TMG 611-1-1. Copies held by author.

[21] Rogers, Minute 5/98, p. 2.

[22] The author reviewed numerous emails and signals from Land Headquarters to 1 JMOVGP and to the Sydney Joint Movements Control Office (JMCO) at the time, drawing attention to 'lost' consignments and the possible need to re-order items of supply from DNSDC if they could not be found. Presumably JMCO staff passed these concerns onto air force staff at ALG, Richmond.

[23] Diary entry, Lieutenant Colonel Paul Rogers, 2 January 1998. Copy held by author.

[24] Rogers, 'Administration for the Truce Monitoring Group', attached tables Sheet 1 and 2. Copy held by the author.

[25] Colonel Jeff B. Wilkinson, Conversations with author in Bougainville in February 1998. The author was in Bougainville conducting research at the time.

[26] Rogers, 'Administration for the Truce Monitoring Group', p. 5.

[27] The author discussed these issues with Lieutenant Colonel Boyd in February 1998.

[28] The author's discussions with Boyd; also the author's personal observations during several visits in Sydney and Bougainville.

[29] Colonel Jerry Mataparae, 'Preparing the TMG for a Reduced NZ Presence', LHQ Operations Log, 4 March 1998. Copy held by author.

30 General John S. Baker in interview with author, 30 August 2005.

31 Colonel Jeff B. Wilkinson, 'Special Commanders SITREP OP BEL ISI', LHQ Operations Log, 1 March 1998; and Colonel Jeff B. Wilkinson, Commander's Diaries, Land Headquarters.

32 Colonel Jeff B. Wilkinson, 'Special Commanders SITREP OP BEL ISI', LHQ Operations Log, 5 March 1998; Colonel Jeff B Wilkinson, 'Special Commanders SITREP OP BEL ISI', LHQ Operations Log, 6 March 1998; and Wilkinson, Commander's Diaries, Land Headquarters.

33 Wilkinson, 'Special Commanders SITREP', 5 March 1998.

34 Wilkinson, 'Special Commanders SITREP', 6 March 1998.

35 Colonel John Culleton in interview with author, 1 November 1997.

36 Major General Jim M. Connolly, 'Rectification of TMG Capability Deficiencies', 12 March 1998; and Wilkinson, Commander's Diaries, Land Headquarters.

37 Major General Jim M. Connolly, 'Directive by Combined Force Commander to 44087 BRIG B. V. Osborn, Commander Peace Monitoring Group for Operation *Bel Isi* Phase II', COMAST Directive No 19/98, HQAST 455/98, 29 April 1998, HQAST 612-10-3, 29 April 1998, HQ AST, Potts Point.

38 Connolly, 'Directive by Combined Force Commander to 44087 BRIG B.V. Osborn, Commander Peace Monitoring Group for Operation *Bel Isi* Phase II', COMAST Directive No 19/98, HQAST 455/98, 29 April 1998, HQAST 612-10-3, 29 April 1998, HQ AST, Potts Point, p. 3.

39 Connolly, 'Directive by Combined Force Commander to 44087 BRIG B.V. Osborn, Commander Peace Monitoring Group for Operation *Bel Isi* Phase II', COMAST Directive No 19/98, HQAST 455/98, 29 April 1998, HQAST 612-10-3, 29 April 1998, HQ AST, Potts Point, p. 3.

40 Major General Frank J. Hickling, 'Directive by Land Commander—Australia Directive to 44087 BRIG B.V. Osborn, Commander Peace Monitoring Group and Commander Joint Task Force 106', Directive 26/98, 5 May 1998, K97-01211; and Brigadier Bruce V. Osborn Commander's Diaries, Land Headquarters.

41 Copies of briefs, minutes and records of conversations are located in Osborn's Commander's Diaries at Land Headquarters. Also Brigadier Bruce V. Osborn in interview with author, 23 July 1998.

42 Copies of letters from Francis Ona to Brigadier Bruce V. Osborn are located in Osborn's Commander's Diaries, Land Headquarters.

43 Brigadier Bruce V. Osborn, 'Concept of Operations—PMG Operations on (sic) Bougainville', 4 June 1998, HQ TMG 611-1-1. Copy held by author.

44 Brigadier Bruce V. Osborn in interview with author, 29 July 1998.

45 Osborn in interview with author, 29 July 1998.

46 Osborn in interview with author, 29 July 1998.

47 Brigadier Bruce V. Osborn, 'OP *Bel Isi* II: Post Operation Report—BRIG B.V. Osborn', Peace Monitoring Group, Arawa Youth Centre, 20 October 1998, pp.7–9, K97-01211, NAA, Sydney.

48 Osborn, 'OP *Bel Isi* II: Post Operation Report—BRIG B.V. Osborn', Peace Monitoring Group, Arawa Youth Centre, 20 October 1998, pp. 6–7.

49 Osborn in interview with author, 29 July 1998.

50 Lieutenant Colonel Gary R. Banister, 'Chief of Staff Post Deployment Report', HQ PMG, 11 August 1998, pp. 1–3. Copy in Brigadier Bruce V. Osborn's Commander's Diaries, Land Headquarters. Banister was Chief of Staff PMG from 1 May 1998 to 31 August 1998. His report summarised the ineffectiveness of specific force preparation and rotation.

51 Major Paul M. Nothard in interview with author, 25 July 1998 (Nothard was the operations officer at Monitoring Team Buin); Corporal Laura Kenny in interview with author, 25 July 1998. (Kenny was a linguist and intelligence operator at Monitoring Team Buin); M.J. Byrne in interview with author, 27 July 1998 (Byrne was an APS peace monitor at Monitoring Team Wakunai); and Major David J. Bartlett in interview with author, 28 July 1998 (Bartlett was operations officer at Monitoring Team Arawa).

52 Brigadier Bruce V. Osborn, 'Discussion Points—LCAUST, 29 Jul 98', 29 July 1998'. Copy located in Osborn's Commander's Diaries. Copy also held by author.

53 Osborn, 'Operation *Bel Isi* II: Post Operation Report', pp. 6–8.

54 Osborn, 'Operation *Bel Isi* II: Post Operation Report', p. 6.

55 Osborn, 'Operation *Bel Isi* II: Post Operation Report', p. 7.

56 Osborn, 'Operation *Bel Isi* II: Post Operation Report', pp. 8–9.

57 Osborn, 'Operation *Bel Isi* II: Post Operation Report', p. 9.

[58] Brigadier Bruce V. Osborn, 'OP *Bel Isi*—Communications Report', PMG 001/98, X687/98, 3 June 1998. Commander's Diaries, Land Headquarters. Osborn wrote a covering letter to a report by his signals officer Captain Stokes entitled 'X6 Post Operational Report' which was submitted unsigned on 28 May 1998. Stokes identified difficulties caused by an unclear relationship between HQ AST and Land Headquarters on the subject of communications, as well as highlighting a number of challenges he faced with *ad hoc* staffing caused by the numbers cap and inexperienced staff. He emphasised that an inefficient resupply of equipment, batteries and parts, 'had a significant effect on operational capability at the time'.

[59] The author conducted these seminars and maintained links on behalf of the LCAUST.

Chapter 11

Projection to East Timor

In August 1942 in New Guinea during the Second World War and in 1966 in Vietnam an accumulation of risks resulted in a small number of Australian troops facing several thousand well-equipped, well-trained and more experienced enemy troops. Fortunately, climate, terrain and the resilience of junior leaders and small teams, as well as effective artillery support in 1966, offset the numerical and tactical superiority of their opponents. Australian troops prevailed against the odds. If either of these two tactical tipping points had gone the other way, there would have been severe strategic embarrassment for Australia. There could have been public pressure for a change in Government and investigations into the competence of the Australian armed forces.

For 48 hours in September 1999, renegade members of the Indonesian military forces and their East Timorese auxiliaries provoked members of an Australian vanguard of the International Force—East Timor (INTERFET) in the streets of the East Timor capital, Dili. Indonesians outnumbered Australians, who carried only limited quantities of ammunition.[1] On the night of 21 September, a 600-strong East Timorese territorial battalion confronted a 40-strong Australian vehicle checkpoint on Dili's main road. Good luck, superior night-fighting technology, the presence of armoured vehicles and discipline under pressure resulted in another historic tactical tipping point going Australia's way. Had there been an exchange of fire that night, there would have been heavy casualties on both sides and several hours of confused fighting between Australian, Indonesian and East Timorese territorial troops. There was also potential for Indonesian and Australian naval vessels to have clashed as Australian ships rushed to deliver ammunition to Australian troops, as well as for Australian transport aircraft and helicopters to have been attacked at Dili airport. Australian and Indonesian relations would have plummeted to an historic low, and Australia's reputation in the region and respect as an American ally would have diminished significantly.

This chapter covers the events and an accumulation of risk that influenced Australia's most significant post-Cold War force projection in September 1999 to East Timor. It examines them from the perspective of Australian military self-reliance and competence at the end of the twentieth century.

Command and Control

The quest for an effective way of planning and conducting operations and campaigns continued in 1998. Close to the second anniversary of Rear Admiral

Chris Oxenbould's submission to the Chiefs of Staff Committee (COSC), Major General Jim Connolly submitted a 'Mid Trial' report on 1 December 1998, as his period as Commander Australian Theatre (COMAST) drew to a close, to demonstrate the efficacy of Theatre Command.[2] He contended that Theatre Command facilitated rapid development of concepts for operations, speedy formation of joint task forces and a unity of command that was previously lacking in the Australian Defence Force (ADF) joint environment.[3] He regretted that operational circumstances during the initial period of the trial had not provided the opportunity to test his concepts. Little did Connolly know that a strategic surprise awaited Australia in 1999 that would not only test the function of force command but also every other function of Australian military force projection.

Connolly did not overlook logistics, but left unexplained why the Service chiefs and their logistic support commanders would comply with his priorities and directives.[4] Based on Operation *Solace*, Operation *Lagoon* and the first 10 months of Operation *Bel Isi*, it was unlikely that either the Maritime or Air Commander would give Connolly or a joint task force commander control over the means of resupply or a guarantee to deliver. It was also just as unlikely, based on the experience of Operation *Bel Isi*, that Major General Des Mueller and his headquarters in Melbourne could guarantee an efficient supply chain to a deployed force.

On 26 May 1999, the new COMAST, Air Vice Marshal Bob Treloar, submitted a progress report on theatre headquarters development with an accompanying document, 'Concept for the Command of the Australian Theatre'.[5] He echoed his predecessor's assessment of the value of Theatre Command.[6] He concluded that Deployable Joint Force Headquarters (DJFHQ) was 'the ADF's only viable potential major JTFHQ [Joint Task Force Headquarters]'.[7] It remained to be seen whether DJFHQ would work. In reality, DJFHQ was not a truly joint headquarters staffed by all three Services. There was not enough day-to-day work at DJFHQ for navy and air force staff, who were needed to support maritime and air operations at their respective environmental headquarters.

Treloar had not sought to change arrangements, except to diminish the operational role of Northern Command (NORCOM).[8] Expectations of sequential and devolved planning and decision-making remained. Indeed, he expected General John Baker's successor as Chief of the Defence Force (CDF), Admiral Chris Barrie, and his staff to issue 'Military Strategic Estimates' for anticipated contingencies, followed by warning orders and possibly execution orders for preliminary operations, before ministerial and cabinet submissions were submitted.[9] This sequence, or one like it, had not been followed since Australia returned to projecting force beyond Australian territorial waters and air space in 1987. Indeed, the theatre planning process added another sequential layer to a cloistered strategic planning process.[10] Treloar's small joint staff groups would still be left to coordinate environmental headquarters staff, who would remain responsive but not necessarily compliant.

While Treloar was comfortable with evolving arrangements, a group of consultants from PricewaterhouseCoopers were not convinced.[11] They concluded that relations between Headquarters Australian Theatre (HQ AST) and its environmental headquarters were dysfunctional and ineffective. HQ AST was not working cohesively, efficiently or effectively and was not ready to assume leadership of joint operations.[12] Overall, there was an emphasis on process, and not on outcomes, as well as 'a lack of common understanding of shared purpose'. Environmental headquarters staff did not regard HQ AST as 'value adding'.[13]

The PricewaterhouseCoopers report was a contrary opinion. The Theatre Command trial had a further six months to go. Exercise *Crocodile 99*, like the *Kangaroo* series of exercises of the 1980s and early 1990s, was intended to test the effectiveness and efficiency of ADF joint command and control arrangements. The jury was still out on Theatre Command.

Projection to East Timor

On 6 February 1999, the Australian Foreign Minister, Alexander Downer, opined that he expected the East Timorese to reject an Indonesian offer of autonomy within the state of Indonesia and that an international military force would be needed to safeguard East Timor's subsequent journey to nationhood.[14] In early March, he flagged a military role for Australia in East Timor after a referendum that was being negotiated by Indonesia, Portugal and the United Nations.[15] Thus, the ADF was faced with the prospect of a neighbourhood operation in East Timor. There was potential for Australian and Indonesian military forces to have to work closely together there. There was a lot at stake for the Indonesian Army (*Tentara Nasional Indonesia*, or TNI).[16] As the institution charged with the protection of the Indonesian nation-state, TNI would lose face if East Timor achieved independence. Since the invasion in 1975, the Indonesian Army had campaigned unsuccessfully to defeat East Timorese pro-independence forces. Like armies throughout history, the Indonesians had a deep desire to vindicate their blood sacrifice by defeating their enemies.[17] Perhaps more importantly, Indonesian generals would have been concerned that an independent East Timor might also set a precedent and encourage secessionist movements in other provinces. In a relatively new country deeply divided by religion, ethnicity, and cultural traditions, the TNI saw itself as the only organisation capable of protecting the unity and integrity of the Indonesian state.[18]

On 27 April 1999, the Australian Prime Minister, John Howard, met with the Indonesian President, Jusuf Habibie, in Bali to discuss the reported massacres of East Timorese civilians in regional centres and in Dili by pro-integration militia during the previous weeks.[19] Howard's intervention in an internal security matter in an Indonesian province was unprecedented.[20] Several days before this meeting, *The Australian* and the *Sydney Morning Herald* published a Defence Intelligence Organisation (DIO) intelligence assessment on East Timor.[21] It identified the role of TNI in instigating violence through militia surrogates. Notwithstanding this leak, Habibie appeared to welcome Howard's visit and affirmed a partnership between Australia and Indonesia to facilitate a solution to East Timor's political status.[22] The two leaders emerged from their talks issuing assurances that the East Timorese would be given the opportunity to decide their political future in a secure environment.[23]

On 5 May 1999, Habibie signed a tripartite agreement between Indonesia, Portugal and the United Nations for a 'popular consultation' in East Timor in August.[24] If the majority of East Timorese voted 'No' in this ballot and the Indonesian Parliament endorsed the result, then the Indonesian Government would invite the United Nations to assist with the transition of East Timor to nationhood. Given competing interests in East Timor and its violent history since 1975, senior ADF officers, Defence officials and analysts in Canberra and Jakarta must have known that the period leading up to the ballot would be violent and that there was potential for an anarchic aftermath. East Timorese pro-integration and pro-independence factions were vying to win popular support for their causes. The pro-integration side, backed by elements of Indonesia's security forces and military intelligence organisations, were already exerting significant coercive power.[25]

In June and early July 1999, first-hand media reports, protests from the newly-deployed UN Assistance Mission—East Timor (UNAMET) and reports from Australian military liaison officers serving with UNAMET, identified an alarming situation.[26] Local Indonesian Army and police units, members of East Timorese territorial battalions and militia groups were intimidating the population to vote for integration. In these circumstances, Indonesian security forces might be too busy either quelling or instigating unrest to provide security for an emergency evacuation of Australian nationals and UN staff.

In secrecy, contingency planning for an ADF-led evacuation operation in East Timor called *Spitfire* began.[27] Following precedents set in the past, Barrie did not authorise inclusion of representatives from lower levels of command in a strategic-level planning compartment.[28] Later, he commented that the political environment in Canberra was most sensitive due to leaks of information about what the Australian Government knew—or did not know—about the situation in East Timor: 'We were reading about our business in the media every day.'[29] For their part, commanders and staff at lower levels of command in Sydney, Townsville and Darwin kept abreast of unfolding events in East Timor in the media and by following reports from Colonel Paul Symon, an ADF officer, who was a senior UN military liaison officer with UNAMET, and national commander for Operation *Faber*, the ADF's participation in UNAMET.[30] Staff at Land Headquarters convened periodic meetings to discuss the situation in East Timor and intelligence staff provided weekly updates.[31] Major General Peter Cosgrove and his staff at DJFHQ assessed that there might be a need for the ADF to evacuate Australian nationals and UN staff. This operation might also include securing protected areas for those fleeing violence. It would take the United Nations some time to assemble and deploy an international force to East Timor to restore public safety, if the Indonesian Government invited foreign troops to do so.[32]

Barrie, Treloar, Major General John Hartley, the Land Commander, Cosgrove and Commodore Mark Bonser at NORCOM in Darwin and their respective staffs became seized by the fate of UNAMET in East Timor. Whereas previous force projections had not benefited from reconnaissance and first hand intelligence, ADF officers participating in Operation *Faber* gave the ADF eyes and ears in East Timor.[33] Symon visited Darwin on 16 July and was able to brief planning staff from all levels of command in Darwin and also in Sydney and Brisbane via video-conferencing facilities. He recalled that this was a pivotal meeting because he realised how little those he spoke to understood the situation in East Timor, the conditions he was working under or the urgent need to support him with independent secure communications. He was also disappointed with the lack of detail in contingency planning. In his view, extant plans had not changed significantly since he left DJFHQ at short notice to serve with UNAMET in mid-June. He was also concerned that he and his fellow Australian observers were being targeted. All had received death threats and knew that they were under surveillance.[34] Hartley took his staff's advice and arranged for Symon to have secure satellite communications.[35]

Logistics would be the major challenge. Mueller was not a member of the Strategic Command Group (SCG). Consequently, he was not privy to contingency planning. Unauthorised preparations had begun among a group of logisticians from each level of command.[36] From Canberra, Colonel Craig Boyd, Director Joint Logistic Operations and Plans, Brigadier Jeff Wilkinson's erstwhile deputy during the first 12 months of Operation *Bel Isi*, kept Wilkinson informed and provided confidential guidance on prospects in East Timor.[37] For his part, Wilkinson and his two force support battalion (FSB) commanders, Lieutenant Colonels Barry McManus, 9 FSB, and Mick Kehoe, 10 FSB, had already studied options for supporting ADF and coalition operations in East Timor. Wilkinson's Logistic Management Centre was managing a supply chain for Operation *Bel Isi*; so it would be a matter of increasing staff numbers and refining processes and procedures for East Timor. They had shared their findings with Lieutenant Colonel Don Cousins, Cosgrove's senior logistic staff officer, who concurred that there would need to be a terminal in Darwin to receive supplies from around Australia, and possibly overseas, for onward movement to East Timor. Joint

Logistics Unit—North (JLU—N) in Darwin, commanded by Mueller, did not have the capacity or capabilities to command terminal operations or to resupply a force deployed to East Timor. The other complicating factor was that Treloar controlled ADF joint movements in support of the force projection to East Timor, not Barrie and his headquarters, or Cosgrove and his headquarters. In addition, Bonser's Headquarters Northern Command (HQ NORCOM) in Darwin was an obvious but unrehearsed headquarters for mounting base and terminal operations there.[38]

Within the context of Australian force projection, July was a paradoxical month. Foreign Minister Downer and the Defence Minister, John Moore, hinted publicly at Australia's military intentions in East Timor.[39] 1st Brigade in Darwin had been brought up to 28 days' notice to move after Moore announced on 11 March 1999 that there was a need to be prepared for 'contingencies that could arise in the region, including East Timor'.[40] Barrie and his staff were involved in secret contingency planning at Australian Defence Headquarters (ADHQ). Elsewhere in the ADF, unauthorised planning had begun without strategic guidance. In a similar way to Operation *Bel Isi*, the strategic, operational and tactical levels of ADF command split into separate uncoordinated planning processes informed by the media; not by the chain of command or intelligence. The *Sydney Morning Herald* echoed widespread expectations that there would be a breakdown in law and order after the ballot result was announced in early September.[41] It did not appear to be difficult for ordinary Australians to connect the new levels of ADF preparedness and the events in East Timor. Presumably this connection did not escape the Indonesian military and civil authorities who were orchestrating violent intimidation in East Timor. Consequently, Australia's military preparedness to intervene and TNI's intimidation to facilitate a 'Yes' vote were open secrets.

By early August 1999, reports by media and UNAMET representatives in East Timor warned an international audience of the strong likelihood of violence after the ballot result was announced in early September.[42] Images and stories of violence had begun to arouse world public opinion in favour of international intervention. General Wiranto, Defence Minister and TNI Commander-in-Chief, soothed that the TNI and the Indonesian police would maintain law and order after the ballot. However, his forces on the ground allowed violence to occur unchecked in the weeks and days leading up to the ballot.

In secrecy, Brigadier Mark Evans, Commander 3rd Brigade, convened a meeting of his local commanders at his headquarters in Townsville on Sunday 22 August. He briefed them on what he knew of Operation *Spitfire* and discussed other scenarios. Kehoe attended, even though he worked for Brigadier Jeff Wilkinson, and was not one of Evans' subordinate commanders. From that day on, with Wilkinson's encouragement, he attended all of Evans' conferences relating to East Timor and provided whatever assistance he could to contingency planning.

Barrie was maintaining close control of contingency planning in Canberra and forbade planning elsewhere. As was the case in 1966 for the deployment of a 4500-strong task force to Vietnam, the government was highly sensitive to leaks. Barrie was forced to tighten operational security.[43] A high-level defence committee noted later that 'planning at all levels had been inhibited by the compartmentalisation of information, implemented due to previous major security leaks. ... At times lower headquarters felt that there was a lack of strategic guidance.'[44]

This 'lock down' not only left Treloar and his staff waiting for strategic guidance and devolution of planning and decision-making from ADHQ, but also bypassed the Service chiefs. They complained later that they had not fulfilled the role of senior environmental advisors and that their input into the compartmented SCG had been ineffective.[45] Treloar commented at the same meeting that compartmentalisation 'introduced additional risk and costs' and compromised operational security, as lower level commanders and staff guessed or acquired information from other sources'.[46] Interestingly, Barrie's centralisation of both the strategic and operational planning for the projection to East Timor unintentionally emulated what the American Commander-in-Chief in the Pacific (CINCPAC) would have done from his headquarters in Hawaii if the Americans had been planning a similar operation. Barrie planned the East Timor campaign with his Head of Strategic Command Division, Major General Mick Keating, and his joint staff. He did not delegate this work to Treloar and his staff groups, who would have coordinated environmental staff effort. By early August, Cosgrove had become a member of the SCG top-secret compartment. Thus, Barrie and Cosgrove integrated the strategic, operational and tactical levels of command and became partners, in conjunction with Keating, in Australia's most strategically significant force projection since 1942.[47]

Deployment

Defence Minister John Moore ordered Barrie to pre-position forces in northern Australia for an evacuation operation (*Spitfire*) on 26 August 1999.[48] Assigned Special Forces and other force elements had less than 12 hours' warning to pack and move.[49] Personnel were warned after arriving at work on the morning of 27 August and were packed, palletised and flying by mid-afternoon.[50] A joint evacuation force assembled at Tindal airbase south of Darwin under Cosgrove's command. It was a joint force comprised of army troops, supported by *Black Hawk* battlefield helicopters and several C-130 *Hercules* transport aircraft.[51] Alongside in Darwin was HMAS *Jervis Bay,* the navy's fast catamaran. From the perspective of generic and specific force preparation, Operation *Spitfire* was mounted at extremely short notice but was an exemplar of what happens in practice when strategic stakes are high. Though there were many uncertainties ahead, the strategic level of command was engaged and ready to direct the tactical level of command. Barrie and his staff were in contact with Brigadier Jim Molan, the Australian Defence Attaché in Jakarta, who was already in Dili with a small staff group to facilitate cooperation with Indonesian security forces for an evacuation operation and to report back to Barrie on the evolving situation.[52] Keating and Cosgrove monitored the situation closely. The ADF was ready. There was still some way to go, however, if it became necessary for a more substantial force projection to follow an evacuation operation.

By this time, Barrie had appointed Treloar as the ADF's national commander to support operations in East Timor.[53] On 30 August, Treloar appointed Wilkinson as his Logistic Component Commander (LOGCC). Wilkinson had already persuaded Hartley to send McManus and an advance party from 9 FSB to Darwin to receive and dispatch stocks to support a projection into East Timor.[54] For the time being, McManus and his staff focused on supporting the burgeoning evacuation force. Wilkinson had also briefed him to plan to support a larger scale operation in the future.[55] Wilkinson also alerted Hartley to the need to raise a Headquarters Force Logistic Support Group (HQ FLSG) to coordinate logistic support in East Timor, should the Indonesian Government invite a larger-scale international intervention. He also directed Kehoe to prepare for deployment to East Timor to set up a terminal in Dili for supplies that McManus and 9 FSB would be forwarding from Darwin, if a larger ADF force deployed into East Timor.[56]

On 30 August 1999 the East Timorese voted.[57] The large turnout was a strong indication that they had rejected autonomy. The withdrawal of international UN volunteers and international election observers began as soon as the ballot boxes were sealed and on their way to Dili. All but essential UN staff began to leave East Timor immediately. Only UN political staff, Military Liaison Officers and UN civilian police remained. Outbreaks of violence resulted in UNAMET staff from some areas withdrawing to Dili.[58] Helicopters flew to outlying areas from Dili picking up staff who had witnessed the growing chaos.[59] While the votes were being counted, East Timorese militia groups intimidated UNAMET and media representatives in Dili while they rampaged through the streets burning houses of suspected pro-independence supporters.[60] From everywhere in East Timor came reports of Indonesian security personnel standing by while militia intimated civilians, looted goods, and burned property.[61] Indications of the mayhem that was about to engulf East Timor were evident as early as Thursday 2 September 1999, when widespread violence broke out in Maliana near the border with West Timor, forcing UNAMET to evacuate its staff urgently and inhabitants to flee.[62] Militia groups and local Indonesian security forces began to loot and burn the town.[63] The United Nations released the ballot result on Saturday 4 September 1999. There was then a period of quiet before the storm. Many East Timorese seemed to know what would be in store. Within a few hours of the announcement, the sacking of East Timor and the terrorising and displacement of its people by marauding militia gangs and East Timorese territorial troops began in earnest.

Following historical precedent, it was the Australian Foreign Minister (Downer) and not the Defence Minister (Moore) who announced on Saturday 4 September 1999 that, in light of the growing violence, Australia would offer to lead an international military force into East Timor, if the Indonesian Government invited the United Nations to intervene.[64] Some were surprised that this announcement triggered 'detailed planning' in the ADF rather than the unfolding events since May which should have signalled that Australia needed to be ready to lead any 'coalition of the willing' into East Timor.[65] At about 10.00 p.m. on Sunday 5 September 1999, Cosgrove called Evans at home and requested him to convene his staff and develop a concept for operations for what by morning would be called Operation *Warden*. His staff at DJFHQ would then have time to review the concept on Monday 6 September before sending it to Treloar's headquarters in Sydney. From there it would be forwarded to Canberra by 7 September for consideration by the SCG and the National Security Committee of Cabinet (NSCC). Evans called in his Brigade Major, Major Marcus Fielding, his senior logistician, Major David Stevens, and his Intelligence Officer, Major John Blaxland. They worked until 4.00 a.m. before dispatching a concept document to meet Cosgrove's early morning deadline.[66] On the same night and morning that Evans, Fielding, Stevens and Blaxland were developing the concept for Operation *Warden*, hundreds of East Timorese climbed the walls around the UNAMET compound in Dili and jumped in to save themselves or just their children from marauding militia. Many of them lacerated themselves and their children on razor wire.[67] The UN Secretary General's Special Representative in East Timor, Ian Martin, began to discuss an evacuation of remaining UNAMET staff.[68]

The SCG compartment approved the Operation *Warden* concept on 7 September and briefed it to the NSCC. Later that same day, Habibie declared martial law in East Timor and issued an ultimatum to Wiranto to restore public safety.[69] Barrie issued his warning order for Operation *Warden* the next day.[70] Concurrently, the United States was exerting increasing pressure on Indonesia to quell violence and arson, but there was no intention of deploying US combat troops to East Timor.[71] Australia would have to lead and support an international intervention alone.[72] Though not specifically intended to do so, Operation *Spitfire* triggered preparations in 3rd Brigade, the only formation trained and capable of rapid deployment. Fortunately, Evans and his staff had been warned informally in April about the likely scenario of having to provide either a protection force for the United Nations in East Timor, or forces to protect an evacuation.[73] Planning for deployment to East Timor had been going on secretly for months. Unlike Operation *Morris Dance*, Operation *Solace* and Operation *Lagoon*, 3rd Brigade would have detailed maps, infrastructure information and recent intelligence estimates for a forthcoming operation.

Barrie now faced the challenge of conducting further evacuation operations in East Timor and preparing for Operation *Warden*. The evacuation force in Tindal, and at the airport and alongside at the port in Darwin, now exceeded 600 personnel from all three Services and involved ships and aircraft. Operation *Spitfire* had begun as a limited protected evacuation operation employing maritime and air force transport assets. It looked like merging into a larger-scale stabilisation operation. Molan and his staff in Dili were Barrie's 'eyes and ears'.[74] Local TNI commanders appeared to have lost control of their rank and file, who were joining East Timorese territorials and militia in looting and ransacking property, and also in terrorising the population, who had fled or were fleeing Dili.[75] This was a volatile and dangerous environment that could lead to the strategic nightmare of an accidental clash between Australian and Indonesian troops. Barrie had warned members of the NSCC that intervention into East Timor under these risky circumstances could lead to war with Indonesia.[76]

While Cosgrove and his headquarters staff would, by their professional inclination and experience, concentrate on projecting land forces into East Timor to stabilise the situation on the ground, there were ominous strategic developments at sea and in the air. Indonesian maritime and air force elements had begun to arrive, ostensibly to facilitate a withdrawal of TNI forces from East Timor. The New Zealand Centre for Strategic Studies reported later that the Indonesian Navy had deployed a T-209 submarine as part of a maritime task group to the waters off East Timor and that the Indonesian Air Force had deployed A-4 *Sky Hawk* and F-16 *Fighting Falcon* aircraft into West Timor.[77] Thus, Barrie had to deter Indonesian interference with an ADF evacuation operation and be ready for anything that might follow if interference occurred. He could do this from his headquarters through Bonser's Headquarters Northern Command (HQ NORCOM) in Darwin to maritime and air force units deployed to northern Australia, or through his headquarters to Treloar who would direct maritime and air force elements deployed to northern Australia. David Horner later confirmed that Barrie decided

> to place F/A-18 fighters, F-111 strike aircraft, forward air control aircraft and aerial tankers on alert during the initial deployment. ... Similarly, warships with a high level of capability in anti-submarine warfare escorted the ships transporting the forces to East Timor. [these forces]

remained under the Commander Australian Theatre [Air Vice Marshal Treloar].[78]

Fortunately for the ADF, probably the strongest deterrent to Indonesian interference was a blunt warning from the United States to Wiranto that law and order should be restored in East Timor as soon as possible.[79]

Concurrently, the ADF had to execute Operation *Spitfire* and prepare for Operation *Warden*. In reality, the two operations were merging as phases of a single-force projection that Cosgrove and his staff had predicted earlier in the year. Operations would begin with a small Operation *Spitfire* force and be followed, given an Indonesian invitation and UN endorsement, by Evans' 3rd Brigade and Cosgrove's DJFHQ, augmented at short notice with *ad hoc* maritime and air force staff groups.[80] For their part, the Indonesian Government, the TNI and their militia surrogates appeared to be executing a preconceived plan.[81] The first phase appeared to be to drive out foreign witnesses to the punishment about to be meted out to the East Timorese for rejecting autonomy.[82] The second phase appeared to be the destruction of infrastructure, looting and population displacement, disguised as an emergency evacuation plan. The final phase appeared to be to leave East Timor abruptly and invite the United Nations and the international community to take over the task. If this was the plan, no TNI opposition would be expected during an evacuation of foreign nationals, but there might be some resistance if international forces interrupted the second more destructive phase.

Operation *Spitfire*

After a close examination of political consequences and increasing pressure on beleaguered UNAMET staff at the UN compound in Dili, the United Nations sought Australian help to evacuate its remaining staff on 9 September 1999.[83] The next day, Molan and Colonel Ken Brownrigg, the Australian Army attaché from Jakarta, met the first C-130 *Hercules* aircraft landing in Dili. Molan and Brownrigg found they had to work very hard to calm Indonesian air force special force troops at the airport.[84] Australia and Indonesia had arrived at a tactical tipping point and the Indonesians cooperated. Fortunately, the ADF had the right people, at the right place and at the right time.

In the early hours of 14 September 1999, in a second evacuation, Martin and the remainder of his staff left East Timor. Soon after, Molan returned to Jakarta with his staff. Molan and Martin left liaison officers at the Australian Consulate building to maintain contact with Indonesian commanders and authorities, and to continue reporting to both Canberra and the United Nations in New York.

Operation *Warden*

Meanwhile, Wiranto had appointed Major General Kiki Syahnakri, his Jakarta-based chief of operations, as the Chief of the Martial Law Authority in East Timor. His plan was to withdraw all locally posted TNI personnel, especially those of East Timorese ethnicity, and replace them with troops from Java. In the meantime, the terror campaign would continue for several days unchecked until there was a sufficient build-up of replacement units and misbehaving units had departed.[85]

The gathering of world leaders in Auckland on 11 September 1999 for the annual meeting of the Asia-Pacific Economic Community (APEC) became the focal point for putting international pressure on Indonesia to allow international intervention. On 12 September, Habibie announced that the Indonesian Government would accept international intervention into East Timor.[86] The United Nations Security Council (UNSC) passed Resolution 1264 on 15 September 1999 authorising what was to become INTERFET, to take all necessary actions to restore peace and security in East Timor.[87] On 16 September, Indonesia cancelled its security agreement with Australia.[88] The scene was set. Barrie, Keating, Treloar, Cosgrove, Evans and Wilkinson, and their respective headquarters and force elements, stood on the threshold. Barrie decided to take command himself:[89]

> This operation will be Operation *Stabilise* and is to be commanded by Major General Cosgrove, *under my command* [author's emphasis]. ... Operation *Stabilise* and *Warden* together represent the most significant military commitment of the Australian Government, on behalf of the Australian people since World War II. Our logistic support must also be a world class performance.[90]

Deployment

Barrie had to synchronise forces from the three Services and their logistic capabilities for a common purpose. The first challenge would be to deploy Cosgrove's land forces safely and efficiently. Treloar, who commanded the joint movements system through 1 JMOVGP, was responsible for the efficient execution of Cosgrove's movement plan and any subsequent movements support he required from Australia. Bonser and his staff in Darwin had the Joint Movement Control Office—Darwin under operational control. Thus, he and Group Captain Ian Jamieson, commander of 1 JMOVGP in Sydney, were in charge of coordinating the movement of personnel and *matériel* staging through Darwin to East Timor, as well as from East Timor. Unlike field exercises conducted in northern Australia since the late 1980s, troops and supplies would have to deploy under operational conditions in a pre-planned tactical order of arrival: this time logistic support would follow and not be pre-positioned for arriving troops.[91]

Cosgrove envisaged a four-phase campaign in East Timor, with specific but limited military objectives. The first phase would be to negotiate with Syahnakri to establish optimum safe preconditions for lodgement. The second phase would be the rapid deployment of as many combat forces as strategic lift would permit. The third phase would be to establish a secure environment in Dili and then throughout East Timor. The final phase would be a transition of INTERFET to a UN peacekeeping operation.[92]

Brownrigg, supported by his maritime and air force counterparts from the Australian Embassy in Jakarta, and Special Forces troops would constitute the first ADF elements on the ground. Brownrigg and his colleagues would reassure Syahnakri and his commanders that INTERFET was a neutral force, only intent on assisting with security while they withdrew miscreant TNI and auxiliary units from East Timor. Brownrigg facilitated a meeting between Cosgrove and Syahnakri at Dili airport on 19 September 1999. Both generals affirmed that they would take every precaution to ensure that those under their command would not be drawn into gun battles through a lack of discipline on either side or through manipulative provocation by third parties.[93] Subsequently, Brownrigg and his colleagues maintained contact with senior TNI and navy and air force commanders after Cosgrove left. Phase 1 was a success.

On the night of 19 September 1999 Phase 2 was poised to begin. Cosgrove's plan depended on the ADF movements system being able to deliver as many combat troops from 3rd Brigade as possible in the first 48 hours so as to create a deterrent effect on the ground in Dili. There would be risks. Cousins did not plan to have substantial reserves of bulky and heavy basic commodities, such as ammunition, rations and water, on hand. He took this risk in order to allow more troops and armoured vehicles to be deployed quickly. His arrangements depended on an efficient air bridge to and from Dili. There was little room for error. He specified logistic and movement arrangements by aircraft load for three weeks.

Group Captain Stewart Cameron controlled the transport aircraft that Cousins would depend on. He established 96 Combined Air Wing Group to coordinate air operations. The core of Cameron's capacity was a force of 12 Australian C-130 *Hercules* transport aircraft and 16 crews. For the air bridge, Canada, France, New Zealand, the Philippines, Britain, the United States and Thailand had provided or promised a further 16 C-130 *Hercules* aircraft and 21 crews.[94]

Seven C-130 *Hercules* aircraft left Townsville for Dili in the early hours of 20 September. While they were inbound, a further five C-130 *Hercules* aircraft flew from northern Australia carrying a vanguard of Special Forces troops and their supplies of fuel and other necessities. They landed at Komoro Airfield ahead of the aircraft from Townsville. Brownrigg, dressed in summer dress uniform, beret and aiguillettes, met his compatriots as if they were arriving for a diplomatic visit: a ploy to ease tension.[95] The TNI officer commanding Indonesian special force troops guarding the airport and his subordinate commanders were polite, cordial and cooperative.

The arrival of the first company from 2nd Battalion, the Royal Australian Regiment (2 RAR), the INTERFET advanced force, was more risky because they ignored orders to leave the aircraft carrying their weapons in a non-threatening manner. The troops ran down the lowered ramp and, in the way that they had trained to do many times before, dispersed at the run, hit the ground and adopted a half moon formation with weapons pointing out—at the ready.[96] Fortunately the benign arrival of the earlier C-130 *Hercules* aircraft and subsequent friendliness had diffused Indonesian suspicion at the airport. However, the environment in the remainder of Dili was hostile. TNI and East Timorese territorials, accompanied by militia sporting red and white bandannas and brandishing weapons, and driving past in trucks, harassed the 2 RAR company assigned to secure the port.[97] The provocateurs yelled out death threats, made cut-throat gestures with their hands and occasionally fired weapons into the air. Initially this was unsettling for the Australians who instinctively readied their weapons for return fire, but they soon assessed that they were not being attacked.[98] They were being tested by undisciplined individuals, who displayed more menacing bravado than bravery.

At sea, Indonesian Navy vessels provoked Australian Navy vessels. Smaller Indonesian craft sailed on collision courses, changing course at the last moment. Larger ships were sailing across the bows of Australian vessels to force them to slow down or to change course. Indonesian captains did not respond to radio calls from Australian commanders. These provocations continued all day and into the night. Like their compatriots in Dili, all the Australian maritime commanders could do was maintain disciplined vigilance and not be drawn into an incident that might provoke an escalation of hostilities.[99]

Unfortunately, the air bridge from Darwin to Dili encountered difficulties after the first aircraft had discharged their loads in Dili and returned to Darwin to load more cargo for the flight back. Unbeknown to Cosgrove, Evans or Cousins and their staffs, there were competing priorities for C-130 *Hercules* aircraft. They assumed that no one else would use C-130 *Hercules* aircraft flights into Dili until 2 RAR, Cosgrove's and Evans' tactical headquarters, vehicles and initial supplies of ammunition, rations and water were on the ground.[100] Risks would increase substantially if there was a time gap between the arrival of troops and their initial supplies. Cousins and his staff had planned each aircraft load meticulously and the order of arrival of tactical and logistics elements into East Timor with

3rd Brigade staff. Evans had directed that all elements would pack 'light' and take a 'Spartan' approach, in accordance with Cosgrove's direction to put as many combat troops on the ground as soon as possible. He planned to insert a 600-strong force from 2 RAR quickly with a minimum of vehicles and supplies. They would carry their water, ammunition and rations on their backs and would wait 24 hours for resupply and more vehicles.[101] Commercial shipping would only operate in a secure environment, so the sea bridge for lodgement would depend on securing Dili quickly and the HMAS *Jervis Bay*, HMAS *Success* and HMAS *Tobruk* shuttling to and from Darwin and Dili on schedule, with other navy vessels positioned offshore holding contingency stocks on board for emergencies.[102]

Even with operational imperatives and 24-hour operations, Komoro Airfield could only handle a finite number of landings and take-offs.[103] Every aircraft load was either contributing to or detracting from Cosgrove's plan and overall force protection. Cousins' movement schedule fell apart by early afternoon on 20 September 1999. After the first sorties that had brought the Special Forces contingent and the first two companies of 2 RAR, the remainder of 2 RAR with vehicles and supplies, including an aircraft bringing bottled water, were delayed while unplanned sorties of media contingents, air force personnel, equipment and supplies, and UNAMET personnel and vehicles were flown in. Consequently, vehicles that Cousins had instructed be brigaded in Dili to distribute water did not turn up. Medical personnel and supplies were delayed at a time when no one knew whether or not there would be casualties. Evans and Cousins at Dili airport watched in dismay as aircraft arrived and did not discharge their expected loads.[104] There was unruly behaviour at Darwin airport as members of 3rd Brigade, who desperately wanted to join their comrades in Dili, were left waiting while they watched journalists, air force staff and supplies as well as UN personnel load and depart ahead of them.[105] They subjected some movements staff to verbal tirades and threatening behaviour.[106]

Confusion and frustration in Darwin increased risk, but did not endanger the initial 24 hours of the lodgement. Australian Special Forces provided force protection with specialist assets. They commandeered scores of abandoned UNAMET vehicles for transport. Thus, sufficient troops were on the ground for high priority tasks. Australian, US and other coalition vessels patrolled offshore near Dili harbour to deter interference. The unplanned use of aircraft forced Cousins to use all of his contingency stocks of water immediately, ordering bottled water to be brought ashore from HMAS *Success*.[107] Later in the afternoon and evening, Company Quartermaster Sergeants from 2 RAR commandeered stocks of bottled water from the airport that had been flown in to build up stock holdings for the air force.[108]

The logistic crisis eased when 3rd Battalion, the Royal Australian Regiment (3 RAR) and a squadron of Australian light armoured vehicles (ASLAVs) and Armoured Personnel Carriers (APCs) arrived aboard HMAS *Jervis Bay* and HMAS *Tobruk* on the morning of 21 September 1999. Once they were aware of 2 RAR's predicament, the arriving paratroopers carried off cartons of bottled water from HMAS *Jervis Bay* and placed them on vehicles at the wharf for their comrades before continuing on to their first objectives in the city.[109] The lodgement was working and 3rd Brigade secured the initial objectives as planned. However, the danger of an accidental clash between Australian and Indonesian forces had not passed. Evans and his two-battalion brigade of about 1500 troops, with limited supplies of water and ammunition on hand, was outnumbered by nearly 15 000 Indonesian troops in Dili, who presumably had plenty of ammunition and other supplies in their barracks.

Overnight on 20 September 1999, the Australians observed new plumes of smoke rise as arsonists lit more fires in the suburbs and in government buildings. They heard the sounds of gunfire as well as explosions of accelerants used to start new fires. Long convoys of TNI soldiers, crammed into trucks with their personal belongings and loot, rolled through the streets, heading towards West Timor. At any time, a truck load of soldiers and militia would drive past groups of INTERFET troops on sentry duty and patrol, shouting and gesturing malevolently.

By the afternoon of 21 September 1999, INTERFET had made its presence felt throughout Dili. Soldiers were patrolling and clearing houses and buildings in which militia were thought to be hiding. There were a number of incidents that could have resulted in a clash between Indonesian and Australian troops. At midday, a group of 300 TNI Marines threatened and tried to intimidate a patrol from 3 RAR.[110] Earlier, a 3 RAR patrol had raised and aimed their weapons at a truckload of TNI personnel, who had raised and aimed their weapons at them.[111] The discipline of Australian troops was commendable, considering that many had only received their training in the Rules of Engagement (ROE) whilst in transit to East Timor, or waiting in Darwin and Townsville for deployment: some of the risks of rushing the tactical level.[112]

Concerned about the mayhem the night before and mindful of the INTERFET mandate to create a secure environment, Evans decided to restrict the movement of trucks of provocateurs and arsonists on the night of 21 September by ordering 2 RAR to set up vehicle check points (VCP) along the main road through Dili.[113] He was setting the conditions for confrontation. Lieutenant Colonel Mick Slater ordered Major Jim Bryant to set up three VCP, several hundred metres apart on the main east-west road through Dili. Slater's intent was to prevent anyone using side streets from passing a single VCP sited on this main route. He was setting a VCP snare to entrap truckloads of arsonists moving at night. Slater ordered

Bryant to stop anyone who was armed, but not in uniform. If they did not have suitable military identification, then they were to be detained for further questioning. Slater allocated six ASLAVs to form two-vehicle herringbone obstacles at each checkpoint that would force vehicles to slow down and zigzag between the vehicles to get through. Truck drivers would not argue with a .50 calibre machine-gun mounted atop an armoured vehicle. Slater strengthened his VCP by reinforcing Bryant's company with his Assault Pioneer Platoon and six pairs of snipers. Bryant allocated an Assault Pioneer section and two pairs of snipers to each of his three rifle platoons.[114]

At around 10.00 p.m., a 600-strong East Timorese territorial battalion, accompanied by TNI personnel, and travelling in a convoy of about 60 trucks, crammed with soldiers, family members and loot, drove into Dili from Baucau. They had murdered, burned and pillaged their way west and were heading directly for Slater's checkpoints.[115] Indonesia and Australia were now approaching another tactical tipping point that could have substantial strategic implications in general, and for the INTERFET campaign in particular. Unfortunately, Slater's VCP operation and Syahnakri's withdrawal operation had not been fully explained at the daily coordination conference at HQ INTERFET. Evans and his staff, and Slater and his staff, were not told of the movement of this battalion either by Syahnakri's staff or by Australian intelligence.[116] The Australians manning checkpoints were unaware that it was in everyone's interest to let this convoy proceed. In the vanguard of this battalion were about 40 outriders on motorbikes. These men wore an assortment of bandannas, T-shirts, singlets and camouflage trousers. Each had a rifle slung over his back.[117] These were the types of people Slater had directed Bryant's men to stop and detain.

Lieutenant Steve Casey's platoon, positioned at the eastern VCP, was the first to encounter these East Timorese outriders. Casey's interpreter, Lieutenant Grant Chisnell, spoke with the leader of the outriders in Bahasa, asking him for his identification and informing him that the Australians had orders to detain any armed persons not in uniform and who did not have suitable TNI identification.[118] While he spoke, the outriders revved their engines and looked on with menace. The leader demanded to be let through immediately. Behind the motorcyclists, trucks began to slow down and stop. Soldiers from the rear trucks began to dismount and move forward, calling out for information on why the convoy was held up. Seconds ticked by—and the tension mounted.

As the leader of the outriders and Chisnell continued to negotiate, the remainder of Casey's platoon and the Assault Pioneers positioned themselves. They were outnumbered and out-gunned. Chisnell and the leader of the outriders raised their voices in argument. Most of the Australians wore night-vision goggles, and all were in flak jackets. They had clear vision of the area. The territorials in the trucks overlooking the scene were in the dark and assumed they could not be seen. They raised their weapons and pointed them at Casey and Chisnell.[119]

The Australian infantrymen held their weapons down at their sides, but pointed their muzzles up at those in trucks who had raised their weapons. They were preparing to fire. Their laser designators formed bright green spots on the chests and heads of the unknowing territorial soldiers. In a split second, a volley of 5.56 mm rounds would follow the laser beams if they showed that they were about to take a sight picture and pull their triggers. The Australian cavalrymen also trained their .50 calibre machine-guns on the line of trucks. Undetected, on top of a bus shelter, the snipers could also see at night through their scopes.[120]

Casey's signaller described the scene over his radio to Bryant, stationed at the next checkpoint, who now had an important decision to make. Would he let the motorbikes and trucks through, or tell Casey to insist on them being pulled over and screened in the search area? Realising that the situation could escalate into a very dangerous standoff or gun battle, Bryant decided to let the convoy through to his VCP, so he could assess the situation personally.[121] This would diffuse the situation at Casey's location, but also give him time to seek guidance from Slater. While Bryant contacted Slater, the motorbikes and trucks zigzagged past the two ASLAVs and drove on.

A second confrontation quickly ensued. This time the outriders were more aggressive and those in the trucks behind them became more resentful at being stopped a second time. In the face of raised voices and raised weapons, Lieutenant Peter Halleday's platoon, the attached Assault Pioneers and the snipers repeated what had occurred at Casey's checkpoint. While laser beams again lit up the territorials, Bryant received word that he was to let the battalion through without further delay.[122] Apparently, Slater had consulted Evans, who assessed the danger immediately, and directed that the territorials should not be delayed any further.[123] Calling out abusively and brandishing their weapons, they drove out of Dili and on to West Timor—a clash with Australian troops having been narrowly avoided.

There were several more provocations from truckloads of TNI soldiers, territorials and militia overnight on 21 September 1999. The Australians maintained their discipline and vigilance. In many cases, their ROE would have permitted them to open fire when weapons were pointed at them, and to have 'mock fired', like in a children's game of 'cowboys and Indians'. It was a dangerous and potentially fatal game. The sounds of a firefight in the dark, that would have soon involved light armoured vehicles, could have escalated as TNI troops spilled out from their barracks, firing at any INTERFET personnel they encountered. Fortunately, there was no firefight and the vast majority of TNI soldiers remained in their barracks or continued moving peaceably to the port for embarkation.

On 27 September 1999, Syahnakri handed over responsibility for the security of East Timor to Cosgrove, leaving only a token TNI presence in Dili. Syahnakri had made the transition work. He had reduced an estimated 15 000-strong security force to a Dili garrison of about 1300 troops. The militia and their controllers were gone. INTERFET had achieved most of its mission in seven days. This first week set the scene for the rest of the campaign. Dili, the political and spiritual centre of East Timor, was secure. UNAMET staff had returned. UN aid agencies, such as the World Food Program and the Office for the Coordination of Humanitarian Aid, had begun facilitating the delivery of humanitarian aid. During this time, a coalition of nations apparently liked what they saw. They confirmed promises of support and began sending contingents of troops. However, several did so in expectation of receiving ADF logistic support. Brigadier Jeff Wilkinson's *ad hoc* supply chain had sustained the 3rd Brigade group during the first critical days of the campaign in Dili near a port and an airfield. Australian military logistics now had to be at force level. Thousands of coalition troops were inbound and 3rd Brigade would need to be supported on the border.

Force Sustainment

The lodgement of sufficient vehicles and stocks to sustain arriving INTERFET forces was delayed for several days and, in some cases, over a week, because of the collapse of movement coordination in Darwin under the weight of competing priorities. There was just not enough transport, movements staff or handling capabilities at Darwin airport or its port to push through the volume of personnel, vehicles, equipment and supplies required. However, Cousins' priority on water, food, fuel and ammunition paid off. Cosgrove and Evans were able to prosecute the campaign in the first seven days without significant logistic limitations. A combination of stocks afloat on navy vessels in Dili harbour, the maritime shuttle of supplies and vehicles on HMAS *Jervis Bay*, HMAS *Tobruk* and HMAS *Success*, and the flexibility to load urgently needed items on aircraft flying around the clock from Darwin, assured supply of the basics of water, food, fuel and ammunition.[124]

Wilkinson and his staff had foreseen the coming requirements to support a force that would climb to over 10 000 personnel, about 50 rotary-wing and fixed-wing aircraft and a fleet of over 1200 vehicles. Their challenge, since beginning planning for Operation *Warden* on the weekend of 8–9 September 1999, had been to mobilise a logistic system, that had been pared back over the previous decade, in just two weeks. Commercial operators had replaced many logistic functions and none would be venturing into danger until INTERFET had secured East Timor. There was also some high-level resistance among senior

ADF officers to using contractors in East Timor.[125] Specialist services, such as movements, stevedoring, water transport, petroleum operations and postal and amenities services, had been cut or no longer existed. There was no deployable logistic force headquarters. Logisticians in Canberra, Brisbane and Sydney had been decimated as a result of the Force Structure Review, Commercial Support Program and the logistic redevelopment projects of the early 1990s.[126] There were also deficiencies in the military logistic infrastructure in Darwin. Joint Logistic Unit—North was structured to support local military units and field exercises. There was no surge capacity to support offshore operations.[127] There was little stock on depot shelves anywhere in Australia in many classes of supply, because ADF force sustainment was based on purchasing items commercially and distributing them to units 'just in time'.[128]

Planning conducted at Headquarters Logistic Support Force (HQ LSF) in Randwick in early September had marked an important logistic milestone during the transition from Operation *Spitfire* to Operation *Warden* and then to the multinational Operation *Stabilise*. For the first time, a formation headquarters that commanded logistic units and was used to solving practical logistic problems, was making plans, taking action and warning units for deployment. Wilkinson and his staff had simultaneous responsibilities to expedite logistic preparations for lodgement of the 3rd Brigade group, as well as to build a supply chain to sustain the main force of international units that were due to arrive in the following weeks. He found staff at short notice to enable HQ LSF and DJFHQ to meet the planning challenge and to establish an INTERFET HQ FLSG. Once word was out among serving and retired logisticians, many offered to help and volunteered to serve in East Timor.[129]

As soon as Habibie announced on 12 September that the Indonesian Government would accept the deployment of an international force into East Timor, Wilkinson ordered a large-scale move of vehicles, equipment and stocks to northern Australia. When Barrie issued his executive order on 14 September 1999 for Operation *Warden*, additional stocks of basic items, such as jerry cans, rations and ammunition were already arriving in Darwin, and more convoys were on their way. Purchasing action had begun for repair parts and essential items that had long lead times.[130] Staff at 1 JMOVGP had begun to charter shipping and to contract commercial road and air transport. For the first time since Australian troops had deployed to the Kokoda Track in 1942, Australian military logisticians were being asked to sustain a major Australian offshore operation by drawing on Australia's military and commercial supply and transport systems.

Wilkinson built the supply chain for INTERFET using his two force support battalions and the newly-raised 60-strong HQ FLSG. The plan was for stocks to be sent to Darwin from the Defence National Supply and Distribution Centre

(DNSDC) at Moorebank in Sydney and other regional base logistic units around Australia. McManus would then arrange for storage and subsequent movement of consignments to East Timor to meet INTERFET needs, using air and sea bridges comprised of ADF, international and Australian commercial assets. Kehoe would receive stocks in Dili at the port and Komoro Airport, and then distribute them to INTERFET units. Thus, the logistic concept was to send as much stock to Darwin as possible and then regulate its flow into East Timor from Darwin. To do otherwise would result in stocks arriving in Dili in bulk without adequate facilities or assets to transport, secure, store or distribute them—a replication of Operation *Hardihood* in Vietnam in 1966.

Colonel Grant Cavenagh, Commander of FLSG in Dili, wrote to Wilkinson on 21 October informing him that there were several 'significant factors that continue to complicate logistic operations in EM [East Timor]'.[131] The strategic level of command in general, and HQ AST in particular, had failed to sign up arriving coalition contingents to implementing agreements for logistic support and to anticipate their logistic support needs. Most contingents arrived needing assistance in unloading and immediate resupply, as well as in catering and transport support.[132]

By late October, after six weeks of arduous operations, there were expectations in Australia and East Timor that it was time to establish more comfortable living conditions for units on the border and elsewhere. By this time, 22 kitchens were offering fresh meals, but many personnel still slept on the ground and there were insufficient tents to accommodate them. There were no laundry facilities and soldiers washed their uniforms in empty ration tins.[133] Since early October, Cousins and his staff had been pressing for camp and accommodation stores to be pre-positioned in Darwin. Mueller's staff was having difficulty responding to these requests amidst their competing priorities.[134]

The ADF supply chain to East Timor was jamming up and difficult to manage. It was unable to improve simultaneously the living conditions of INTERFET troops in the field, satisfy demands for water, food, fuel, spare parts and other items, keep construction stores flowing to the engineers and build up stocks before the coming wet season.[135] The pressure on the logistic system supporting Operation *Stabilise* did not go unnoticed. Hartley visited East Timor on 4 and 5 November 1999. He spoke with commanders and staff and, upon his return to Australia, distributed a highly critical assessment to Treloar and Mueller.[136] Hartley ascertained that, despite appointing Wilkinson as logistics component commander at HQ AST, there was a need for an over-arching logistic coordination agency.[137] What he failed to mention was that Wilkinson in Australia and Cavenagh in Dili had not been given operational control over maritime or air force logistic units and assets, or over the joint movements system. He also commented that little effort had been made to forecast major logistic and engineering requirements. Compounding these two major weaknesses, Hartley assessed that there were signs of an imminent logistic disaster, especially with the wet season only weeks away. He pointed to the backlog of unsatisfied demands for resupply, a lack of visibility of items within the movements system, a deficit of logistic and engineer assets in East Timor, and insufficient shipping.[138] His report also contained examples of commanders taking into their own hands the resupply of spare parts to keep their vehicles and equipment going and of them commandeering camp stores from depots to improve the living conditions of their troops.[139]

Hartley's report produced a number of strong reactions. Treloar sought an explanation from Wilkinson.[140] Hartley had brought to the surface the gap between customer expectations and what the supply chain was delivering. This distraction from the task of solving the problem caused uproar amongst logistic commanders and staff supporting Operation *Stabilise*. They felt that their efforts were being criticised at a time when they could do no more to satisfy Cosgrove's priorities.[141]

Throughout November 1999, logisticians at all levels worked long hours to reduce the backlog of supplies, to build stocks before the wet season set in and to push through camp stores and other amenities to improve the living conditions of those in the field. For example, 2 RAR received a full complement of stretchers, tents, camp stores, such as chairs and tables, and duckboards by 12 November, eight weeks after they had landed in Dili.[142] The week before, backlogs in demands for spare parts and other critical items had been overcome. Mail was regular. A canteen service and showers were available every day in Balibo and Maliana, the two major Australian bases on the border.[143] The Joint Amenities Unit, operating in Dili provided stock for canteens at all the major bases, a duty-free service for returning troops, an Interflora service and video hire. Local labour had been hired in most locations to launder clothes, and to clean kitchens, toilets, accommodation and working areas. All kitchens produced high-quality food and were supported by an efficient fresh-food resupply system.[144] By 15 December 1999, Mueller and Support Command had taken over logistic responsibilities for Operation *Stabilise* and a more conventional logistic system replaced Wilkinson's interim arrangements. Though there were still nine weeks to go before INTERFET would be relieved by UN forces on 23 February 2000, the mission had been accomplished by mid-December. Indeed, INTERFET had been a garrison force since mid-October. Based on its outcomes, the intervention was an outstanding success. Based on its processes, there was much for the ADF to reflect on.

ENDNOTES

[1] A 'first line' of ammunition was limited to the amount of ammunition ordered to be carried by each individual and vehicle. The amount of ammunition is limited by the capacity of individuals to carry ammunition as well as other commodities such as water. Australian armoured vehicles not only carry their own ammunition, but may also carry quantities of small arms ammunition for combat troops. A second line of ammunition is normally located with a sub-unit headquarters.

[2] Major General Jim M. Connolly, 'Mid Trial Report for COSC on Theatre Command', HQAST 261-8-2, 1 December 1998, p. 1. HQAST, Potts Point.

[3] Connolly, 'Mid Trial Report for COSC on Theatre Command', HQAST 261-8-2, 1 December 1998, p. 8.

[4] Connolly, 'Mid Trial Report for COSC on Theatre Command', HQAST 261-8-2, 1 December 1998, p. 6; and Major General Jim M. Connolly, 'Concept for Command of the Australian Theatre', 1 December 1998, p. 6, HQ AST 261-8-2, HQ AST, Potts Point.

[5] Air Vice Marshal Bob Treloar, 'COSC Agendum 19/1999, Progress Report on Theatre Headquarters Development', HQ AST 716/99, 26 May 1999, 623-11-1; and Air Vice Marshal Bob Treloar, 'Concept for the Command of the Australian Theatre', 26 May 1999, HQ AST 261-8-2, HQ AST, Potts Point.

[6] Treloar, 'COSC Agendum 19/1999', pp. 1 and 5.

[7] Treloar, 'COSC Agendum 19/1999', p. 2.

[8] Major General Peter J. Cosgrove in interview with author, 3 January 2000.

[9] Treloar, 'COSC Agendum 19/99', Annex B—The Strategic Planning Process and Theatre Planning.

[10] This process had been reviewed and made more efficient, but secrecy isolated this refined strategic planning process from lower levels of command. Commodore Jim S. O'Hara, Air Commodore Angus G. Houston and Brigadier Brian G. Stevens, 'Report of Review of the Strategic/Operational Relationship', 14 October 1998, HQAST 623-11-1, HQ AST, Potts Point.

[11] Price Waterhouse Coopers, *Defence HQAST Business Process Re-engineering (BPR) Scoping Study, vol. 1: report*, 14 July 1999. Copy held by author. The authors based their criticisms on a comparison of HQ AST and HQ CINCPAC [Headquarters Commander in Chief—Pacific] in Hawaii, as well as first-hand research in Sydney with staff at HQ AST and Maritime, Land and Air Headquarters.

[12] Price Waterhouse Coopers, *Defence HQAST Business Process Re-engineering (BPR) Scoping Study, vol. 1: report*, 14 July 1999, Executive Summary.

[13] Price Waterhouse Coopers, *Defence HQAST Business Process Re-engineering (BPR) Scoping Study, vol. 1: report*, 14 July 1999, pp. 14–16.

[14] Geoff Kitney, 'Downer: UN force needed in transition', *Sydney Morning Herald*, 6 February 1999, p. 5.

[15] Alexander Downer, 'We stand ready to help in any way we can', *Sydney Morning Herald*, 2 March 1999, p. 17; Robert Garran, 'Military destined for Timor', *The Australian*, 2 March 1999, p. 1; Greg Sheridan, 'No alternative but to take the risk', *The Australian*, 2 March 1999, p. 1; and Paul Kelly, 'East Timor on the road to chaos', *The Australian*, 3 March 1999, p. 13.

[16] The author has used the acronym TNI (*Tentara Nasional Indonesia* or Indonesian Army). This title applied after 1 April 1999. Before then, the Indonesian armed forces incorporated the policing function, and were known as ABRI (*Angkatan Bersenjata Republik Indonesia* or Indonesian Armed Forces).

[17] Harold Crouch assessed that, 'An overwhelming majority of army officers had served in East Timor at one time or another and some had served three or four tours of duty there. Many officers also felt a deep emotional attachment to East Timor as the place where several thousand Indonesian soldiers had died'. Harold Crouch, 'The TNI and East-Timor Policy', in (eds) James J. Fox and Dionisio Babo Soares, *Out of the Ashes: Destruction and Reconstruction of East Timor*, C. Hurst and Co., London, 2000, p. 138.

[18] Crouch, 'The TNI and East-Timor Policy', in (eds) Fox and Soares, *Out of the Ashes: Destruction and Reconstruction of East Timor*, pp. 137–38 and 146. Also, Colonel Ken A. Brownrigg, Comments by email on draft chapter on Operation *Spitfire* in Bob Breen, *Mission Accomplished, Australian Defence Force participation in International Force East Timor*, Allen and Unwin, Sydney, 2001. Copies of emails held by author. Brownrigg was the Australian Army attaché in Jakarta in 1999 and monitored the attitudes of senior Indonesian officers to events in East Timor in 1999.

[19] On 5 April 1999 there was an attack on civilians sheltering in a priest's house in Liquica and, on the weekend 17–18 April, militia gangs killed and injured a number of civilians in Dili. See Lindsay Murdoch and Peter Coleman-Adams, 'Freedom Slaughtered, Howard outrage as military shoot down peace process', *Sydney Morning Herald*, pp. 1 and 9; Lindsay Murdoch, 'Revealed: Our Timor role', *Sydney Morning*

Herald, 21 April 1999, pp. 1 and 9; Mark Dodd, Peter-Coleman-Adams and Hamish McDonald, 'Massacre shatters brief day of peace', *Sydney Morning Herald*, 24 April 1999, p. 1; Don Greenlees, 'Militias murder, kidnap during truce signing', *Weekend Australian*, 24–25 April 1999, p. 12; and Mark Dodd, 'Militia Law', *Sydney Morning Herald*, 24 April 1999, p. 39.

[20] Greg Sheridan, 'High-risk Howard throws caution to the wind', *The Australian*, 21 April 1999, p. 8; and Robert Garran and Don Greenlees, 'PM's bid to stop thugs', *The Australian*, 20 April 1999, p. 1, pp. 16–17.

[21] Mark Dodd, Peter-Coleman-Adams and Hamish McDonald, 'Defence report warning of violence', *Sydney Morning Herald*, 24 April 1999, pp. 1 and 17; and Richard McGregor and Alan Stokes, 'PM told of Timorese slaughter', *Weekend Australian*, 24–25 April 1999, pp. 1 and 12. The DIO report referred to was Defence Intelligence Organisation, 'ABRI backing violence', *Current Intelligence Brief*, 4 March 1999.

[22] Paul Kelly, 'Habibie's signal to the army', *The Australian*, 21 April 1999.

[23] Don Greenlees, 'A full and free choice', *The Australian*, 28 April, p. 1; and Greg Sheridan, 'The vital questions left unanswered', *Australian*, 28 April, p. 1.

[24] United Nations, 'Agreement between the Republic of Indonesia and the Portuguese Republic on the Question of East Timor', 5 May 1999. Copy of text included as Appendix 3 to Ian Martin, *Self Determination in East Timor, The United Nations, the Ballot and International Intervention*, International Peace Academy Occasional Papers series, Lynne Rienner Publishers, London, 2001.

[25] While there may still be some debate about interpreting evidence and confirming causal relationships between Indonesian security forces and militia violence, the balance of evidence shows that there was a strong link. See Peter Bartu, 'The militia, the military, and the people of Bobonaro', in (eds) Richard Tanter, Mark Selden, and Stephen R Shalom, *Bitter flowers, sweet flowers: East Timor, Indonesia and the world community*, Rowman & Littlefield, New York, 2001, pp. 73–90; Hamish McDonald, Desmond Ball, James Dunn, Gerry van Klinken, David Bourchier, Douglas Kammen, and Richard Tanter, *Masters of Terror: Indonesia's Military and Violence in East Timor in 1999*, Canberra Papers on Strategy and Defence, no. 145, Strategic and Defence Studies Centre, The Australian National University, Canberra, 2002; (eds) Freek Colombijn and J. Thomas Lindblad, *Roots of violence in Indonesia; contemporary violence in historical perspective*, KITLV Press, Leiden, 2002; and Freek Colombijn, 'Explaining the violent solution in Indonesia', *The Brown Journal of World Affairs*, vol. 9, no. 1, 2002, pp. 49–56.

[26] Colonel Paul B. Symon, 'OP *Faber*, Australian Service Contingent I Sitreps and Orders June—October 1999', Undated. Copy held by author.

[27] Cosgrove in interview with author, 3 January 2000.

[28] Cosgrove in interview with author, 3 January 2000.

[29] Admiral Chris A. Barrie in interview with author, 6 September 2005.

[30] Symon, 'OP *Faber*, Australian Service Contingent I Sitreps and Orders June—October 1999'.

[31] The author attended these meetings and was present at weekly briefings at Land Headquarters and daily video-conferences between HQ AST and each environmental headquarters.

[32] Cosgrove in interview with author, 3 January 2000.

[33] Operation *Faber* covered ADF participation in UNAMET.

[34] Lieutenant Colonel Paul B. Symon in interview with author, 21 August 2000.

[35] The author had personal involvement in this decision. He also had discussions with Colonel Stephen J. Dunn, Colonel (Operations) Land Headquarters and Lieutenant Colonel Mark Hoare, SO1 Intelligence, LHQ, at the time.

[36] Brigadier Jeff B. Wilkinson in interview with author, 6 May 2005.

[37] Colonel Craig W. Boyd in discussions with author at the time and subsequently. Also Colonel Craig W. Boyd, 'OP *Warden*: Draft Concept of Logistic Support', Version 3, 11 September 1999. 'This concept has no official status. It was developed by DJLOP [Boyd] from earlier planning with input from HQAST, LHQ [Land Headquarters] and LSF.'

[38] *terminal operations*: Activities related to receiving, unloading, storing, preparing and then loading and dispatching *matériel* to an area of operations (AO). These activities can involve sea, land and air transport.

[39] Robert Garran, 'Troops on Timor alert, Military numbers doubled in readiness for urgent move', *The Australian*, 7 July 1999, pp. 1 and 7. The front page of *The Australian* contained a photograph of HMAS *Jervis Bay*, a large, fast catamaran alongside in Darwin. This vessel had been leased by Defence in April

1999 and was able to accommodate 500 personnel comfortably, a further 300, less comfortably, or a mix of personnel, vehicles and supplies (See David Horner, *The Making of the Australian Defence Force*, The Australian Centenary History of Defence, Volume V, Oxford University Press, Melbourne, 2001, pp. 11–12) The accompanying article contained information on the state of readiness of the ADF to deploy to East Timor.

[40] Horner, *The Making of the Australian Defence Force*, p. 11.

[41] Lindsay Murdoch, 'Fears of after-vote bloodbath increase', *Sydney Morning Herald*, 10 July 1999, p. 4.

[42] David Jenkins, 'All over bar the shooting', *Sydney Morning Herald*, 26 August 1999, p. 11; Mark Dodd, 'Fear, squalor and the breach of faith', *Sydney Morning Herald*, 28 August 1999, p. 25; Hamish McDonald, 'Island of fear and faith', *Sydney Morning Herald*, 28 August 1999, p. 39; and Martin, *Self Determination, The United Nations, the Ballot and International Intervention*, pp. 81–82.

[43] Barrie in interview with author, 6 September 2005.

[44] Classified source.

[45] Classified source.

[46] Classified source.

[47] Cosgrove in interview with author, 3 January 2000.

[48] Brigadier Steve H. Ayling, Discussions with author in May 2000. Ayling was appointed Director General INTERFET in September 1999. He was privy to strategic level planning and orders for Operation *Spitfire* in August 1999.

[49] Major James F. McMahon in interview with author, 15 December 1999. McMahon was Officer Commanding 3rd Squadron, SASR. See (ed.) Captain Craig Stockings, *Paratroopers as Peacekeepers , 3rd Battalion, The Royal Australian Regiment, East Timor 1999–2000*, Imprint, Sydney, October 2000, p. 8.

[50] McMahon in interview with author, 15 December 1999. See also (ed.) Stockings, *Paratroopers as Peacekeepers , 3rd Battalion, The Royal Australian Regiment, East Timor 1999–2000* , p. 8. Major Peter C. Steel in interview with author, 15 December 1999. Steel was Officer Commanding 5 Aviation Squadron Group.

[51] For further detail see David Horner, *SAS: Phantoms of War, A History of Australian Special Air Service*, updated edition, Allen and Unwin, Sydney, 2002.

[52] Brigadier Jim Molan, Comments by email on draft chapter on Operation *Spitfire* in Bob Breen, *Mission Accomplished, Australian Defence Force participation in International Force East Timor*. Copies of emails held by author.

[53] Barrie in interview with author, 6 September 2005.

[54] Brigadier Jeff B. Wilkinson, 'Brief to G84 Steering Group. Logistic Lessons from Operations in East Timor 1999–2000', HQLSF, 7 February 2000. Copy held by author.

[55] The author was privy to these arrangements at the time.

[56] Lieutenant Colonel Mick C. Kehoe in interview with author, 3 February 2000.

[57] Martin, *Self Determination in East Timor, The United Nations, the Ballot and International Intervention*, Appendix 6.

[58] Don Greenlees and Robert Garran, *Deliverance: The Inside Story of East Timor's Fight for Freedom*, Allen and Unwin, Sydney, 2002, pp. 197–200.

[59] Major John Gould, Situation Report as at 5 September 1999. Gould worked for Lieutenant Colonel Paul Symon in UNAMET headquarters. Copy held by author.

[60] Martin, *Self Determination in East Timor, The United Nations, the Ballot and International Intervention*, p. 92.

[61] Martin, *Self Determination in East Timor, The United Nations, the Ballot and International Intervention*, pp. 94–97.

[62] Martin, *Self Determination in East Timor, The United Nations, the Ballot and International Intervention*, pp. 89–101. See also Tim Fischer, *Seven Days in East Timor*, Allen and Unwin, Sydney, 2000, pp. 99–102.

[63] Gould, Situation Report as at 5 September 1999.

[64] Greenlees and Garran, *Deliverance: The Inside Story of East Timor's Fight for Freedom*, p. 238.

[65] Greenlees and Garran, *Deliverance: The Inside Story of East Timor's Fight for Freedom*, p. 236.

[66] Brigadier Mark Evans in interview with author, 6 February 2000.

[67] Martin, *Self Determination in East Timor, The United Nations, the Ballot and International Intervention*, p. 98.

[68] Martin, *Self Determination in East Timor, The United Nations, the Ballot and International Intervention*, p. 98.

[69] Greenlees and Garran, *Deliverance: The Inside Story of East Timor's Fight for Freedom*, p. 239.

[70] ADHQ, CDF WNGO [Warning Order], 13/99 OP Warden, SIC 14X, 100830ZSEP99. Copy held by author.

[71] Classified source, Defence Archives, Queanbeyan.

[72] Greenlees and Garran, *Deliverance: The Inside Story of East Timor's Fight for Freedom*, pp. 242–44.

[73] The author met with Evans and his subordinate commanders and headquarters staff in April and briefed them based on UN planning documents that he had been received from Australian staff at the United Nations in New York and his assessment of the course of events in East Timor.

[74] Barrie in interview with author, 6 September 2005.

[75] Brownrigg, Comments by email on draft chapter on Operation *Spitfire* in Bob Breen, *Mission Accomplished, Australian Defence Force participation in International Force East Timor*.

[76] Barrie in interview with author, 6 September 2005.

[77] Centre for Strategic Studies, *Strategic and Military Lessons from East Timor*, CSS Strategic Briefing Papers, vol. 2, part 1, Victoria University of Wellington, February 2000, p. 1, available at <http://www.victoria.ac.nz/css/docs/Strategic_Briefing_Papers/Vol.2%20Feb%202000/East%20Timor.pdf>, accessed 1 August 2008. See also Horner, *The Making of the Australian Defence Force*, p. 24.

[78] Horner, *The Making of the Australian Defence Force*, pp. 24–25.

[79] See Garran and Greenlees, *Deliverance: The Inside Story of East Timor's Fight for Freedom*, Chapter 12.

[80] Horner, *The Making of the Australian Defence Force*, pp. 19–20.

[81] There were reports that the Indonesian Cabinet was split between a liberal elite that had gained influence after the demise of the Suharto regime in 1998 and 'old-guard nationalists'. The nationalists probably supported the razing of East Timor and the displacement of thousands of East Timorese population and at least condoned the actions of TNI. See Don Greenlees, 'Rogue element', *Weekend Australian*, 11–12 September 1999, p. 29. John Martinkus in *A Dirty Little War*, Random House, Sydney, 2001 claims to have discovered a copy of the TNI plan two months before its execution. See also Hamish McDonald, 'Australia's bloody East Timor secret, spy intercepts confirm Government knew of Jakarta's hand in massacres', *Sydney Morning Herald*, 14 March 2002. McDonald quotes from material from radio intercepts from the Defence Signals Directorate (alleged to have been leaked to him by Defence officials) that point to a TNI plan to drive East Timorese out of the territory and lay waste to its infrastructure. See also Greenlees and Garran, *Deliverance: The Inside Story of East Timor's Fight for Freedom*, chapter 11.

[82] Martin, *Self Determination in East Timor, The United Nations, the Ballot and International Intervention*, p. 94.

[83] Martin, *Self Determination in East Timor, The United Nations, the Ballot and International Intervention*, p. 100.

[84] Martin, *Self Determination in East Timor, The United Nations, the Ballot and International Intervention*, p. 100.

[85] Brownrigg, Notes on draft. See also Greenlees and Garran, *Deliverance*, pp. 228–29.

[86] Greenlees and Garran, *Deliverance: The Inside Story of East Timor's Fight for Freedom*, pp. 258–61.

[87] Martin, *Self Determination in East Timor, The United Nations, the Ballot and International Intervention*, Appendix 5.

[88] See Horner, *The Making of the Australian Defence Force*, p. 13, for a summary of the tensions between Australia and Indonesia at the time.

[89] According to David Horner, Admiral Chris Barrie decided to bypass COMAST and HQAST and take command himself because of 'the international nature of the force'[INTERFET]. David Horner, *The Evolution of Australian Higher Command Arrangements*, Command Paper 3/2002, Centre for Defence Leadership Papers, Australian Defence College, p. 29. Copy held by author.

[90] Admiral Chris A. Barrie, Chief of the Defence Force and Commander in Chief, Operation *Stabilise*, ADHQ, 'Operation Stabilise', I4X CDF/440, 190700Z SEP99. Copy held by author.

[91] Bob Breen, 'Australian Military Force Projection in the late 1980s and the 1990s: what happened and why', PhD thesis, The Australian National University, 2006, pp. 81–86 (Exercise *Kangaroo* 89), pp. 104–107 (Exercise *Kangaroo* 92) and pp. 177–82 (Exercise *Kangaroo* 95).

[92] Cosgrove in interview with author, 3 January 2000.

[93] Brownrigg, Comments by email on draft chapter on Operation *Spitfire* in Bob Breen, *Mission Accomplished, Australian Defence Force participation in International Force East Timor*.

[94] Group Captain Stewart R. Cameron, Interview with author, 20 February 2000.

[95] **aiguillettes**: an ornamental tagged cord or braid, typically gold in colour, worn on a uniform around the shoulder and armpit with a cord extension attached to a middle button of a shirt or jacket.

[96] Major Robert V. Parker in interview with author, 19 December 1999. Parker commanded this company.

[97] Major Jim L. Bryant in interview with author, 23 December 1999. Bryant commanded this company.

[98] Bryant in interview with author, 23 December 1999.

[99] Commander Daryl W. Bates in interview with author, 18 February 2000. Bates was Chief of Staff, Maritime Component at HQ INTERFET.

[100] Evans in interview with author, 6 February 2000; and Lieutenant Colonel Don Cousins in interview with author, 23 February 2000.

[101] Evans in interview with author, 6 February 2000. After the first 12 sorties had come and gone on the morning of 20 September 1999, there was only capacity for 13 more sorties that day. A total of 25 C–130 *Hercules* sorties flew in and out of Dili on 20 September. Details of these were in a table provided by Group Captain Stewart R. Cameron during his interview with author on 20 February 2000. Copy held by author.

[102] Commodore B.D. Robertson in interview with author, 18 February 2000. Robertson was Maritime Component Commander HQ INTERFET from December 1999 until 23 February 2000 after Commodore J. Stapleton.

[103] Cameron in interview with author, 20 February 2000.

[104] Evans in interview with author, 6 February 2000; and Cousins in interview with author, 23 February 2000.

[105] Captain Lawrence T. Sargeant in interview with author, 21 December 1999. Sargeant was a nursing officer waiting at Darwin Airport on 20 September. He recalled incidents of booing, jeering and shouting.

[106] Captain Kate L. Saunders in interview with author, 7 February 2000. Saunders worked at Joint Movement Control Office—Darwin during the initial deployment of INTERFET and was subjected to several tirades.

[107] Cousins in interview with author, 23 February 2000.

[108] Warrant Officer Class One, Peter F. Mele in interview with author, 9 January 2000. Mele was Regimental Quarter Master Sergeant, 2 RAR.

[109] Mele in interview with author, 9 January 2000.

[110] Stockings, *Paratroopers as Peacekeepers, 3rd Battalion, The Royal Australian Regiment, East Timor 1999–2000*, p. 28.

[111] Stockings, *Paratroopers as Peacekeepers, 3rd Battalion, The Royal Australian Regiment, East Timor 1999–2000*, p. 23.

[112] Stockings, *Paratroopers as Peacekeepers, 3rd Battalion, The Royal Australian Regiment, East Timor 1999–2000*, p. 20. Lieutenant Colonel Nick W. Welch, notes on draft chapter of Bob Breen, *Mission Accomplished, Australian Defence Force participation in International Force East Timor*, May 2000. Copy held by author. Welch was Commander Officer of 3 RAR. Also Lieutenant Colonel Mick D. Slater in interview with author, 9 January 2000. Slater was Commanding Officer of 2 RAR.

[113] Evans in interview with author, 6 February 2000.

[114] Slater in interview with author, 9 January 2000; and Bryant in interview with author, 23 December 1999.

[115] McDonald, Ball, Dunn, van Klinken, Bourchier, Kammen, and Tanter, *Masters of Terror Indonesia's Military and Violence in East Timor in 1999*. The activities of 745th Territorial Battalion are covered in this publication. See also Cameron Barr, 'A brutal exit', *Christian Science Monitor*, 13 March 2000.

[116] Evans in interview with author, 6 February 2000. Major Marcus C. Fielding in interview with author, 6 February 2000. Fielding was Brigade Major for 3rd Brigade.

[117] Lieutenant Steve M. Casey in interview with author, 23 December 1999.

[118] Lieutenant Grant A. Chisnell in interview with author, 28 December 1999.

[119] Corporal Michael D. Cooke in interview with author, 28 December 1999. Cooke was a member of Assault Pioneer Platoon.

[120] Private P.A. Francis in interview with author, 28 December 1999. Francis was a member of Sniper Section, 2 RAR.

[121] Bryant in interview with author, 23 December 1999.

[122] Bryant in interview with author, 23 December 1999.

[123] Evans in interview with author, 6 February 2000.

[124] Cousins in interview with author, 23 February 2000.

[125] Contrary to Major General Mueller's 'concept of civilianising logistic support wherever possible', 'there are some senior Army officers who refuse to entertain any notion of allowing contractors to totally control the log support of certain items into EM [East Timor], eg fresh food. The rationale is that it is a war zone'. Lieutenant Commander R. Van Geelen, 'Future Force Spt in Darwin—Op Warden', Minutes of a meeting convened by Brigadier Jeff B. Wilkinson, LOGCC, 3 October 1999. Copy held by author.

[126] Brigadier Jeff B. Wilkinson, 'Brief to SCA (A) Conference—Logistic Observations in East Timor 1999–2000', 24 February 2000. Copy held by author.

[127] Lieutenant Colonel Alan A. Murray, 'From SCA LO—Arrangements in Darwin', email to Commander M. McKeith, Headquarters Support Command—Australia, 26 September 1999. Murray was a liaison officer from SCA located with HQ LSF. In this e-mail, he describes his efforts to have interim logistic support arrangements continue for several more weeks because JLU (N) 'was flat out supporting normal dependency [local Darwin-based ADF units] and that SCA was not easily able to reinforce JLU (N)'. Copy held by author.

[128] Murray, 'From SCA LO—Arrangements in Darwin', email to McKeith, 26 September 1999.

[129] Wilkinson in interview with author, 6 May 2005.

[130] Wilkinson, 'Brief to SCA (A) Conference'.

[131] Colonel Grant D. Cavenagh, 'Logistic Capability Issues—Op *Stabilise*', INTERFET, 21 October 1999. Copy held by author.

[132] Cavenagh, 'Logistic Capability Issues—Op *Stabilise*', INTERFET, 21 October 1999, pp. 1–4.

[133] Mele in interview with author, 9 January 2000.

[134] Cousins in interview with author, 23 February 2000.

[135] Major General P.J. Cosgrove in interview with author, 30 January 2000.

[136] Major General John C. Hartley, 'Logistic Problems—East Timor', LCAUST OU05279/99, 6 November 1999, K99-00405, NAA, Sydney. Copy held by author.

[137] Hartley, 'Logistic Problems—East Timor', LCAUST OU05279/99, 6 November 1999, p. 2.

[138] Hartley, 'Logistic Problems—East Timor', LCAUST OU05279/99, 6 November 1999, p. 2.

[139] Hartley, 'Logistic Problems—East Timor', LCAUST OU05279/99, 6 November 1999, p. 1.

[140] Brigadier Jeff B. Wilkinson in discussions with author during November 1999.

[141] Cavenagh in interview with author, 17 January 2000; Cousins in interview with author, 23 February 2000; Kehoe in interview with author, 3 February 2000; and Lieutenant Colonel Barry McManus in interview with author, 8 December 1999.

[142] Mele in interview with author, 9 January 2000.

[143] Mele in interview with author, 9 January 2000.

[144] Cousins in interview with author, 23 February 2000.

Chapter 12

Reflections and Observations

Reflections

In November 1999, senior Australian Defence Force (ADF) officers and Defence officials reflected on pre-deployment preparation, deployment and initial INTERFET operations.[1] The major issues were command and control and the performance of the ADF logistic system. From the perspective of command and control, the consensus was that *ad hoc* and secretive planning processes and a late change to command and control arrangements were unhelpful. There was a call for a review of the role of Headquarters Australian Theatre (HQ AST) and criticism of the uneven flow of information from the Strategic Command Group (SCG). There were also criticisms of intelligence collection and evaluation. One Service chief commented that the Defence Intelligence Organisation (DIO) only offered 'classified news' readily available in the media and that the 'intelligence requirements of the SCG had never been communicated to DIO'.[2] There was evidence that logistic and communications staff functions at Australian Defence Headquarters (ADHQ) were dysfunctional. Staff capability and crisis management structures, as well as communications and information security within Defence and from Defence to other Government departments, proved unsatisfactory.[3] One report commented that 'the transition from a foreign policy crisis to a whole of Government crisis was not well handled and Defence's lead role in managing a peace enforcement operation was not recognised by other departments'.[4]

On 24 November 1999, Air Vice Marshal Bob Treloar submitted a report on Theatre Command for higher level consideration.[5] He affirmed that Theatre Command was working well and would work even better when component commanders were collocated in one building, 'a logical outcome of current ADF capability evolution. ... The co-located Headquarters will be structured for war but adapted for peace'.[6] He also emphasised that 'the importance of the DJFHQ [Deployable Joint Force Headquarters] cannot be overstated'.[7] He noted, however, that 'other than a liaison officer from Air Force and Navy there are currently no non-Army personnel in DJFHQ's joint staff; the core of the HQ and of any JTFHQ [Joint Task Force Headquarters]'.[8]

There was also consensus among senior ADF officers that there was room for improvement of logistic support. Higher-level logistic planning processes had also proved to be inadequate.[9] There was a strong case for appointing a permanent strategic logistic component commander at ADHQ in Canberra.[10] There was also comment that Brigadier Jeff Wilkinson had been more of a joint logistic coordinator, rather than a joint logistic commander.[11] He never had authority over maritime or air force logistic units or assets. In effect, the navy and the air force had operated their own supply chains to their force elements, using their own vessels and aircraft, while also endeavouring to meet Wilkinson's requirements for land forces. Once again, the joint movements system (1 JMOVGP) had acted as a booking agent and coordination centre rather than a regulatory agency that managed priorities on behalf of commanders. Thus, Wilkinson had neither control of the means to move personnel and supplies to the right places at the right time, nor control over mounting base operations in Darwin.

The ADF contemplated its experiences from Operations *Spitfire*, *Warden* and *Stabilise* over the following months of 2000. There were several events organised to examine logistic lessons.[12] By September 2000, the newly appointed Commander Joint Logistics (CJLOG), Major General Peter Haddad, and Air Vice Marshal Colin Hingston, Head National Support, had written a paper entitled, 'National Support and Theatre Sustainment—Lessons from East Timor'. It addressed command and control, logistic management systems, combat service support capabilities, supply chain performance, civil support capability and international arrangements and agreements.[13] In sum, Haddad and Hingston blamed the strategic level of command for not properly warning and including Major General Des Mueller and logisticians at Support Command in the initial planning for the force projection to East Timor. This exclusion left extant logistic arrangements unable to respond effectively and resulted in Wilkinson having to set up *ad hoc*, inefficient and complicated arrangements. In effect, Haddad and Hingston were stating that those same Melbourne and Sydney-based logistic organisations that had failed to manage the supply chain satisfactorily for operations in Somalia in 1993, and for Operations *Lagoon* and *Bel Isi* would have delivered a superior service for Operation *Stabilise* if there had been more time to plan at the beginning.[14]

Reflections on command and control and logistic support arrangements for Operations *Warden* and *Stabilise* were thorough. However, there were trends that echoed the failed efforts of the past to learn from operational experience and apply lessons to future operations. One trend was to change the form but not the substance. For example, past operations demonstrated conclusively that there were fundamental problems with force sustainment of deployed forces. These problems were not cited in reports to justify changes. Another trend was not to review previous operations to verify what worked well and what needed to be changed. Senior defence committees seemed to examine and note what happened in the most recent operation, but not the cumulative evidence of problems from past operations to inform their deliberations on what might need to be done. The ADF did not appear to have a mechanism or organisation for analysing its operational performance objectively over time and identifying and acting on persistent systemic problems. In short, the ADF did not audit its operations.

Observations

After Operation *Stabilise*, the ADF did not substantially adjust command and control arrangements for operations in 2000. The theatre level of command was left in place awaiting the co-location of the environmental commanders and their staffs in one building with Commander Australian Theatre (COMAST) and his staff. Concerns remained. Would there be sufficient time for the strategic level of command to delegate planning and conduct of campaigns and operations to COMAST and his staff? If there was sufficient time, would political circumstances allow the theatre level to conduct campaigns and operations without undue interference? Would the Australian Government wait for the passage of information from the tactical level through to the strategic level, via an intermediate level of command, when it was instantaneous from the tactical level to the world?

The ADF did change arrangements for logistics more substantially, but left historical weaknesses. The new CJLOG was left to compete for, but not command, enabling logistic resources. He had no assigned deployable logistic support headquarters or units. He commanded the Defence National Supply and Distribution Centre (DNSDC) (a commercialised and joint distribution centre in Sydney) but not the means, such as navy vessels or service aircraft, to move stock along supply chains to deployed forces. Joint Logistic Command (formerly Support Command–Australia) consolidated force sustainment arrangements, but left CJLOG in charge of supporting too many functions simultaneously. There would be competing priorities within these functions as well as for the use of navy vessels and service aircraft.

So, despite ending the twentieth century with one of Australia's most strategically important and risky military force projections, the lessons were not applied again. Intuitively, one might have expected that a force-projecting island nation like Australia would have become increasingly proficient, having had opportunities for both rehearsal and practice for more than a century. The reverse was true—especially when allies were not in a position to help. During the decade leading up to Operation *Stabilise*, the ADF was neither as proficient as it believed it was, nor as competent as it should have been. Operation *Stabilise* once again exposed historically persistent weaknesses in the enabling functions of force projection. Australia had depended on good luck and the resilience of junior leaders and small teams at tactical tipping points in 1942, on the Kokoda Track, and in 1966, at Long Tan in Vietnam, and had to do so again in the streets of Dili in 1999. For Operations *Lagoon* and *Bel Isi*, deficiencies in force projection increased risk. The same increase in pressure occurred for Operation *Stabilise*.

Why was this so? Why were there still problems after 115 years of participation in the military emergencies and campaigns of allies as well as several operations in the near region?

Force of Habit

In 1987, the government announced that Australia's defence would be based on self reliance and joint operations.[15] At that time, Australia and its armed forces had been conditioned by just over a century of dependence on allies for the functions of force projection. Overcoming the legacy of this conditioning was the major challenge. Following the habits of 100 years, the ADF did not design, develop or rehearse all of the enabling functions—especially those that had been provided by allies, such as deployment, protection and force sustainment, during the late 1980s and the 1990s. The ADF preferred to rehearse force employment after arrival, rather than pre-deployment functions that would optimise arrival and subsequent employment and sustainment. The major impediment to joint operations was allies employing Australian contingents from the three Services separately for over 100 years. The Services clung to the experiences of the previous decades by preferring to exercise and operate separately, and resisting joint arrangements for their command, employment and sustainment.

Preference for Good News

Faulty force projection increased risk on operations in the late 1980s and the 1990s. While tactical-level reports described the risks, the higher levels of command appeared to be out of touch, favouring good news over bad. After all, operational outcomes were excellent and these operations enhanced Australia's military reputation. Consequently, there appeared to be only a passing interest in the increased pressure put on the tactical level of command. There also appeared to be little enthusiasm or mechanisms for applying lessons. The ADF became a victim of its own success. Even when Australian Governments decreased official warning time to an average of four weeks, force elements appeared to deploy on time and in good order, and accomplish their missions. Fortunately, no capable opponents awaited them that might have taken advantage of the unhelpful circumstances of their preparation, loading, deployment and subsequent supply chain management.

Was Strategic Guidance at Fault?

An alternate hypothesis is to link strategic guidance with deficiencies in force projection, and play down 100 years of conditioning and inter-Service rivalry. Though it is not the purpose of this monograph to explore strategic level decision-making and policy development, an examination of the *Defence of Australia 1987* does not reveal a direct link. The architect of that White Paper, Paul Dibb, correctly assessed that 'Australia is one of the most secure countries in the world' and faces 'no identifiable military threat'.[16] However, he did not advocate continental defence or isolationism. The White Paper left all three Services with generic capabilities for force projection.

In respect to land forces, it specified that 'more emphasis will be given to highly mobile forces capable of rapid deployment'.[17] Dibb saw Australia's geography as both a boon and a 'daunting task' for force projection.[18] Remoteness from centres of global conflict and the sea and air gap around the continent, as well as self-sufficiency in basic commodities, were blessings for Australian defence because they posed significant force projection challenges for enemies.[19] However, the 'daunting task' for the ADF would be self-reliant defence of Australian territorial sovereignty. Dibb envisioned Australia having to project military force over thousands of kilometres from the southern and eastern heartlands to the western and northern hinterlands.[20] To achieve this, he recommended an emphasis on projecting maritime and air power with support from ground forces able to operate over 'vast distances'—within continental Australia—to defeat 'raiding groups'.[21] While the *Defence of Australia 1987* assessed that the primary purpose of land force projection would be national, there were sufficient land force capabilities to enable both regional and international projection. Dibb recognised that logistics would underwrite force projection. He recommended pre-positioning both combat forces and 'integral ADF logistic capacities within operational areas in the north'.[22] He also identified the need for 'sustained exercises in the north, supported by bases in the south, to test and identify weaknesses in our logistic train'.[23]

Practice Makes Perfect

The problems encountered during the four weeks before deployment originated in a lack of practice. The crux was slow responses down the chain of command. Orders and instructions arrived too late to influence tactical- level preparations and deployment. The ADF did not rehearse the use of warning time, planning processes, joint command and control, force protection, tactical deployment or force sustainment under simulated operational conditions. Flawed rehearsal became defective performance. The strategic and operational levels of command shrouded warning time in secrecy and then rushed planning. Planners imposed arbitrary and disruptive caps on numbers for land forces and made *ad hoc* command arrangements. There was insufficient preparation and reconnaissance. Though a small unit assisted pre-deployment preparations after 1991, tactical commanders had to rely on their own initiative and resourcefulness to prepare land forces, and on special pleading to secure additional resources for force preparation and capability enhancements before deployment.

Lead joint commanders nominated mounting authorities and mounting headquarters. However, the army did not have doctrine or practiced procedures for mounting base operations. There was no over-arching ADF machinery for synchronising joint logistic preparation or personnel administration, except through collegial cooperation at the tactical level. Logisticians were under pressure to concentrate stocks for ship loading at short notice, often at great expense and always with unsatisfactory coordination. The consequence of rushing planning, preparation and deployment was increased risk at sea off Fiji in May 1987 and off Bougainville in October 1994. For land projections to Bougainville and East Timor, troops arrived tired, under-rehearsed and with an unnecessarily incomplete understanding of what lay ahead. Yet they were required to perform well immediately under intense media scrutiny. The results of increasing risk could have been casualties, diminution of Australia's military reputation, and some political and diplomatic embarrassment. Fortunately, ADF force elements were not facing opponents or circumstances on arrival that took advantage of their fatigue and lack of situational awareness.

Tribal Differences

The challenge for each Chief of the Defence Force (CDF) in the late 1980s and the 1990s was to overcome the impediments of a century of conditioned dependence on allies for some functions as well as inter-Service rivalry. The Australian Services maintained separate command and sustainment systems, and trained for independent employment until the early 1980s. Sir Philip Bennett's successors did their best to exercise their statutory authority to command assigned forces from the Services for operations. The Services resisted. Successive *Kangaroo* Exercises failed to bring the three Services under joint command or to establish efficient joint movements and sustainment arrangements. There was no testing of the logistic train. Once again, faulty rehearsal contributed to defective supply chain performance on operations. The navy and the air force did not support a land operation in Somalia satisfactorily in 1993, despite General Peter Gration ordering them to provide vessels and aircraft for sustainment.[24] Major General Murray Blake had responsibility for operational outcomes in Somalia, but not the enabling authority over navy vessels and service aircraft to support his deployed force. Major General Peter Arnison had no control over the means for supply for Operation *Lagoon* in 1994.

After experimenting with improvised arrangements in 1992 and 1995 on *Kangaroo* Exercises, General John Baker appointed a permanent theatre commander and raised a theatre headquarters in Sydney in 1996. The aim was to create a separate, as well as a geographically separated, operational level of command to plan and conduct joint campaigns and operations. The assumption was that interaction under a theatre commander would encourage the development of a culture of inter-Service cooperation among environmental commanders. Indeed, the eventual aim was to co-locate environmental headquarters under the theatre commander in one facility. The problem was that there was insufficient time for development of strategic guidance and subsequent devolution of planning and decision-making to a theatre level of command. Experience showed that four weeks was not long enough for another level of command, between the strategic, operational and tactical levels, to receive and convert strategic guidance into orders and instructions and prepare force elements for deployment. Collegial cooperation between staff at the environmental headquarters and small coordinating staff groups at the theatre headquarters neither facilitated prompt force projection nor better logistics. Major General Frank Hickling, the lead joint commander for operations in Bougainville in 1997, could not rely on HQ AST to give him sufficient guidance and warning time before deployment. Subsequently, he could not rely on his environmental colleagues to provide his desired rate of maritime or air resupply effort or effect.

Failure of Theatre Command

The projection to East Timor in 1999 also demonstrated that, when time was short and political and strategic stakes were high, there would be circumscribed devolution of command to a theatre level. The CDF, Admiral Chris Barrie, delegated national, not operational command, to his theatre commander, Air Vice Marshal Bob Treloar. Arguably, his successors would most likely do so again in similar circumstances. Media scrutiny of this projection also epitomised the instantaneous visibility of the tactical level to a worldwide audience and scores of commentators. The operational commander in East Timor, Major General Peter Cosgrove, communicated directly to this audience, as well as directly to Barrie and his senior staff. There was a limited role for Treloar and his headquarters. The argument that having Treloar and his headquarters in the chain of command freed Barrie to command this strategically important operation by continuing to command 22 ongoing operations was thin. In reality, the three environmental headquarters had a closer relationship to those operations than theatre staff. There is some substance in an argument that Treloar commanded ADF assets that were on standby in case there was interference with the INTERFET deployment, but it would have been most unlikely that he would have had the freedom to respond to a threat. Barrie and Prime Minister John Howard would most likely have exercised command and control of operations against renegade Indonesian forces.

The other problematic argument justifying a separate and separated theatre level of command was that Treloar coordinated logistics for the East Timor projection. In reality, neither he, nor his logistic counterpart in Melbourne, Mueller, meaningfully coordinated force sustainment, which largely reverted to service control. Improvised and unrehearsed logistic arrangements applied for three months during the most critical period of the INTERFET projection. The Land Commander, Major General John Hartley, and Treloar's Logistic Component Commander, Wilkinson, had to make *ad hoc* arrangements during this period for managing mounting and forward operating bases, as well as the supply chain.

Failure of Joint Logistics

Joint force commanders, who were usually army officers, were unable to control logistic priorities or the vessels and aircraft they needed to deploy and sustain their forces. For their part, ADF logisticians and the navy and the air force did not rehearse short notice tactical deployment of land forces or joint supply chain management. The ADF movements system moved troops and *matériel* administratively for major field exercises and for offshore operations. Deploying troops were passengers on haphazardly loaded navy vessels and air force and commercial aircraft. Fortunately, for these projections, there was time to unload and reorganise after arrival, and to move tactically thereafter. It did not matter that commanders, who were responsible for operational outcomes, did not control loading or the means for deployment. There was no substantial military contest awaiting their forces on arrival.

The penalties for joint operational commanders not having firmer control over logistic priorities and the means of deployment and resupply could have been high in September 1999. The projection to East Timor required efficient and precise tactical loading and deployment. While the navy and the air force did not have competing priorities for previous projections, both Services did for the INTERFET deployment because of the posture of Indonesian maritime and air force elements in general, and limited airport infrastructure in Dili in particular. Fortunately, the navy had the capacity to assign transport vessels exclusively in support of the INTERFET deployment. The leasing of HMAS *Jervis Bay* was a master stroke. However, there were competing priorities for the use of service aircraft flying into Dili. Neither Cosgrove nor his tactical land force commander, Brigadier Mark Evans, had control of these priorities. Consequent delays in getting troops and initial supplies to Dili increased risk significantly. If outnumbered Australian troops had become involved in an accidental escalation of hostilities in Dili on 20 or 21 September 1999, they would have run out of ammunition and potentially taken and inflicted heavy casualties—a tactical setback that would have had significant strategic, diplomatic and political repercussions.

Control of the enablers was the root problem for deploying and sustaining deployed land forces. Service chiefs and their logistic support commanders were not in the chain of command for ADF operations; yet they controlled logistics. This was not a major issue for the navy and the air force. These Services owned transport assets to support their organic logistic capabilities. They routinely practised force sustainment under operational conditions. Both Services were competent in independent deployment and distant logistic support, including supply of spare parts. The army was a dependent service bereft of the means for deployment and resupply, and under-rehearsed in supply chain management. After Defence established the DNSDC as well as joint logistic units (JLU) around Australia in the 1990s, the army lost control of much of its organic logistic infrastructure and became another customer. Offshore land operations competed for logistic support with navy and air force priorities as well as with the needs of domestic training and national base-to-base supply. Accordingly, force sustainment was not pushed to land operations by commanders responsible for operational outcomes, but had to be pulled from Service chiefs, their logistic commanders and departmental fleet managers, amidst competing priorities.

Thus, at the end of the twentieth century, after over a century of dependence on allies for sustainment and independent Service employment, and just under 30 years aspiring to self-reliance and a joint and commercial logistic culture for operations, ADF logistics was still not working satisfactorily. New arrangements that were put in place in 2000, following the projection to East Timor, awaited testing in the new century.

All of the Australian force projections of the twentieth century were successful and enhanced Australia's military reputation. Arguably, if Australia continued as a dependent ally and did not aspire to self-reliant defence and joint operations, the status quo would suffice. However, circumstances in 1942 and 1966, and during the late 1980s and the 1990s, required Australia to project force independently and demanded inter-Service cooperation. This monograph shows that independent projections in the late 1980s and the 1990s were successful, but that there was room for improvement. The challenge for the twenty-first century would be to reduce the level of difficulty the ADF was having with force projection in the final two decades of the twentieth century.

ENDNOTES

[1] Classified sources.
[2] Classified sources.
[3] Classified sources.
[4] Classified source.
[5] Air Vice Marshal Bob Treloar, 'Theatre Headquarters', HQAST 01568/99, 24 November 1999, 623-11-1.HQ AST, Potts Point.
[6] Air Vice Marshal Bob Treloar, 'The Form and Function of HQAST', HQ AST 01570/99, 24 November 1999, p. 14, 623-11-1, HQ AST, Potts Point.
[7] Treloar, 'The Form and Function of DJFHQ', HQAST 01569/99, 24 November 1999, p. 1, 623-11-2, HQ AST, Potts Point.
[8] Treloar, 'The Form and Function of DJFHQ', HQAST 01569/99, 24 November 1999, p. 4.
[9] Classified sources.
[10] Classified source.
[11] Classified source.
[12] HQ AST, Augmented Theatre Commanders' Meeting, 21 February 2000. The agenda item was 'Logistic Lessons from Operations in East Timor', Support Command—Australia Conference, 24 February 2000, Presentation 'Logistic Observations for Operations in East Timor 1999 to 2000'. HQ AST, 'OP Stabilise—Lessons Learnt Seminar', 1 March 2000.

[13] Major General Peter F. Haddad and Air Vice Marshal Colin M. Hingston, 'National Support and Theatre Sustainment—Lessons from East Timor', 6 September 2000, classified file, Defence Archives Queanbeyan. Copy held by author. (Note: The reference itself is not classified.)

[14] Headquarters Logistic Command (HQ LOGCOMD) in Melbourne and the Moorebank Logistic Group in Sydney had supported Operation *Solace* unsatisfactorily in 1993. For Operation *Lagoon*, Moorebank Logistic Group had become the Defence National Supply and Distribution Centre (DNSDC), and it was this centre and HQ LOGCOMD that provided unsatisfactory support. For Operation *Bel Isi*, HQ LOGCOMD had become Headquarters Support Command—Australia (HQ SCA), and this headquarters and DNSDC provided unsatisfactory support.

[15] Department of Defence, *The Defence of Australia 1987*, presented to the Parliament by the Minister for Defence, the Honourable Kim. C. Beazley, MP, Australian Government Publishing Service, Canberra, 1987, pp. 1–2, 60–62.

[16] Paul Dibb, *Review of Australia's Defence Capabilities*, Report to the Minister for Defence by Mr Paul Dibb, Australian Government Publishing Service, Canberra, March 1986, p. 1.

[17] Department of Defence, *Defence of Australia 1987*, p. 63.

[18] Department of Defence, *Defence of Australia 1987*, p. 3.

[19] Department of Defence, *Defence of Australia 1987*. See p. 1 for geographic advantages and p. 2 for economic advantages of self sufficiency in basic commodities.

[20] Department of Defence, *Defence of Australia 1987*, p. 3.

[21] Department of Defence, *Defence of Australia 1987*. See pp. 7–9 for emphasis on projecting and defending with maritime and air power and p. 10 for organisation, disposition and mobility of ground forces.

[22] Department of Defence, *Defence of Australia 1987*, p. 12.

[23] Department of Defence, *Defence of Australia 1987*, p. 12.

[24] See *A Little Bit of Hope, Australian Force—Somalia*, Allen and Unwin, Sydney, 1998, chapter 6.

Chapter 13

Conclusion

> Australia is a lucky country run mainly by second-rate people who share its luck. It lives on other people's ideas, and although it's ordinary people are adaptable, most of its leaders (in all fields) so lack curiosity about the events that surround them that they are often taken by surprise.
>
> Donald Horne, *The Lucky Country*, 1964[1]

> The historian has actual men and women, real characters, crowds and choruses as the subject of his work; and it seems to me that if he cannot see that their qualities, motives and ideas in interplay combine to produce vast actual drama in the rise and fall and other vicissitudes of nations, then he is inadequate for his real task. Surely, especially at times such as the present, men and women look to the historian to tell them, as far as possible, not the partisan view of a period or an episode; it is difficult for them to shut their ears to the din of party propaganda, both honest and charlatan. The guidance which they seek is surely that of someone who will at least attempt to exhibit to them events, causes and results as they actually happened on the world stage. And if the historian cannot write that drama in its full truth, with the interplay of good and ill, wisdom and folly, all parties working to its complex conclusion, then so much less the historian he.
>
> C.E.W. Bean, 22 February 1938.[2]

From the perspective of military force projection, Australia's luck and time is running out. When Donald Horne wrote *The Lucky Country*, he had in mind that, while other nations were becoming cleverer, Australia was still relying for its prosperity on the luck of its geographic, climatic, agricultural and geological circumstances. He called for Australia to become more innovative and proactive in shaping its future and making decisions in its national interests.[3] Militarily, Australia has also been lucky rather than clever. At two historic tactical tipping points in 1942 and 1966, the nation depended on good fortune prevailing over incompetence. Since the end of the Cold War in 1989, the Australian Defence Force (ADF) has been fortunate that more capable opponents or more demanding circumstances have not put deployed land forces under more pressure. Operations that should have been trouble-free dry runs for force projection have been bedevilled by persistent deficiencies and unnecessary risks. Good luck and the resilience of junior leaders and small teams avoided strategic and political embarrassment.

Time is running out because Australia's geographic advantages are no longer as significant in protecting the nation from attack as they used to be. The worldwide jihadist threat to Western interests and moderate Islam does not depend on invading maritime and air armadas for success. Jihadists are sophisticated learning enemies who employ barbaric but astute tactics that produce strategic effects. The terrorist attacks in New York city and Washington, DC on 11 September 2001 are evidence of this. They infiltrate borders, as well as nesting in the homelands of their adversaries before striking unexpectedly. The London Underground attacks in July 2005 are the result of such tactics. They learn from their operations and strike again, as shown by the terrorist attacks in Bali in October 2002 and October 2005 and the ongoing bombing campaign in Iraq and Afghanistan. They need to be fought by learning organisations and capable intelligence systems within 'whole-of-nation' security efforts. This monograph concludes that, from the perspective of force projection, the ADF was not a learning organisation and did not have capable intelligence systems at the turn of the century. The need for several inquiries into Australian intelligence in recent years suggests that this monograph is not alone in this assessment.[4]

Time is also running out because Australia's security circumstances are likely to change.[5] So far, Australian Governments have been able to offer allies token contributions to campaigns against jihadists in Iraq and Afghanistan. There may come a time when the United States Government insists on more substantial Australian commitments in more dangerous settings against jihadists, or in response to other military emergencies in countries such as Iran, North Korea and Taiwan.[6] Regional emergencies may also require Australia to respond rapidly into dangerous and volatile environments.[7] At the time of writing, jihadists have not attacked Australia. There may come a time when the Australian Government orders a prompt, strong and smart response to an attack on the homeland. The government may also require the ADF to pre-empt an attack at short notice that is being mounted regionally or internationally. Based on this monograph, the ADF may be found wanting, because it has continually failed to apply lessons from its own operational history.

In 2003, the Chief of the Defence Force (CDF), General Peter Cosgrove, opined that 'the Australian Defence Force has come a long way in recent years. In my view, we have positioned ourselves as a modern, professional military organisation through the quality of our work'.[8] He announced that the vision for the future was encapsulated in a Future Warfighting Concept that emphasised and enhanced previous concepts contained in another Defence guidance document, *Force 2020*, of the Seamless Force, effects-based operations and network centric warfare.⁹ The accompanying booklet to Cosgrove's covering letter offered:

> This approach seeks to apply strength against weakness. It values surprise and deception. It requires an ability to act fast, to reach out to the critical place at the right time, and create simultaneous problems that an adversary cannot resolve. In order to fight this way, the ADF will need the ability to be deployed and sustained at home and at a distance. ... The ADF's ability to project power within Australia and its adjacent air and sea space remains vital; but the need to be capable of deploying forces overseas—generally as part of a coalition—remains important.[10]

This is the credo of modern force projection as echoed in an earlier Defence publication, *The Australian Approach to Warfare*, which stated that 'whilst Australia's posture is defensive, we should seek to attack hostile forces as far from our shores as possible'.[11] The importance of force projection in support of allies was stated in *National Security: A Defence Update* in 2003 that was produced in response to the changing world security environment, precipitated in part by the jihadist attacks in New York and Washington on 11 September 2001.[12] In 2005, at the inaugural Australian Strategic Policy Institute International Conference, 'Australia's Defence and Security: Challenges and Opportunities at the Start of the 21st Century', the Defence Minister, Senator Robert Hill, stated:

> The role of the expeditionary force might have changed, but the need to be able to project our military forces—in meeting today's security challenges, is as vital as ever—possibly more so. This was recognised by the Howard Government in its 2000 White paper which endorsed a program to significantly enhance our joint force expeditionary capacity.[13]

However, in 2003, three years after its last lucky force projection to East Timor and the publication of *Defence 2000: Our Future Defence Force*, the ADF demonstrated once again that its structure, processes and procedures were impediments to acting fast, reaching out to the critical place at the right time, and deploying and sustaining at a distance.[14] Post-operational reports from Operation *Anode*, a regional projection of a 2500-strong Australian-led combined force to the Solomon Islands to support a restoration of law and order, confirms this monograph's conclusion that the ADF is not a learning organisation and has the wrong structures and processes for force projection.[15] The government gave the ADF four weeks to prepare and deploy in July 2003 after contemplating its options in secrecy for several months. There was a familiar and lamentable pattern of the government and the ADF not using warning time effectively, followed by rushed planning, reconnaissance and preparation, haphazard ship loading, number capping and raising *ad hoc* headquarters.[16] Orders and instructions took too long to produce and did not influence preparations and deployment.[17] Good luck favoured this operation. No capable opponents awaited arrival. There were no substantial consequences from what were now becoming traditional problems with logistics, except that Australian and regional troops were inconvenienced and endured unnecessarily austere living conditions for four weeks.[18]

Is this monograph too fastidious? Will there always be difficulties and risks with military operations? Indeed, do military operations always depend for their success on the resilience of junior leaders and small teams? Should a middle-ranking power like Australia aspire to self-reliance? Allies have and will continue to underwrite Australia's defence. Is it understandable and unremarkable that Australia began the twentieth century as a dependent British ally and finished 100 years later as a dependent American ally? Does the monograph over-emphasise the opinions of eyewitnesses at the tactical level and their post-operations reports as well as other evidence from departmental files? Surely these are minority views lacking a broader perspective? The majority view, endorsed by both senior Defence committees and successive governments, is that the ADF performed very well on operations during the late 1980s and the 1990s, and will continue to do so in the twenty-first century.[19]

Military operations are dangerous and difficult to manage. However, the imperative should be to minimise risk to one's own forces and maximise the risk to one's opponents. It is also important to ease the inevitable pressure on people who are being sent into harm's way, not the reverse. Junior leaders and small teams deserve the best advantages they can get. The media will soon notice if these are not forthcoming. Relying on allies to cover gaps in Australia's proficiency in force projection is not only folly, but also demeaning to Australia's nationhood. Australia is obligated to develop a self-reliant defence. Not doing so invites the unsatisfactory circumstances of the defence of New Guinea in 1942, the battle of Long Tan in 1966 and the dangers in Dili in 1999 to repeat in some form next time the ADF is required to lead or operate alone. Reports from the tactical level are neither minority opinions nor the views of institutional dissenters. Evidence of eyewitnesses and first-hand research adds credibility. Although the Defence Department has an obligation to manage its public reputation, it must not ignore reports from those who faced danger simply because the documents contain inconvenient observations.

This monograph follows the historiography of Australia's first official military historian, C.E.W. Bean. He favoured first-hand research, frontline sources and descriptive tactical detail. However, the monograph has adopted his research method, not his commemorative intent or heroic, Homeric style. Indeed, the monograph reverses his style. It examines and criticises rather than commemorates and inspires. Its narrative is aligned to a framework of the 10 enabling functions of force projection and follows the chronologies of four case studies. It is akin to an historical audit of contemporary ADF operations. Like an audit, it devotes more words to breaches of best practice than compliance. While there are books and articles critical of the conduct of Australian military operations and campaigns, it was neither Bean's intention nor possibly the intent of most Australian military historians to audit or critique Australia's armed forces on technical proficiency.[20] Arguably, military history audits, like their corporate counterparts, would not attract a wide and admiring readership. However, an audit approach to history not only gets closer to the plain and absolute truth—the objective of good scholarship—but can also become important for the nation's future defence.

Thus, this monograph departs from the laudatory and commemorative style of Bean's histories and some contemporary popular histories.[21] It follows the more technical and objective style of the official histories of the Second World War, Korea, and of Australia's involvement in Southeast Asian conflicts between 1948 and 1975. Dudley McCarthy describes the carnage and misfortunes of the Kokoda Campaign in 1941–42.[22] Robert O'Neill points out that 3 RAR was 'under-strength, under-equipped and collectively poorly prepared for war' before telling the story of the battalion's hasty deployment to the Korean Peninsula in 1950.[23] Peter Dennis and Jeffrey Grey record the poor preparation of battalions moving to Malaya in the 1950s and 1960s.[24] They point out that 2 RAR was in a 'parlous state' and 'did not reach its establishment until just before leaving Australia' and that several years later 3 RAR was not ready for operations when it embarked.[25] Ian McNeill leaves the reader in no doubt about the mismanagement that preceded the battle of Long Tan and the luck that had to prevail for the Australians to avoid a military disaster.[26]

There would not be a significant difference between this monograph and official interpretations if the ADF audited its operations independently. In the late 1980s and the 1990s, tactical-level reporting did not move up the ADF chain of command without modification. Self-congratulatory and optimised reports from higher levels of command, typically from headquarters that commanded operations, did not encourage senior ADF committees to take action to apply lessons.[27] An exception was the reporting on logistics in 1999 for the projection to East Timor. This Operation did attract the interest of the Australian National Audit Organisation. The resultant audit report identified many of the difficulties that the ADF was having in deploying and sustaining land forces.[28] A useful innovation might be for the ADF to conduct audits of its operations, within the framework of the functions of force projection, employing an organisation or board comprised of suitably qualified and experienced persons that is outside the chain of command, but reports to the Defence Minister and the CDF.

The ADF has an institutional obligation to tell its story as part of Australia's national story. It also has a duty to record, retain and analyse operational performance and apply corporate memory to the planning and conduct of future operations. Alan Ryan points out that it would be useful to employ historians on operations both for telling the story and to provide useful operational analysis and corporate memory from past operations.[29] Thus historians, who would not be in the chain of command, could conduct first-hand research and write histories of operations soon after they occur. The result would be satisfaction of imperatives to record as well as to learn from history simultaneously. These accounts would be the first draft of official histories, enriching them with eyewitness reports while history was being made. However, Captain Sir Basil Liddell Hart highlighted one of the problems identified in this monograph when he wrote in *Thoughts on War* in 1944 that 'the discovery of uncomfortable facts had never been encouraged in armies, who treated their history as a sentimental treasure rather than a field of scientific research'.[30]

This monograph is a constructed narrative of events as well as a dissertation. Though not setting out to do so, it has made the case for consolidating ADF joint command and control and the ways and means of force projection. The three Services and their environmental commanders and their staffs are not positioned organisationally to contribute effectively. The separate and separated theatre level of command does not work. The ADF logistics system is still not functioning well for force projection.[31] It is certainly not 'joint'. And intelligence organisations have failed to deliver at the tactical level—where it counts.

Senator Hill announced a new Joint Operations Command on 16 March 2004 and there have been further refinements in 2005.[32] Reflecting the advice of General Peter Cosgrove, his intentions were 'to simplify and streamline the ADF's command structure and allow more effective control of forces on operations'.[33] Based on the historical analysis in this monograph, he did not go far enough in 2004. However, the appointment of a Chief of Joint Operations (CJOPS) to exercise command through an integrated joint headquarters (Headquarters Joint Operations Command or HQ JOC) located at Bungendore near Canberra, rather than one comprised of co-located environmental staff, almost completes the transformation required to facilitate prompt, strong and smart Australian force projection for the future.[34]

The final step is to match responsibility with the ways and means to deploy, sustain and manoeuvre. As the officer ultimately responsible for ADF operations, the CDF needs CJOPS and HQ JOC to incorporate joint command of operations, a strategic joint logistics component commander, joint movements and a deployable joint force headquarters. The CJOPS should provide options and advice, both upwards to government and across to other departments and allies via the CDF, as well as direction and advice to both Service chiefs and environmental commanders.

Conclusion

The CJOPS has responsibility to deliver specified military effects at the right place at the right time. Based on historical precedents, he will be allowed about four weeks or less to do so. In 2004, Cosgrove recognised that, to fulfil this role, the CJOPS had to have authority over environmental commanders and their staffs. In 2005, the newly appointed CDF, Air Chief Marshal Angus Houston, recognised that it would be more effective to integrate rather than just co-locate environmental staff groups and environmental commanders in one facility. The step yet to be taken, however, is to consolidate high-readiness ADF force elements, intelligence assets, mounting bases and the means for force sustainment and joint movements—the enablers.

The ADF's operational experiences of the late 1980s and the 1990s make a case for the formation of an ADF rapid response command under the CJOPS. This command would be comprised of permanently assigned combat and logistic formations and units from the three Services, intelligence assets, vessels, service aircraft and infrastructure.[35] This would change the paradigm for ADF joint operations from 'pulling' assets and support from the Services to 'pushing' assets and support to deployed forces that are under operational control and have been rehearsed thoroughly for force projection. Service chiefs and Defence equivalents would still retain technical and administrative control of personnel and assets assigned to rapid response command, but not operational control.[36]

Most importantly, a rapid response command would rehearse the functions of force projection under simulated operational conditions and develop a joint force projection ethos and culture. This type of rehearsal could facilitate whole-of-nation responses to regional and world events requiring some form of military action, as well as efficient specific force preparation, deployment and sustainment. Thus, warning time would equal preparation time. Planning compartments could be vertical down to the tactical level of command rather than just horizontal across organisations and departments in Canberra. Reconnaissance could include each level of command and a range of specialists belonging to the one organisation. Forward elements could practise tactical deployment, preceded and accompanied by force protection elements, and followed by responsive joint logistics, with stamina as well as intelligence that would blend human and technical capabilities.

In summary, the history of Australian military operations until the end of the twentieth century was mostly about national, regional and international force projection. After the first projection to the Sudan in 1885, Australian forces, fostered by allies, participated in international military emergencies and wars, as well as Southeast Asian and Pacific area campaigns for the next 87 years. By 1972, Australia's military posture was evolving to include national force projection. In the 1976 White Paper, *Australian Defence*, the emphasis moved to self-reliant defence of the homeland and near region.[37] The ADF spent the next 11 years periodically rehearsing national force projection. During the late 1980s and the 1990s, Australian Governments returned to responding militarily to particular regional and international emergencies and events, mostly in the company of allies, while still continuing to rehearse nationally. In the twenty-first century, this trend has continued.

This monograph tells the story of Australia's military force projection in the late 1980s and the 1990s and analyses proficiency within the framework of 10 enabling functions. It concludes that all was not well. The ADF has to consolidate rather than divide command and control arrangements. At the same time, the ADF has to divide into a rapid response command for operations and assign Service chiefs the crucial tasks of raising, training and maintaining their environmental capabilities. They would retain technical and administrative command of forces assigned to rapid response command. At the time of writing, a rapid response command does not exist. Its formation awaits a victory for commonsense under the present Defence senior leadership group, a major terrorist attack on Australian soil or on Australian interests overseas, or a military disaster.

ENDNOTES

[1] Donald Horne, *The Lucky Country*, Terra Nova, Melbourne, 1964, p. 220.

[2] C.E.W. Bean, 'The Writing of the Australian Official History of the Great War—Sources, Methods and Some Conclusions,' (Read before the Royal Australian Historical Society, 22 February 1938) in *Despatch*, Journal of the New South Wales Military Historical Society, vol. XXXVI, no. 2, April/June 2001. First published in the Royal Australia Historical Society, *Journal and Proceedings*, vol. XXIV, 1938, part 2, p. 21.

[3] For some views on Donald Horne's legacy of ideas, see Macgregor Duncan, Andrew Leigh and David Madden, 'Wise Hedgehogs and Clever Foxes', 19 September 2005, ON-line Opinion, available at <http://www.onlineopinion.com.au/view.asp?article=195>, accessed 14 November 2007; Anne Henderson, 'Still the Lucky Country, Never Was, Still Isn't', Address to National Archives, 2 March 2003; and John Mulvaney, 'Still A Lucky Country?', Presentation to National Archives, 15 April 2003.

[4] Inquiries in 2003 and 2004 by successive Inspector Generals Intelligence and Security, Mr William Blick and Mr Ian Carnell. *Inquiry into Australian Intelligence Agencies* by Mr Philip Flood in 2005. For documentation and correspondence, see <http://www.defence.gov.au/publications.cfm>, accessed 14 November 2007. For the report of the Inquiry into *Australian Intelligence Agencies*, see <http://www.dpmc.gov.au/publications/intelligence_inquiry/docs/intelligence_report.pdf>, accessed 31 July 2008,

[5] While it is useful to examine Australian Government documents related to Australia's security circumstances and expectations for the future, it is also instructive to examine US and British assessments of global security issues and the consequent US and British strategic postures under the present administrations in documents such as, George W. Bush, *The National Security Strategy of the United States of America*, The White House, March 2006, available at <http://www.comw.org/qdr/fulltext/nss2006.pdf>, accessed 1 August 2008; George W. Bush, *The National Security Strategy of the United States of America*, The White House,17 September 2002, available at <http://www.whitehouse.gov/nsc/nss.pdf> accessed 1 August 2008; United States Department of Defense, *Quadrennial Defense Review Report*, Department of Defense, Washington, DC, 6 February 2006, available at <http://www.defenselink.mil/qdr/report/Report20060203.pdf>, accessed 1 August 2008; United States Department of Defense, *The National Defense Strategy of the United States of America*, Department of Defense, Washington, DC, March 2005, available at <http://www.comw.org/qdr/fulltext/0503nds.pdf>, accessed 1 August 2008; US Joint Chiefs of Staff, *The National Military Strategy of the United States of America: A Strategy for Today; A Vision for Tomorrow*, Department of Defense, Washington, DC, March 2004, available at <http://www.defenselink.mil/news/Mar2005/d20050318nms.pdf>, accessed 1 August 2008; United

States Department of Defense, *Annual Report to Congress, The Military Power of the People's Republic of China 2005*, Office of the Secretary of Defence, Washington, DC, 2005, available at <http://www.globalsecurity.org/military/library/report/2006/2006-prc-military-power.htm>, accessed 1 August 2008; and UK Ministry of Defence, *Delivering Security in a Changing World*, Defence White Paper, The Stationary Office, London, December 2003, available at <http://www.premier-ministre.gouv.fr/IMG/pdf/whitepaper2003.pdf>, accessed 1 August 2008.

[6] At a recent conference on 'Next Generation Threats', Professor Robert J. O'Neill, former Chichele Professor of the History of War, All Souls College, University of Oxford, former Chairman of the Council of Institute of Strategic Studies and inaugural Chairman of the Australian Strategic Policy Institute, offered that it was possible that Australian forces could be asked to participate in US-led operations in Iran, North Korea and Taiwan. Patrick Walters, 'Our troops "facing three wars"', *The Australian*, 26 October 2005.

[7] Australian Government views on Australia's concerns for the South Pacific region are described in Department of Defence, *National Security: A Defence Update*, Canberra, 2003, pp. 19–22, available at <http://www.defence.gov.au/ans2003/Report.pdf>, accessed 1 August 2008.

[8] Department of Defence, *Future Warfighting Concept*, Foreword, Australian Defence Doctrine Publication—D.02, Canberra, 2003, available at <http://www.defence.gov.au/publications/fwc.pdf>, accessed 31 July 2008.

[9] See Department of Defence, *Force 2020*, Canberra, June 2002, available at <http://www.defence.gov.au/publications/f2020.pdf>, accessed 31 July 2008; and Department of Defence, *Future Warfighting Concept*, Foreword and p. 1, available at <http://www.defence.gov.au/publications/fwc.pdf>, accessed 31 July 2008.

[10] Department of Defence, *Force 2020*, June 2002, pp. 2 and 16, available at <http://www.defence.gov.au/publications/f2020.pdf>, accessed 1 August 2008. Also see pp. 36–37 for descriptions of the requirements for force deployment, force protection and force generation and sustainment.

[11] Department of Defence, *Force 2020*, June 2002, available at <http://www.defence.gov.au/publications/f2020.pdf>, accessed 1 August 2008. See pp. 15 and 18 for 'Internal Benchmarks' of force projection. The quote is from Department of Defence, *The Australian Approach to Warfare*, Canberra, 2002, p. 20, available at <http://www.defence.gov.au/publications/taatw.pdf>, accessed 1 August 2008.

[12] Department of Defence, *National Security: A Defence Update*, Canberra, 2003, pp. 13 and 23, available at <http://www.defence.gov.au/ans2003/Report.pdf>, accessed 1 August 2008.

[13] Senator Robert Hill, Speech to Australian Strategic Policy Institute Inaugural International Conference, 'Australia's Defence and Security: Challenges and Opportunities at the Start of the 21st Century', 14 September 2005, available at <http://www.defence.gov.au/media/index.cfm>, accessed 14 November 2007.

[14] Department of Defence, *Defence 2000: Our Future Defence Force*, presented to Parliament by the Minister of Defence the Hon. John Moore, Australian Government Publishing Service, Canberra, 2000, available at <http://www.defence.gov.au/whitepaper>, accessed 10 January 2008.

[15] Lieutenant Colonel John J. Frewen, 'Combined Joint Task Force 635 (CTF 635) Post Operation Report (POR)—OP Anode, 24 Jul–18 Nov 03', Guadalcanal Beach Resort, Solomon Islands, 21 January 2004, Addressed to COMAST (Rear Admiral Mark F. Bonser). Frewen was Commander Combined Task Force 635 from 24 July–19 November 2003. Copy held by author. Air Commodore D.G. Green, 'Operation *Anode* Evaluation Report', ADFWC 120-21-1, January 2004. Copy held by author. This was a report drafted for Green by Lieutenant Colonel Phillip R. Tyrell, who led a Theatre Evaluation Team from the ADF Warfare Centre during the pre-deployment and deployment phase of Operation *Anode*. Tyrell submitted it for signature in January 2004 before departing on long service leave. It is a frank critique. To the author's knowledge, Tyrell's report was not signed and distributed. Army Headquarters, 'Operational Evaluation of the Tactical Level Land Specific Aspects of Operation *Anode*', 12 December 2003. Copy held by author.

[16] Frewen, 'Combined Joint Task Force 635', pp. 3–12. Tyrell, 'Operation *Anode* Evaluation Report', pp. 1–8. Army Headquarters, Operational Evaluation of the Tactical Level, Executive Summary, pp. 1–8.

[17] Frewen, 'Combined Joint Task Force 635', p. 7.

[18] Frewen, 'Combined Joint Task Force 635', pp. 8–9.

[19] See Department of Defence, *The War in Iraq: ADF Operations in the Middle East 2003*, Canberra, 2003, available at <http://www.defence.gov.au/publications/lessons.pdf>, accessed 1 August 2008;

and Department of Defence, *Winning in Peace Winning in War: The Australian Defence Force's Contribution to the Global Security Environment*, Canberra, 2004, available at <http://www.defence.gov.au/media/download/2004/Aug/250804/Defence_Winning%20Peace_War.pdf>, accessed 1 August 2008.

[20] Examples of critiques of Australian military operations are Terry Burstall, *Vietnam: The Australian Dilemma*, University of Queensland Press, Brisbane, 1993; and Matthew Gubb, *The Australian Military Response to the Fijian Coup: An Assessment*, SDSC Working Paper, no. 171, Strategic and Defence Studies Centre, The Australian National University, Canberra, November 1988.

[21] Patsy Adam-Smith, *The Anzacs*, Claremont Penguin, Melbourne, 1978; and Peter FitzSimons, *Kokoda*, Hodder Headline, Sydney, 2004.

[22] Dudley McCarthy, *South-West Pacific Area—First Year Kokoda to Wau*, Official History of Australia in the War of 1939–1945, Series 1, vol. V, Australian War Memorial, 1959. See pp. 46–48 for assessment of the quality of units deployed to New Guinea in 1942 and pp. 117–18, pp. 131–32 and pp. 265–68 for descriptions of logistic support and air resupply.

[23] Robert O'Neill, *Australia in the Korean War 1950–53, Volume II, Combat Operations*, The Australian War Memorial and the Australian Government Publishing Service, Canberra, 1985, chapter 1, The Australian Army Enters the War.

[24] Peter Dennis and Jeffrey Grey, *Emergency and Confrontation: Australian Military Operations in Malaya and Borneo 1950–1966*, The Official History of Australia's involvement in Southeast Asian Conflicts 1948–1975, Allen and Unwin in association with the Australian War Memorial, Sydney, 1996.

[25] Dennis and Grey, *Emergency and Confrontation*, p. 90. The authors cite members of the battalion complaining that too much time was spent rehearsing for a pre-embarkation parade when weapons training for reinforcements would have been a wiser use of time. Subsequent marksmanship on operations was poor, pp. 98–99. Comments on 3 RAR, p. 222.

[26] Ian McNeill, *To Long Tan: The Australian Army and the Vietnam War 1950–1966*, The Official History of Australia's involvement in Southeast Asian Conflicts 1948–1975, Allen and Unwin in association with the Australian War Memorial, Sydney, 1993, pp. 174–342.

[27] An example is Land Headquarters, 'Operation *Lagoon*—Post Operation Report, Combined Force Peace Support Operations on Bougainville, PNG, Oct 94', Plans 120/941, November 1994, K94-0132528. Copy held by author.

[28] Australian National Audit Office, Audit Report No.38, *Management of Australian Defence Force Deployments to East Timor*, 2001–02 Performance Audit, Australian National Audit Office, Canberra, 2002, available at <http://www.anao.gov.au/uploads/documents/2001-02_Audit_Report_38.pdf>, accessed 1 August 2008.

[29] Alan Ryan, *Thinking Across Time: Concurrent Historical Analysis on Military Operations*, Land Warfare Studies Centre, Working Paper no. 114, July 2001, available at <http://www.defence.gov.au/army/lwsc/docs/wp%20114.pdf>, accessed 1 August 2008.

[30] Captain Sir Basil H. Liddell Hart, *Thoughts on War*, Faber and Faber, London, 1944. Quoted in Anthony H. Cordesman, 'Iraq, Grand Strategy, and the Lessons of Military History', 2004 S.T. Lee Lecture on Military History, Center for Strategic and International Studies, Washington, DC, 19 October 2004, p. 4, available at <http://www.csis.org/media/csis/pubs/iraq_grandstrat.pdf>, accessed 1 August 2008.

[31] Brigadier Wayne Jackson, 'An Evaluation of Australian Defence Force Logistics Support to Operation *Anode* for the Chief of Joint Operations', September 2004. Copy held by author.

[32] Senator Robert Hill, 'Changes to Defence Force Higher Command Arrangements', Media Release 54/2005, 16 March 2005.

[33] Hill, 'Changes to Defence Force Higher Command Arrangements', Media Release 54/2005, 16 March 2005.

[34] Author discussed these new arrangements with Lieutenant General Ken J. Gillespie, VCDF and Chief of Joint Operations on 5 August 2005.

[35] The British Government recognised the need for consolidating force projection capabilities into a Joint Rapid Reaction Force (JRRF) in August 1996. The British armed forces solved the problem of only assigning a lead joint commander just before deployment by appointing a Chief of Joint Operations (CJO) and establishing a Permanent Joint Headquarters (PJHQ) as well as the JRRF. However, they demurred on permanent assignment of high readiness force elements and a direct relationship between CJO and Chief of the Defence Services (CDS). See Richard M. Connaughton, 'Organizing British Joint Rapid Reaction Forces', *Joint Force Quarterly*, Autumn 2000, available at

<http://www.dtic.mil/doctrine/jel/jfq_pubs/1726.pdf>, accessed 1 August 2008. See also the Permanent Joint Headquarters website at <http://www.armedforces.co.uk/mod/listings/l0006.html#PJHQ>, accessed 1 August 2008.

[36] **technical control**: It also covers specialised and professional authority for the proper management of assets including technical standards and regulations for maintenance, repair and use of vehicles, weapons, equipment and other *matériel*. *administrative control*: This term covers the non-operational administrative responsibility, such as personnel management, including individual training.

[37] In 1976 the Government issued a Defence White Paper, *Australian Defence*, that explained Australia's changed strategic circumstances and emphasised force projection into the 'neighbourhood' rather than 'some distant or forward theatre'. Department of Defence, *Australian Defence*, White Paper presented to Parliament by the Minister for Defence, the Hon. D.J. Killen, November 1976, Australian Government Publishing Service, Canberra, 1976, p. 10.

Glossary

administrative control
This term covers the non-operational administrative responsibility, such as personnel management, including individual training.

aiguillettes
an ornamental tagged cord or braid, typically gold in colour, worn on a uniform around the shoulder and armpit, with a cord extension attached to a middle button of a shirt or jacket.

area of direct military interest
According to *Defence of Australia 1987*, Australia's area of direct military interest included Australia, its territories and proximate ocean areas, Indonesia, Papua New Guinea, New Zealand and other nearby countries in the Southwest Pacific. It stretches over 7000 kilometres from the Cocos Islands to New Zealand and the islands of the Southwest Pacific and 5000 kilometres south to 'the Southern Ocean'.

Bahasa
Official language of the Republic of Indonesia.

capability
Combination of force structure and its preparedness that encompasses equipment, trained personnel to operate the equipment, and the total support required to operate both efficiently and effectively.

chain of command
The succession of commanding officers from a superior to a subordinate through which command is exercised. Also called 'command channel'. (DOD, NATO)

combined
Between two or more forces or agencies of two or more allies. (DOD)

command and control
The exercise of authority and direction by a properly designated commander over assigned and attached forces in the accomplishment of the mission. Command and control functions are performed through an arrangement of personnel, equipment, communications, facilities, and procedures employed by a commander in planning, directing, coordinating, and controlling forces and operations in the accomplishment of the mission. Also called C2. (DOD)

command, control, communications and computer systems	Integrated systems of doctrine, procedures, organisational structures, personnel, equipment, facilities, and communications designed to support a commander's exercise of command and control across the range of military operations. Also called C4 systems. (DOD)
command relationships	The interrelated responsibilities between commanders, as well as the operational authority exercised by commanders in the chain of command; defined further as combatant command (command authority), operational control, tactical control, or support. See also chain of command. (DOD)
Concept of Intelligence Operations	A verbal or graphic statement, in broad outline, of an intelligence directorate's assumptions or intent in regard to intelligence support of an operation or series of operations. The concept of intelligence operations, which complements the commander's concept of operations, is contained in the intelligence annex of operation plans. The concept of intelligence operations is designed to give an overall picture of intelligence support for joint operations. It is included primarily for additional clarity of purpose. See also concept of operations. (DOD)
Concept of Operations	A verbal or graphic statement, in broad outline, of a commander's assumptions or intent in regard to an operation or series of operations. The concept of operations frequently is embodied in campaign plans and operation plans; in the latter case, particularly when the plans cover a series of connected operations to be carried out simultaneously or in succession. The concept is designed to give an overall picture of the operation. It is included primarily for additional clarity of purpose. Also called commander's concept or CONOPS. (DOD)
deployment	1. In naval usage, the change from a cruising approach or contact disposition to a disposition for battle. 2. The movement of forces within areas of operations. 3. The positioning of forces into a formation for battle. 4. The relocation of forces to desired areas of operations. (NATO)

doctrine	A set of principles describing how the Australian Defence Force will support the attainment of national objectives.
fire support coordination centre	A single location in which are centralised communications facilities and personnel incident to the coordination of all forms of fire support. Also called FSCC. (DOD)
force	An aggregation of military personnel, weapon systems, equipment, and necessary support, or combination thereof. (DOD)
force activity designators	Numbers used in conjunction with urgency of need designators to establish a matrix of priorities used for supply requisitions. Defines the relative importance of the unit to accomplish the objectives of the Department of Defence. Also called FADs. (DOD)
force projection	The ability to project the military element of national power from the continental United States (CONUS) or another theatre, in response to requirements for military operations. Force projection operations extend from mobilisation and deployment of forces to redeployment to CONUS or home theatre. (DOD)
force protection	Activities such as gathering, evaluating and communicating intelligence and employing counter-intelligence and protective agents and groups, such as Special Forces, to protect individuals, groups and force elements from hostile interference, including protection from the vicissitudes of operational environments, such as disease and harsh climates, through preventive health measures, clothing and equipment and conducive living conditions. (New definition)
force sustainment	The science of planning and carrying out the movement and maintenance of deployed forces through a supply chain. In its most comprehensive sense, those aspects of military operations that deal with: (a) design and development, acquisition, storage, movement, distribution, maintenance, evacuation, and disposition of *matériel*; (b) movement, evacuation, and hospitalisation of personnel; (c)

	acquisition or construction, maintenance, operation, and disposition of facilities; and (d) acquisition or furnishing of essential services. Also logistics. (DOD)
forcible entry	Seizing and holding of a military lodgement in the face of armed opposition. (DOD)
forward operations base	In special operations, a base usually located in friendly territory or afloat that is established to extend command and control or communications or to provide support for training and tactical operations. Facilities may be established for temporary or longer duration operations and may include an airfield or an unimproved airstrip, an anchorage, or a pier. A forward operations base may be the location of a special operations component headquarters or a smaller unit that is controlled and/or supported by a main operations base. Also called FOB. See also advanced operations base; main operations base. (DOD)
joint	Connotes activities, operations, organisations and arrangements, in which elements of two or more services participate. (adapted from DOD)
land power	The ability to project military force by or from individuals and groups operating on land either on foot or from land, sea or aerial platforms, normally accompanied by application of direct and indirect fire support. (Air Marshal M.J. Armitage and Air Commodore R.A. Mason, *Air Power in the Nuclear Age, 1945–85: Theory and Practice*, Urbana, New York, 1985)
littoral power	The ability to combine maritime, land and air power to project military force simultaneously on or below water, on land and in the air in a prescribed area. (Air Marshal M.J. Armitage and Air Commodore R.A. Mason, *Air Power in the Nuclear Age, 1945–85: Theory and Practice*, Urbana, New York, 1985)
maritime power	The ability to project military force by or from a platform on or below water, normally the sea. *air power*: The ability to project military force by or from a platform in the third dimension above the surface of the earth. (Air Marshal M.J. Armitage and Air

Commodore R.A. Mason, *Air Power in the Nuclear Age, 1945–85: Theory and Practice*, Urbana, New York, 1985)

military capability	The ability to achieve specified strategic effects. It includes four major components: *force structure*: numbers, size, and composition of the force elements that comprise the Australian Defence Force; e.g., divisions, ships, air squadrons; *modernisation*: technical sophistication of forces, units, weapon systems, and equipments; *readiness*: the ability to provide capabilities required by the commanders to execute their assigned missions. This is derived from the ability of each unit to deliver the outputs for which it was designed; and *sustainability*: the ability to maintain the necessary level and duration of operational activity to accomplish missions. Sustainability is a function of providing for and maintaining those levels of ready forces, *matériel*, facilities and consumables necessary to support military effort. (DOD)
operation	1. A military action or the carrying out of a strategic, operational, tactical, service, training, or administrative military mission. 2. The process of carrying on combat, including movement, supply, attack, defence, and manoeuvres needed to gain the objectives of any battle or campaign. (DOD)
operation order	A directive issued by a commander to subordinate commanders for the purpose of effecting the coordinated execution of an operation. Also called OPORD. (DOD)
operational art	The employment of military forces to attain strategic and/or operational objectives through the design, organisation, integration, and conduct of strategies, campaigns, major operations, and battles. Operational art translates the joint force commander's strategy into operational design and, ultimately, tactical action, by integrating the key activities at all levels of war.
operational level of war	The level of war at which campaigns and major operations are planned, conducted, and sustained to accomplish strategic objectives within theatres or

other operational areas. Activities at this level link tactics and strategy by establishing operational objectives needed to accomplish the strategic objectives, sequencing events to achieve the operational objectives, initiating actions, and applying resources to bring about and sustain these events. These activities imply a broader dimension of time or space than do tactics; they ensure the logistic and administrative support of tactical forces, and provide the means by which tactical successes are exploited to achieve strategic objectives. See also strategic level of war; tactical level of war. (DOD)

operationally ready A unit, ship, or weapon system capable of performing the missions or functions for which it is organised or designed. Incorporates both equipment readiness and personnel readiness; that is, personnel available and qualified to perform assigned missions or functions. See also readiness. (DOD)

posture Combination of capability and intent.

pre-position To place force elements, equipment, or supplies at or near the point of planned use or at a designated location to reduce reaction time, and to ensure timely support of specific force elements during initial phases of an operation. (DOD, NATO)

reconnaissance A mission undertaken to obtain, by visual observation or other detection methods, information about the activities and resources of hostile forces and groups and influential stakeholders, or to secure data concerning the meteorological, hydrographical, or geographic characteristics of a particular area. (DOD, NATO)

redeployment The relocation of forces to advantageous areas of operations and locations and return of forces to the homeland.

Rules of Engagement Directives issued by competent military authority which specify the circumstances and limitations under which Australian forces will initiate and/or continue combat engagements with other forces encountered. (Australian Defence Force Publication 101, Glossary, 1994)

strategic level of war	The level of war at which a nation, often as a member of a group of nations, determines national or multinational (alliance or coalition) security objectives and guidance, and develops and uses national resources to accomplish these objectives. Activities at this level establish national and multinational military objectives; sequence initiatives; define limits and assess risks for the use of military and other instruments of national power; develop global plans or theatre war plans to achieve these objectives; and provide military forces and other capabilities in accordance with strategic plans. See also operational level of war; tactical level of war. (DOD)
tactical level of war	The level of war at which battles and engagements are planned and executed to accomplish military objectives assigned to tactical units or task forces. Activities at this level focus on the ordered arrangement and manoeuvre of combat elements in relation to each other and to the enemy to achieve combat objectives. See also operational level of war; strategic level of war.
task group	The second highest level in a task organisation, a task group is a grouping of units under one commander subordinate to task force commander, formed for the purpose of carrying out specific functions. (DOD)
technical control	It also covers specialised and professional authority for the proper management of assets including technical standards and regulations for maintenance, repair and use of vehicles, weapons, equipment and other *matériel*.
terminal operations	Activities related to receiving, unloading, storing, preparing and then loading and dispatching *matériel* to an area of operations. These activities can involve sea, land and air transport.
theatre	A designated geographic area for which an operational level joint or combined commander is appointed and in which a campaign or series of major operations is conducted. A theatre may contain one or more joint areas of operation.

Bibliography

Notes on Sources

Files

Departmental files are listed with prefixes, such as Land Headquarters (LHQ), HQ ADF, ADHQ, and LOGOMD. These files were examined in Sydney (LHQ), Canberra and Queanbeyan (HQ ADF, ADHQ), or Melbourne (LOGCOMD). Files beginning with a two-digit prefix, or 'K' followed by a two-digit prefix, belong to the Commonwealth Record series A6721. Files beginning with four-digit prefixes belong to the Commonwealth Record series A11502.

Classified Sources

Classified sources were examined at either in Russell Offices, Canberra, or at the Defence Archives, Queanbeyan.

Copies held by author

Copies of documents listed in footnotes as being held by the author are located in the repository of the Official History of Australian Peacekeeping and Post-Cold War Operations Project at the Australian War Memorial.

Interviews

Recordings of interviews are located in the repository of the Official History of Australian Peacekeeping and Post Cold War Operations Project at the Australian War Memorial.

Author as a Source

The author conducted research with Australian forces in Somalia (April–May 1993) and, periodically, in Bougainville (1998–2000) and East Timor (2000–2002). His journals contain interview notes, records of conversations and meetings as well as observations, both professional and personal. Copies of these journals are currently held by the author and will be located in the repository of the Official History of Australian Peacekeeping and Post Cold War Operations Project at the Australian War Memorial in due course.

Ranks

Sometimes there is a difference between the military ranks of individuals mentioned in the text and identified as sources in footnotes and in the Bibliography, usually as interviewees. The rank used in the text and when the person has been used as a source is the one worn at the time.

Official Records

Australian Defence Force

Australian Army, *An Australian Army for the 21st Century*, Directorate of Army Public Affairs, October 1996

Chief of Army Directive 5/99, Mobilisation Directive—Expansion of the Ready Deployment Force, 29 April 1999

Chiefs of Staff Committee, *Report on the Study into ADF Command Arrangements*, by Brigadier John S. Baker, Headquarters Australian Defence Force, Canberra, 1988

Department of Defence, Chief Information Officer, The Australian Defence Glossary, The Defence Language Management System, available at <http://dlms.dcb.defence.gov.au/> (Restricted)

The Fundamentals of Land Warfare, LWD 1, Defence Publishing Service, Canberra, 2000

Joint Warfighting, Capstone Series, Australian Defence Force Doctrine Publication ADDP-D-4, Defence Publishing Service, Canberra, June 2004

Land Command Concept of Operations, Land Headquarters, Sydney, 2002

The Report on the Structural Review of Higher ADF Staff Arrangements, by Major General John M. Sanderson, Canberra, 1989

Royal Australian Air Force, *Fundamentals of Australian Aerospace Power*, AAP1000, Fourth Edition, Aerospace Centre, Defence Publishing Service, Canberra, 2002

Royal Australian Navy, *Australian Maritime Doctrine*, RAN Doctrine 2000, Defence Publishing Service Canberra, 2000

Support Command–Australia, A Framework for Strategic and Operational Level Logistic Support of Joint Operations, Headquarters, Support Command Australia, Melbourne, 1999

Australian Government

Successive annual *Defence Reports* from 1987 to 1999/2000

Audit Report No. 16, Defence Reform Program Management and Outcomes, Australian National Audit Office, Canberra, 2001

Audit Report No. 38, Management of Australian Defence Force Deployments to East Timor, Australian National Audit Office, Canberra, 2001, available at <http://www.anao.gov.au/uploads/documents/2001-02_Audit_Report_38.pdf>, accessed 1 August 2008

Bibliography

'Australia's Regional Security', Ministerial Statement by Senator the Hon Gareth Evans QC, Minister for Foreign Affairs and Trade, Department of Foreign Affairs and Trade, Canberra, December 1989

Australia's Strategic Planning in the 1990s, Australian Government Publishing Service, Canberra, 1989

Australia's Strategic Planning in the 1990s, Australian Government Publishing Service, Canberra, 1992

Australia's Strategic Policy 1997, Directorate of Publishing and Visual Communications, Canberra, December 1997

The Australian Approach to Warfare, Canberra, 2002, available at <http://www.defence.gov.au/publications/taatw.pdf>, accessed 1 August 2008

Australian Defence, presented to Parliament by the Minister of Defence the Hon. D.J. Killen, November 1976, Australian Government Publishing Service, Canberra, 1976

Australian Defence: Report on the Reorganisation of the Defence Group of Departments, November 1973, by Sir Arthur Tange, Australian Government Publishing Service, Canberra, 1974

The Australian Defence Force: Its Structure and Capabilities, Australian Government Publishing Service, Canberra, 1984 *Key Elements in the Triennial Review of Strategic Guidance since 1945*, Submission by the Department of Defence to the Joint Standing Committee of Foreign Affairs, Defence and Trade, April 1986

Australian Senate, Ministerial Statement, 'Defence into the 21st Century', by the Hon Robert Ray, Minister of Defence, 30 May 1991

The Bougainville Crisis: An Australian Perspective, by the Hon. Alexander Downer, MP, Minister for Foreign Affairs, Department of Foreign Affairs and Trade, Canberra, 2001

Defence 2000: Our Future Defence Force, presented to Parliament by the Minister of Defence the Hon John Moore, Australian Government Publishing Service, Canberra, 2000, available at <http://www.defence.gov.au/whitepaper/>, accessed 10 January 2008

The Defence of Australia 1987, presented to the Parliament by the Minister for Defence, the Hon. Kim C. Beazley, MP, Australian Government Publishing Service, Canberra, 1987

Defending Australia, Defence White Paper 1994, Australian Government Publishing Service, Canberra, 1994

Force 2020, Canberra, 2002, available at <http://www.defence.gov.au/publications/f2020.pdf>, accessed 31 July 2008

From Phantom to Force: Towards a More Efficient and Effective Army, The Parliament of the Commonwealth of Australia, Canberra, August 2000

Funding Australia's Defence, Australian Government Publishing Service, Canberra, 1998

Future Directions for the Management of Australia's Defence, Addendum to the Report of the Defence Efficiency Review, Secretariat Papers, Department of Defence, Canberra, 1997

Future Warfighting Concept, Canberra, 2003, available at <http://www.defence.gov.au/publications/fwc.pdf>, accessed 31 July 2008

Government Response by Senator the Hon Gareth Evans QC, Minister for Foreign Affairs, to the Report of the Parliamentary Delegation to Bougainville, 8 June 1994

House of Representatives, Ministerial Statement, 'Defence Policy', by the Hon Ian McLachlan, AO, MP, Minister of Defence, 15 October 1996

In the National Interest, Australia's Foreign and Trade Policy White Paper, by Senator Gareth Evans, Minister for Foreign Affairs, Department of Foreign Affairs and Trade, Canberra, 1997

The Management of Australia's Defence Force, Australian Government Publishing Service, Canberra, 1987

National Security: A Defence Update, Canberra, 2003, available at <http://www.defence.gov.au/ans2003/index.htm>, accessed 1 August 2008

Peacekeeping Policy: The Future Australian Defence Force Role, Departmental Publications, Canberra, June 1993

Report of the Visit of the Australian Parliamentary Delegation to Bougainville 18–22 April 1994, *Bougainville: A Pacific Solution*, Australian Government Publishing Service, Canberra, 1994

Restructuring the Army, Directorate of Publishing and Visual Communications, Canberra, 1996

Review of Australia's Defence Capabilities, Report to the Minister for Defence by Mr Paul Dibb, Australian Government Publishing Service, Canberra, March 1986

Stockholding and Sustainability in the Australian Defence Force, Australian Government Publishing Service, Canberra, 1992

Strategic Review 1993, Defence Publications, Canberra, 1993

A Visit to East Timor, 2 December 1999, presented to President of the Senate on 20 December 1999

The War in Iraq: ADF Operations in the Middle East 2003, Department of Defence, Canberra, 2003, available at <http://www.defence.gov.au/publications/lessons.pdf>, accessed 1 August 2008

Winning in Peace Winning in War: The Australian Defence Force's Contribution to the Global Security Environment, Department of Defence, Canberra, 2004, available at <http://www.defence.gov.au/media/download/2004/Aug/250804/Defence_Winning%20Peace_War.pdf>, accessed 1 August 2008

International Military Publications and Strategic Reports

Bush, George W., *The National Security Strategy of the United States of America*, The White House, March 2006, available at <http://www.comw.org/qdr/fulltext/nss2006.pdf>, accessed 1 August 2008

————, *The National Security Strategy of the United States of America*, The White House, 17 September 2002, available at <http://www.whitehouse.gov/nsc/nss.pdf>, accessed 1 August 2008

UK Ministry of Defence, *British Defence Doctrine*, JWP-0-01, 2nd Edition, The Stationary Office, London, 2001

UK Ministry of Defence, *Delivering Security in a Changing World*, Defence White Paper, The Stationary Office, London, December 2003, available at <http://www.premierministre.gouv.fr/IMG/pdf/whitepaper2003.pdf>, accessed 1 August 2008

UK Ministry of Defence, *Joint Operations*, JWP 3-00, The Stationary Office, London, 2001. Royal Navy, *British Maritime Doctrine*, Second Edition, BR1806, The Stationary Office, London, 1999

US Department of the Army, *Decisive Force: The Army in the Theater of Operations*, FM 100-7, Headquarters Department of Army, Washington DC, 31 May 1995

US Department of the Army, *Theater Distribution*, FM 100-10-1, Headquarters Department of Army, Washington DC, 1 October 1999

US Department of Defense, *Quadrennial Defense Review Report*, Department of Defense, Washington DC, 6 February 2006, available at <http://www.defenselink.mil/qdr/report/Report20060203.pdf>, accessed 1 August 2008

US Department of Defense, *The National Defense Strategy of the United States of America*, Washington DC, March 2005, available at <http://www.comw.org/qdr/fulltext/0503nds.pdf>, accessed 1 August 2008

US Department of Defense, *Annual Report to Congress, The Military Power of the People's Republic of China, 2005*, Office of the Secretary of Defense, Washington DC, 2005, available at <http://www.globalsecurity.org/military/library/report/2006/2006-prc-militarypower.htm>, accessed 1 August 2008

US Department of Defense, *Dictionary of Military and Associated Terms*, JP 1-0212, Department of Defense, Washington DC, April 2001

US Department of Defense Dictionary of Military Terms available at <http://www.dtic.mil/doctrine/jel/doddict/>, accessed 10 January 2008

US Joint Chiefs of Staff, *The National Military Strategy of the United States of America, A Strategy for Today; A Vision for Tomorrow*, Department of Defense, March 2004, available at <http://www.defenselink.mil/news/Mar2005/d20050318nms.pdf>, accessed 1 August 2008

Books and Book Chapters

Adam-Smith, Patsy, *The Anzacs*, Claremont Penguin, 1978

Andrews, Eric, The Department of Defence, *The Australian Centenary History of Defence*, vol. V, Oxford University Press, Melbourne, 2001

Atkinson, James J., *Australian Contingents to the China Field Force 1900–1901*, New South Wales Military Historical Society and The Clarendon Press, Sydney, 1976

Austin, Victor, *To Kokoda and Beyond: The Story of the 39th Battalion 1941–1943*, Melbourne University Press, Melbourne, 1988

Ball, Desmond, *The Politics of Defence Decision-making in Australia: The Strategic Background*, Research School of Pacific Studies, The Australian National University, Canberra, 1979

Ball, Desmond and Pauline Kerr, *Presumptive Engagement: Australia's Asia-Pacific Security Policy in the 1990s*, Allen and Unwin, Sydney, 1996

Bartu, Peter, 'The militia, the military, and the people of Bobonaro', in Richard Tanter, Mark Selden, and Stephen R Shalom (eds), *Bitter flowers, sweet flowers: East Timor, Indonesia and the world community*, Rowman & Littlefield, New York, 2001

Bean, C.E.W, *The Australian Imperial Force in France during the Allied Offensive, 1918*, The Official History of Australia in the War of 1914–1918, vol. VI, Angus and Robertson, Sydney, 1942

———, *The Story of ANZAC, Official History of Australia in the War of 1914–1918*, vol. 1, Angus and Robertson, Sydney, 1939

Brands, H.W. (ed.), *The Use of Force after the Cold War*, Texas A&M University Press, College Station, 2000

Breen, Bob, *A Little Bit of Hope, Australian Force—Somalia*, Allen and Unwin, Sydney, 1998

———, *The Battle of Kapyong: 3rd Battalion, The Royal Australian Regiment in Korea 25–24 April 1951*, Training Command, Sydney, 1992

———, *The Battle of Maryang San, 3rd Battalion, The Royal Australian Regiment in Korea 1–6 October 1951*, Training Command, Sydney, 1993

———, *First to Fight: Australian Diggers, NZ Kiwis and US Paratroopers in Vietnam 1965–66*, Allen and Unwin, Sydney, 1988

———, *Mission Accomplished, Australian Defence Force Participation in International Force East Timor*, Allen and Unwin, Sydney, 2001

Brigg, Stan and Les, *The 36th Australian Infantry Battalion 1939–1945*, The 36th Battalion Association, Sydney, 1967

Brune, Peter, *Gona's Gone*, Allen and Unwin, Sydney, 1993

———, *Those Ragged Bloody Heroes: From the Kokoda Trail to Gona Beach 1942*, Allen and Unwin, Sydney, 1991

Budden, Frank M., *That Mob!—The Story of the 55/53 Australian Infantry Battalion, A.I.F.*, self published, Ashfield, New South Wales, 1973

Burstal, Terry, *Vietnam: The Australian Dilemma*, University of Queensland Press, Brisbane, 1993

Cheeseman, Graeme, *The Search for Self-Reliance: Australian Defence since Vietnam*, Longman Cheshire, Melbourne, 1993

Cheeseman, Graeme and Robert Bruce (eds), *Discourses of Danger and Dread Frontiers: Australian Defence and Security Thinking after the Cold War*, Allen and Unwin, Sydney, in association with the Department of International Relations, Research School of Pacific and Asian Studies, The Australian National University, Canberra, 1996

Clark, Rex, *First Queensland Mounted Infantry Contingent in the South African War 1899–1900*, The Military Historical Society of Australia, ACT Branch, Canberra, 1971

Coates, John, *Suppressing Insurgency, An Analysis of the Malayan Emergency, 1948–1954*, Westview Studies in Regional Security, Boulder, 1992

Colombijn, Freek and J. Thomas Lindblad (eds), *Roots of violence in Indonesia; contemporary violence in historical perspective*, KITLV Press, Leiden, 2002.

Cotton, James and John Ravenhill (eds), *Seeking Asian Engagement: Australia in World Affairs 1991–1995*, Oxford University Press, Melbourne, 1997.

Cranston, Fred, *Always Faithful: The History of the 49th Battalion*, Boolarong Publications, Brisbane, 1983

Day, David, *The Politics of War—Australia at War, 1939–45: From Churchill to MacArthur*, Harper Collins Publishers, Sydney, 2003

D'Costa Tony (ed.), *Bougainville: The Forgotten War*, Pax Christi International, Brussels, 1995

Dennis, Peter and Jeffrey Grey, *Emergency and Confrontation: Australian Military Operations in Malaya and Borneo 1950–1966*, The Official History of Australia's involvement in Southeast Asian Conflicts 1948–1975, Allen and Unwin in association with the Australian War Memorial, Sydney, 1996

Dennis, Peter, Jeffrey Grey, Ewan Morris and Robin Prior, *The Oxford Companion to Australian Military History*, Oxford University Press, Melbourne, 1995

Dexter, David, *The New Guinea Offensives*, Official History of Australia in the War of 1939–1945, series 1, vol. VI, Australian War Memorial, Canberra, 1961

Dibb, Paul, *Planning a Defence Force Without a Threat: A Model for Middle Powers*, Strategic and Defence Studies Centre, The Australian National University, Canberra, 1996

Dinnen, Sinclair, Ron May and Anthony J. Regan, *Challenging the State: the Sandline Affair in Papua New Guinea*, Pacific Policy Paper 30, State, Society and Governance in Melanesia, National Centre for Development Studies, Research School of Pacific and Asian Studies and Department of Political and Social Change, Research School of Pacific and Asian Studies, The Australian National University, Canberra, 1997

Dorney, Sean, *The Sandline Affair*, Allen and Unwin, Sydney, 1998

Eather, Steve, *Desert Sands, Jungle Lands: A biography of Major Ken Eather, CB, CBE, DSO, DSC*, Allen and Unwin, Sydney, 2003

Edwards, Peter (with Gregory Pemberton), *Crises and Commitments: The Politics and Diplomacy of Australia's involvement in Southeast Asian Conflicts 1948–1965*, The official history of Australia's involvement in South East

Asian Conflicts 1948–1975, Allen and Unwin in association with the Australian War Memorial, Sydney, 1992

Field, Laurence M., *The Forgotten War: Australian involvement in the South African Conflict of 1899–1902*, Melbourne University Press, Melbourne, 1979

Fischer, Tim, *Seven Days in East Timor*, Allen and Unwin, Sydney, 2000

FitzSimons, Peter, *Kokoda*, Hodder Headline, Sydney 2004

Fox, James J. and Dionisio Babo Soares (eds), *Out of the Ashes: Destruction and Reconstruction of East Timor*, C. Hurst and Co, London, 2000

Gammage, Bill, *The Broken Years: Australian Soldiers in the Great War*, Penguin Books, Melbourne, 1975

Gillison, Douglas, *Royal Australian Air Force 1939–1942*, Official History of Australia in the War of 1939–1945, series 3, vol. 1, Australian War Memorial, Canberra, 1962

Greenlees, Don and Robert Garran, *Deliverance:; The Inside Story of East Timor's Fight for Freedom*, Allen and Unwin, Sydney, 2002

Grey, Jeffrey, *A Military History of Australia*, Studies in Australian History, Cambridge University Press, Cambridge, 1990

———, *The Australian Army*, The Australian Centenary History of Defence, vol. I, Oxford University Press, Melbourne, 2001

Hasluck, Paul, *Diplomatic Witness: Australian Foreign Affairs 1941–1947*, Melbourne University Press, Melbourne 1980

Henderson, W., *The New South Wales Contingents to South Africa, From October 1899 to March 1900 with a "Roll Call of Honour", Being the Names of our Officers and Men at the Front*, Turner and Henderson, Sydney, 1900. Located in the Royal United Services Institute of New South Wales Library, Pitt Street, Sydney

HMAS Tobruk, 'Tobruk's Solace', Pictorial Record, n.d.

Horner David M., *Crisis of Command: Australian Generalship and the Japanese Threat 1941–1943*, The Australian National University Press, Canberra, 1978

———, *Defence Supremo, Sir Fredrick Shedden and the making of Australian defence policy*, Allen and Unwin, Sydney, 2000

———, (ed.), *Duty First: The Royal Australian Regiment in War and Peace*, Allen and Unwin, Sydney, 1990

———, *The Gulf Commitment: The Australian Defence Force's First War*, Allen and Unwin, Sydney, 1992

———, *The Gunners: A History of Australian Artillery*, Allen and Unwin, Sydney, 1995

———, *Inside the War Cabinet: Directing Australia's War Effort 1939–45*, Allen and Unwin in association with the Australian Archives, Sydney, 1996

———, *The Making of the Australian Defence Force*, The Australian Centenary History of Defence, Volume V, Oxford University Press, Melbourne, 2001

———, *SAS: Phantoms of War, A History of Australian Special Air Service*, updated edition, Allen and Unwin, Sydney, 2002

———, *Strategic Command: General Sir John Wilton and Australia's Asian Wars*, Oxford University Press, Melbourne, 2005

Inglis, Kenneth S., *The Rehearsal: Australians at war in the Sudan 1885*, Rigby Publishers, Adelaide, 1985

Keogh, E.G., *The South West Pacific 1941–1945*, Grayflower Productions, Melbourne, 1965

Keown-Boyd, Henry, *A Good Dusting: The Sudan Campaigns 1883–1899*, Book Club Associates, London, 1986

Liria, Yauka Aluamba, *Bougainville Campaign Diary*, Indra Press, Melbourne, 1993

Londey, Peter, *Other People's Wars: A History of Australian Peacekeeping*, Allen and Unwin, Sydney, 2004

Long, Gavin, *The Six Years War: Australia in the 1939–45 War*, Australian War Memorial and Australian Government Publishing Service, Canberra, 1973

Malik, J. Mohan (ed.), *Australia's Security in the 21st Century*, Allen and Unwin, Sydney, 1999

Martin, Ian, *Self Determination in East Timor, The United Nations, the Ballot and International Intervention*, International Peace Academy Occasional Papers series, Lynne Reinner Publishers, London, 2001

Martinkus, John, *A Dirty Little War*, Random House, Sydney, 2001

McCarthy, Dudley, *South-West Pacific Area—First Year Kokoda to Wau*, Official History of Australia in the War of 1939–1945, Series 1, vol. V, Australian War Memorial, 1959

McCauley, Lex, *The Battle of Coral-Balmoral*, Hutchinson, Melbourne, 1988

McKernan, M. and M. Browne (eds), *Australia: Two Centuries of War and Peace*, Australian War Memorial in association with Allen and Unwin, Sydney, 1988

McLean-Williams, Iain, *Vietnam: A Pictorial History of the 6th Battalion, The Royal Australian Regiment*, Printcraft Press, Brookvale, New South Wales, 1967

McNeill, Ian, *The Team: Australian Army Advisers in Vietnam 1962–1972*, Australian War Memorial, Canberra, 1984

———, *To Long Tan: The Australian Army and the Vietnam War 1950–1966*, The Official History of Australia's involvement in Southeast Asian Conflicts 1948–1975, Allen and Unwin in association with the Australian War Memorial, Sydney, 1993

McNeill, Ian and Ashley Ekins, *On the Offensive: The Australian Army in the Vietnam War 1967–1968*, The Official History of Australia's involvement in Southeast Asian Conflicts 1948–1975, Allen and Unwin in association with the Australian War Memorial, Sydney, 2003

Mordike, John, *An Army for a Nation: A history of Australian military developments 1880–1914*, Allen and Unwin in association with The Directorate of Army Studies, Department of Defence, Sydney, 1992

Nicolls, Bob, *Blue Jackets and Boxers*, Allen and Unwin, Sydney, 1986

O'Callaghan, Mary-Louise, *Enemies Within*, Double Day Australia, Sydney, 1999

O'Neill, Robert, *Australia in the Korean War 1950–53, Volume I, Strategy and Diplomacy*, Australian War Memorial and Australian Government Publishing Service, Canberra, 1981

———, *Australia in the Korean War 1950–53, Volume II, Combat Operations*, Australian War Memorial and Australian Government Publishing Service, Canberra, 1985

———, *Vietnam Task: The 5th Battalion, the Royal Australian Regiment*, Cassell, Melbourne, 1968

Oliver, Douglas, *Black Islanders: A Personal Perspective of Bougainville 1937–1991*, Hyland House, Melbourne, 1991

Pedersen, Peter A., *Monash as Military Commander*, Melbourne University Press, Melbourne, 1985

Pemberton, Gregory, *All the Way: Australia's Road to Vietnam*, Allen and Unwin, Sydney, 1987

Regan Anthony J., *The Bougainville Conflict: Origins and Development, Main Actors, and Strategies for Resolution*, Mimeo, Port Moresby, 1996

———, 'The PNG Policy-making Environment as a Window on the Sandline Controversy', in Dinnen, May and Regan (eds), *Challenging the State: the Sandline Affair in Papua New Guinea 1997*, Research School of Pacific and Asian Studies, The Australian National University, Canberra, 1998

Ryan, Alan, *From Desert Storm to East Timor, Australia, the Asia-Pacific and the 'New Age'*, Study Paper No 302, Land Warfare Studies Centre, Canberra, January 2000, available at <http://www.defence.gov.au/Army/lwsc/Publications/SP/SP_302.pdf>, accessed 14 November 2007

———, *Primary Responsibilities and Primary Risks: Australian Defence Force Participation in the International Force East Timor*, Study Paper No 304, Land Warfare Studies Centre, Canberra, November 2002, available at <http://www.defence.gov.au/Army/lwsc/Publications/SP/SP_304.pdf>, accessed 14 November 2007

Shepherd, Allan, *Trends in Australian Defence: A Resources Survey*, Australian Defence Studies Centre, ADFA, University of New South Wales, Canberra, 1999

Smith, Hugh (ed.), *Australia and Peacekeeping*, Australian Defence Studies Centre, ADFA, University of New South Wales, Canberra, 1990,

———, *Peacekeeping Challenges for the Future*, Australian Defence Studies Centre, ADFA, University of New South Wales, Canberra, 1993

Stephens, Alan, *The Royal Australian Air Force*, The Australian Centenary History of Defence, Volume II, Oxford University Press, Melbourne, 2001

Stevens, David (ed.), *The Royal Australian Navy*, The Australian Centenary History of Defence, Volume III, Oxford University Press, Melbourne, 2001

Stockings, Craig, *Paratroopers as Peacekeepers, 3rd Battalion, The Royal Australian Regiment, East Timor 1999–2000*, Imprint, Sydney, October 2000

Sutton, Ralph, *Soldiers of the Queen: War in the Soudan*, New South Wales Military Historical Society and The Royal New South Wales Regiment, Sydney, 1985

———, (ed.), *For Queen and Empire: A Boer War Chronicle*, 75th Anniversary Commemorative Edition, New South Wales Military Historical Society, Sydney, 1974

Sullivan, Gordon R., *Land warfare in the 21st century*, Strategic Studies Institute, U.S. Army War College, 1993

Sullivan, Gordon R. and James M. Dubik, *Envisioning Future Warfare*, U.S. Army Command and General Staff College Press, Fort Leavenworth, Kansas, 1995

Sullivan, Gordon R. and Michael V. Harper, *Hope is Not a Method*, Broadway Books, New York, 1997

Tanter, Richard, Mark Selden and Stephen R. Shalom (eds), *Bitter flowers, sweet flowers: East Timor, Indonesia and the world community*, Rowman & Littlefield, New York, 2001

Van Creveld, Martin, *The Transformation of War*, Free Press, New York, 1991

Wehner, Monica and Donald Denoon (eds), *Without a gun, Australia's Experiences Monitoring Peace in Bougainville, 1997–2001*, Pandanus Books, The Australian National University, Canberra, 2001

Wilcox, Craig, *Australia's Boer War*, Oxford University Press, Melbourne, 2002

Articles and Papers

Barber, David, 'Bougainville rebels free five soldiers in goodwill gesture', *Sydney Morning Herald*, 23 July 1997

Barber, David and Craig Skehan, 'PNG pact with rebels', *Sydney Morning Herald*, 11 October 1997

Barker, Geoffrey, '$100m in extra PNG aid but troops not on the agenda, *Australian Financial Review*, 26 August 1997

Bean, C.E.W., 'The Writing of the Australian Official History of the Great War—Sources, Methods and Some Conclusions', (Read before the Royal Australian Historical Society, 22 February 1938) in *Despatch*, Journal of the New South Wales Military Historical Society, Volume XXXVI, no. 2, April/June 2001. First published in the Royal Australia Historical Society, *Journal and Proceedings*, vol. XXIV, 1938, Part 2

Beasley, Kent, *Information Operations during Operation Stabilise in East Timor*, Working Paper no. 120, Land Warfare Studies Centre, Canberra, August 2002 available at <http://www.defence.gov.au/Army/lwsc/Publications/WP/WP_120.pdf>, accessed 14 November 2007

Blaxland, John, *Information-era Manoeuvre, The Australian-led Mission to East Timor*, Working Paper no. 118, Land Warfare Studies Centre, Canberra, June 2002, available at <http://www.defence.gov.au/Army/lwsc/Publications/WP/WP_118.pdf>, accessed 14 November 2007

Breen, Bob, *Giving Peace a Chance, Operation Lagoon, Bougainville 1994: A Case Study of Military Action and Diplomacy*, Canberra Papers on Strategy and Defence no. 412, Strategic and Defence Studies Centre, The Australian National University, Canberra, 2001

———, 'Problems of an Expeditionary Force—First Battalion, the Royal Australian Regiment in 1965', *Defence Force Journal*, no. 60, September/October, 1986

Centre for Strategic Studies, 'Strategic and Military Lessons from East Timor', *CSS Strategic Briefing Papers*, vol. 2: part 1 Victoria University of Wellington, February 2000, available at <http://www.victoria.ac.nz/css/docs/Strategic_Briefing_Papers/Vol.2%20Feb%202000/East%20Timor.pdf>, accessed 1 August 2008

Colombijn, Freek, 'Explaining the violent solution in Indonesia', *The Brown Journal of World Affairs*, vol. 9, no. 1, 2002

Correspondent in Wellington, 'Anzac force on cards for Bougainville', *Weekend Australian*, 23–24 August 1997

Cotterill, Daniel, 'ANAO Examines ADF's East Timor Logistics', *Australian Defence Magazine*, August 2002

Crouch, Harold, 'The TNI and East-Timor Policy', in James J. Fox and Dionisio Babo Soares (eds), *Out of the Ashes: Destruction and Reconstruction of East Timor*, C. Hurst and Co, London, 2000

Barrie, Chris A., Change, 'People and Australia's Defence Capability for the New Century,' *Australian Defence Force Journal*, no. 134, January/February 1999

Davis, Paul K., 'Observations on the Rapid Deployment Joint Task Force', Paper prepared for 23rd Annual Convention of the American International Studies Association held on 24–27 March 1982, *The RAND Paper series*, June 1982, available at <http://www.rand.org/publications/P/P6751/P6751.pdf>, accessed 14 November 2007

Dennis, Peter and Jeffrey Grey (eds), *The Second Fifty Years, The Australian Army 1947–1997*, Proceedings of the Chief of Army's History Conference held at the Australian Defence Force Academy, 23 September 1997, School of History, University College, Australian Defence Force Academy, Canberra, 1997

De Somer, Greg, *The Capacity of the Australian Army to Conduct and Sustain Land Force Operations*, Working Paper no. 106, Land Warfare Studies Centre Canberra, August 1999

D'Hage, Colonel Adrian S., 'Operation Morrisdance: An Outline History of the Involvement of the Australian Defence Force in the Fiji Crisis of May 1987', *Defence Force Journal*, no. 80, January/February 1990

Dibb, Paul, 'Defence Force Modernisation in Asia: Toward 2000 and Beyond', *Contemporary South East Asia*, vol. 18, no. 4, March 1997

———, 'The Relevance of the Knowledge Edge', *Australian Defence Force Journal*, no. 134, January/February 1999

——, 'The Revolution in Military Affairs and Asian Security', *Survival*, vol. 39, no. 4, Winter 1997–98

Dunbar, Jane, 'Bougainville truce creates climate for lasting peace treaty', *Weekend Australian*, 11–12 October 1997

Dupont, Alan, 'Transformation or Stagnation: Rethinking Australia's Defence', *Australian Journal of International Affairs*, vol. 57, no. 1, April 2003

Evans, Michael, *Conventional Deterrence in the Australian Strategic Context*, Working Paper no. 103, Land Warfare Studies Centre, Canberra, September 1998

——, *The Role of the Army in a Maritime Concept of Strategy,* Working Paper no. 101, Land Warfare Studies Centre, Canberra, September 1998

——, *The Tyranny of Dissonance, Australia's Strategic Culture and Way of War 1901–2005*, Study Paper no. 306, Land Warfare Studies Centre, Canberra, February 2005

Freedman, Lawrence, 'The Changing Forms of Military Conflict', *Survival*, vol. 40, no. 4, Winter 1998–99

——, *The Revolution in Strategic Affairs,* Adelphi Paper 318, Oxford University Press for International Institute of Strategic Studies, Oxford, 1998

Fry, Greg, *Australia's South Pacific Policy: From 'Strategic Denial' to 'Constructive Commitment'*, Working Paper 1991/8, Department of International Relations, Research School of Pacific Studies, The Australian National University, Canberra, 1991

Gubb, Matthew, *The Australian Military Response to the Fijian Coup: An Assessment*, Working Paper no. 171, Strategic and Defence Studies Centre, The Australian National University, Canberra, November 1988

Harnwell, M.L., 'Supporting Hope-Logistic Support to 1 RAR BN GP Operation SOLACE', *Army Ordnance*, June 1993

Hartley, Keigh, 'Can the UK Afford a Rapid Deployment Force?', *Royal United Services Institute Journal for Defence Studies*, no. 127, March 1982

Hirst, Megan, 'Narrative in the War Histories of C.E.W. Bean', Academic Essays, Access: History, vol. 2, no. 2 (Summer 1999), *The History Journals Guide*, Department of History, University of Queensland, Brisbane, 2005

Hookey, Helen and Roy Denny (eds), *Australian Defence Planning: Five Views of Policy Makers*, Canberra Papers on Strategy and Defence no. 120, Strategic and Defence Studies Centre, The Australian National University, Canberra, 1988

Hopkins, Major General R.N.L., 'History of the Australian Occupation in Japan 1946–50', *Journal of the Royal Australian Historical Society*, vol. XL. Part II, 1954

Horner, David, 'The ADF in the Gulf War', *Journal of the Royal United Services Institute of Australia*, October 1992

———, *Australian Higher Command in the Vietnam War*, Canberra Papers on Strategy and Defence no. 40, Strategic and Defence Studies Centre, The Australian National University, Canberra, 1986

———, 'Defending Australia in 1942', *War and Society*, vol. 11, no. 1, May 1993

Hurley, David J., 'Operation Solace', *Defence Force Journal*, January/February 1994

Isenburg, David, 'The Rapid Deployment Force: The Few, the Futile and the Expendable', *Cato Policy Analysis*, no. 44, The Cato Institute, Washington DC, 8 November 1984, available at <http://www.cato.org/pubs/pas/pa044.html>, accessed 14 November 2007

James, N.F., 'A Brief History of Australian Peacekeeping', *Defence Force Journal*, January/February 1994

Jenson, A.H., 'FSPB Coral', *Australian Infantry*, May–June 1973

Kirkwood, Richard, 'Towards 2000—DNSDC: A Logistic Odyssey', *Support Command Australia*, Summer 1999

Martin, Ian, *Self Determination in East Timor, The United Nations, the Ballot and International Intervention*, International Peace Academy Occasional Papers series, Lynne Reinner Publishers, London, 2001

May, Ron J., *The Situation on Bougainville: Implications for Papua New Guinea, Australia and the Region*, Parliamentary Research Service, *Current Issues Brief*, no. 9, Canberra, 1996–97

McDonald, Hamish, Desmond Ball, James Dunn, Gerry van Klinken, David Bourchier, Douglas Kammen and Richard Tanter, *Masters of Terror: Indonesia's Military and Violence in East Timor in 1999*, Canberra Papers on Strategy and Defence no. 145, Strategic and Defence Studies Centre, The Australian National University, Canberra, 2002

Médicins Sans Frontières, 'Life, Death and Aid', *MSF Annual Report*, 1993

Mellor, W.J.A., 'Operation Restore Hope: The Australian Experience', US Army War College, Fort Carlisle, 23 May 1995

Morrice, A.J., 'The Mogadishu Express', *Defence Force Journal*, January/February 1994

Murdoch, Lindsay, 'Troops may join PNG mission', *Age*, 21 August 1997

———, 'Australia flies rebels from Bougainville', *Age*, 30 September 1997

New Zealand Press Association, Australian Foreign Press and Australian Associated Press correspondents, 'NZ talks aim at ending Bougainville crisis', *The Australian*, 3 July 1997

O'Callaghan, Mary-Louise, 'Hidden Agenda', *Australian Weekend Magazine*, 14–15 August 1999

Peterson, G.M., 'Human Intelligence and Somalia', *Defence Force Journal*, January/February 1994

———, 'Psyops and Somalia', *Defence Force Journal*, January/February 1994

Regan, Anthony J., Submission to the Foreign Affairs Sub-Committee of the Joint Standing Committee on Foreign Affairs, Defence and Trade Inquiry, *Bougainville: The Peace Process and Beyond*, State, Society and Governance in Melanesia Project, Research School of Pacific and Asian Studies, The Australian National University, Canberra, 1999

Roberts, Greg, 'PNG and rebel leaders to meet at historic summit', *Sydney Morning Herald*, 25 November 1997

Ryan, Alan, *Thinking Across Time: Concurrent Historical Analysis on Military Operations*, Working Paper no. 114, Land Warfare Studies Centre, Canberra, July 2001, available at <http://www.defence.gov.au/army/lwsc/docs/wp%20114.pdf>, accessed 1 August 2008

Segal, David, 'Whatever Happened to Rapid Deployment?', *Armed Forces Journal*, March 1991

Skehan, Craig, '$100m to rebuild war-torn island', *Sydney Morning Herald*, 26 August 1997

Stanley, Peter, 'Reflections on Bean's Last Paragraph', *Sabretache*, vol. XXIV, July/September 1983

Stewart, Cameron, 'Australians asked to join operation', *The Australian*, 10 December 1992

Stockings, Craig (ed.), *Paratroopers as Peacekeepers*, 3 RAR, Sydney, 4 October 2000

Thompson, Alan, *Australia's Strategic Defence Policy: A Drift Towards Neo-Forward Defence*, Working Paper no. 29, Australian Defence Studies Centre, ADFA, University of New South Wales, Canberra, 1994

Tucker, David, 'Fighting Barbarians', *Parameters*, vol. 28, no. 2, Summer 1998

Journals (held by author)

Breen, Bob, no. 1, Bougainville Operation *Bel Isi*, November 1996–April 1997

———, no. 2, Bougainville Operation *Bel Isi*, 21 April 1996–7 May 1996

———, no. 3, Bougainville Operation *Bel Isi*, July–August 1998

———, no. 4, Bougainville Operation *Bel Isi*, November 1998–March 1999

———, no. 5, Bougainville Operation *Bel Isi*, East Timor, Operation *Faber*, March–September 1999

———, no. 6, Bougainville Operation *Bel Isi*, East Timor Operation *Spitfire*, Operation *Warden*, September–November 1999

———, no. 7, East Timor, Operation *Stabilise*, November–December 1999

———, no. 8, East Timor, Operation *Stabilise*, 30 December 1999–19 January 2000

———, no. 9, East Timor, Operation *Stabilise*, 20 January 2000–15 February 2000

———, no. 10, East Timor, Operation *Tanager*, April–May 2000

Commanders Diaries (located at Land Headquarters, Victoria Barracks, Sydney)

Colonel Steve K. Joske, Operation *Bel Isi I*, November 1997–January 1998

Brigadier Bruce V. Osborn, Operation *Bel Isi II*, May–October 1998

Major Gary J. Stone, Operation *Morris Dance*, 21 May–7 June 1987

Colonel Jeff B. Wilkinson, Operation *Bel Isi I*, February–April 1998

Case Study Fiji

Files

Defence Archives Queanbeyan

HQ ADF, Fiji Coup 1987—ADFCC Aspects, 87 22646

HQ ADF, Communications related to second Fijian Coup, 87 22646

HQ ADF, Contingency Plan, Australian Defence Force ADF Involvement in United Nations Peace Keeping, 89 12253

NAA Sydney

LHQ Duty Officer's Log, 21 May 1987–3 June 1987

LHQ OP Morris Dance Duty Log, 291-K1-9

LHQ OP Morris Dance General, 291-K1-11

LHQ OP Morris Dance Movements and Flights, 291-K1-12

LHQ OP Morris Dance—Navy, 291-K1-15

LHQ, OP Picaresque, 570-K1-182

LHQ Operation Morris Dance (Sitreps), 291-K1-10

Interviews

Brigadier Brian R. Dawson, 29 September 2004, Staff Officer Grade 3 (Operations) LHQ, Operation *Morris Dance*

General Peter C. Gration AC, OBE (Retd), 19 August 2005, CDF, Operation *Morris Dance*

Lieutenant Colonel K.W. Pippard (Ret), 20 December 2004, Operations Officer UNTAG-1, Operation *Picaresque*

Chaplain Gary J. Stone, 17 May 1997, Army Commander, Operation *Morris Dance*

Case Study Bougainville 1994

Files

HQ ADF Administrative Support to Operation *Lagoon*—Director Personnel Plans-Army Aspects, 94 29080

HQ ADF Australia Defence Force (ADF) Health Support to Operation *Lagoon*, 94 26515

HQ ADF Bougainville Peace Conference—Operation *Lagoon*, 94 29423

HQ ADF Bougainville Peace Conference (BPC), Operation *Lagoon*, 94 29423

HQ ADF, Costing Aspects—Operation *Lagoon* (Bougainville) Logistic Support for Peacekeeping Forces DCOST, 94 27740

HQ ADF Operation *Lagoon*—ADF Support to the Bougainville Peace Conference—Legal Advice, 94 28537

HQ ADF Operation *Lagoon*—ADF Support to Bougainville Peace Talks—Joint Logistic Operations and Plans (JLOP) Aspects, 94 27354

HQ ADF Operation *Lagoon*—Bougainville—Logistic Support for Peacekeeping Forces—Costing Aspects, 96 36639

HQ ADF Operation *Lagoon*—CNS Aspects, 94 30589

HQ ADF Operation *Lagoon*—Communications—Director General Joint Communication and Electronic Aspects, 98 18439

HQ ADF Operation *Lagoon*—Defence Public Relations Aspects, 94 28493

HQ ADF Operation *Lagoon*—Director Communications Group Aspects, 94 29849

HQ ADF Operation *Lagoon*—Director General Defence Force Legal Services Aspects, 94 35372

HQ ADF Operation *Lagoon*—Joint Communications and Electronics (JCE) Branch Issues, 98 17955

HQ ADF Operation *Lagoon*—Legal Services Branch Aspects, 94 26461

HQ ADF Operation *Lagoon*—Navy Office Contingency Co-ord Centre (NOCCC) Aspects, 94 30588

HQ ADF Operation *Lagoon*, Australian Support to Bougainville Peace Talks, Joint Logistics Aspects, 94 27354

HQ ADF Operation *Lagoon*, Bougainville, Administrative Support, 98 17231

HQ ADF Operation *Lagoon*, Bougainville, Out Traffic, 98 17229

HQ ADF Operation *Lagoon*, Post Operation Reports, Special Forces and Expenditure, 98 18173

HQ ADF Operation *Lagoon*, Support for PNG Peace Talks—DJOPS Aspects, 94 26303

HQ ADF Operation *Lagoon*, Support to Papua New Guinea Peace Talks, DJOPS Aspects, 94 26303

HQ ADF Operations *Lagoon* and *Capon-Bougainville*—Conditions of Service Directorate of Personnel Service and Conditions-Army Aspects, 94 34599

HQ ADF Overseas Deployment—South Pacific Peace Keeping Force (SPPKF) Operation *Lagoon*, Bougainville, 94 28989

HQ ADF Security, Operation *Lagoon*, 97 34183

HQ ADF South Pacific Regional Peacekeeping Force, OP *Lagoon*, 2002 7992

NAA, Sydney

LHQ Financial Management of OP *Lagoon*, K94 02007

LHQ OP *Lagoon* Administration Aspects, K94 01361

LHQ OP *Lagoon* CIS Operations/Communications Aspects, K94 01440

LHQ Op *Lagoon*, Comms Aspects, K94 01444

LHQ Op *Lagoon* General Int Aspects, K94 01400

LHQ Op *Lagoon*, Joint INTSUMs, K94 02438

LHQ Op *Lagoon*, Log Aspects, K94 01393

LHQ Op *Lagoon* Logistic Aspects, K94 01393

LHQ Op *Lagoon* Medical Aspects, K94 01424

LHQ Op *Lagoon* Personnel Aspects, K94 01409

LHQ Op *Lagoon* Planning Aspects, K94 01325

NAA, Melbourne

LOGCOMD Logistics Support to Operation *Lagoon* (16 September 1994–22 September 1994), Operations Branch, LOGC 950131

LOGCOMD Logistic Support to Operation *Lagoon* (22 September 1994–7 December 1994), Operations Branch, LOGC 950151

Interviews

Major General Peter J. Abigail, 18 March 1997, Commander Combined Force

Colonel M.J. Bird, 9 April 1997, former Chief Engineer PNGDF

Major S.C. Castle-Burns, 16 May 1997, Liaison officer

Major John O. Cronin, 31 December 1997, Liaison officer

Lieutenant Colonel J.A.T. Dunn, 15 May 1997, Legal Officer, Combined Force

Lieutenant Colonel Roger A. Hill, 31 October 1997, SO1 Intelligence, LHQ

Lieutenant Colonel Ian K. Hughes, 23 October 1997, DQ, 3rd Brigade

Brigadier David J. Hurley, 3 March 1997, Liaison Officer

Joseph Kabui, Discussions in Bougainville during visits in 1998 and 1999 (President, Bougainville Interim Government)

Sam Sirivi-Kauona, 16 January 2001, Commander, Bougainville Revolutionary Army

———, Discussions in Bougainville during visits in 1997 and 1998

Brigadier Phil J. McNamara, 29 October 1997, (Colonel (Operations), LHQ)

Lieutenant Colonel David L. Morrison, 24 October 1997, BM, 3rd Brigade

Captain Jim S. O'Hara, RAN, 13 November 1996, Maritime Component Commander

Warrant Officer Class Two, M. Pert, 15 May 1997, Liaison WO

Captain Russ W. Sharp, RAN, 19 March 1997, Director Joint Logistic Operations, HQ ADF

Lieutenant Colonel Robert W. Shoebridge, 31 May 1997 SO1 Joint Operations (Land), HQ ADF

Case Study Bougainville 1997–98

Files

Defence Archives, Queanbeyan

HQ ADF Committees—Higher Defence Committees—Chiefs of Staff Committee (COSC)-Operation Bel Isi—Concept of Operations, 97 40217

HQ ADF Committees—Higher Defence Committees—Chiefs of Staff Committee (COSC)—BEL ISI II Concept of Operations (CONOPS)-COSC Consideration, 9 April 1998, 98 12352

HQ ADF Committees—Higher Defence Committees—Chiefs of Staff Committee (COSC)—Operation SIERRA/ Operation Terrier Consideration, 97 39034

HQ ADF Committees, Higher Defence Committees, Chiefs of Staff Committee (COSC), Bel Isi II Contribution, 98 12352

HQ ADF Committees, Higher Defence Committees, Committee, Strategic Command Group (SCG) Post Operation Report-Operation Bel Isi, Phase One, 99 5103

HQ ADF Finance, Operation Bel Isi Finance Guidelines, 1997-98, 98 2107

HQ ADF Operation Bel Isi, ADF Support to Papua New Guinea (PNG)—DJLOP Aspects, 97 37914

HQ ADF Operation Bel Isi (Terrier) Phase 1, Australian Defence Force (ADF) Support to Bougainville Peace Process, 97 38602

HQ ADF Operation Bel Isi (Terrier) Phase 1-ADF Support to BGV Talks-Costing Aspects FASRFP, 97 38602

HQ ADF Operation Terrier/Operation Bel Isi, Australian Defence Force (ADF) Support to Papua New Guinea, 97 15413

HQ JOC, Potts Point Sydney

HQ AST Organisation, Form and Function, HQ AST, 623-11-1

Interviews

General John S. Baker, AC (Retd), 30 August 2005, CDF, Operation *Bel Isi*

Major David J. Bartlett, 28 July 1998, Operations Officer, Monitoring Team Arawa, Peace Monitoring Group

Michael J. Byrne, 27 July 1998, APS peace monitor, Monitoring Team Wakunai, Peace Monitoring Group

Lieutenant Colonel Richard P. Cassidy, 8 February 1998, Chief Negotiator, Truce Monitoring Group

Colonel John J. Culleton, Discussions, November–December 1997, Colonel (Operations), LHQ

Lieutenant Colonel Ashley L. Gunder, Discussions November–December 1997, SO1 Plans, LHQ

Major John G. Howard, 10 February 1998, Operations Officer, Truce Monitoring Group

Colonel David J. Hurley, 3 March 1998, Member of Resources Group, Operation *Bel Isi*

Corporal Laura Kenny, 25 July 1998, Linguist and intelligence operator, Monitoring Team Buin, Peace Monitoring Group

Colonel Clive W. Lilley, 25 October 1998, Commander Reconnaissance Group, Truce Monitoring Group

Brigadier Roger C. Mortlock, 27 October 1998, Commander, Truce Monitoring Group, December 1997–January 1998.

Major Paul M. Nothard, 25 July 1998. Operations Officer, Monitoring Team Buin, Peace Monitoring Group

Brigadier Bruce V. Osborn, 29 July 1998, Commander, Peace Monitoring Group, May–October 1998

Personal Diary

Lieutenant Colonel Paul M. Rogers, November 1997–31 January 1998, Commander Logistic Support Team, Truce Monitoring Group

Case Study East Timor

Files

Defence Archives, Queanbeyan

ADHQ Committees Higher Defence Committee—Chiefs of Staff Committee (COSC)—Review of East Timor Operations, 99 35225

ADHQ Committees Higher Defence Committee—Strategic Command Group–East Timor, 99 5095

ADHQ Committees, Higher Defence Committees, Chiefs of Staff Committee (COSC), Review of East Timor Operations, Communications, 99 35225

ADHQ Committees, Higher Defence Committees, Committee, Strategic Command Group (SCG), East Timor, 99 5095

ADHQ Committees, Higher Defence Committees, Committee, Strategic Command Group (SCG) Review of East Timor Operations, 99 5099

ADHQ Committees, Higher Defence Committees, Committee, Strategic Command Group (SCG), Post Operations Reports East Timor, 99 5106

ADHQ Committees, Higher Defence Committees, Strategic Command Group (SCG), Post Operational Report INTERFET, 99 5103

ADHQ Corporate Support Operation *Warden*, 2000 3239

ADHQ Logistic Issues, Op *Warden*, 2000 2604

ADHQ Operations, Contingency Planning Op *Spitfire*, 99 25025

ADHQ Operation *Spitfire*, SC Aspects, 2000 26205

ADHQ Operation *Stabilise*, INTERFET, Directorate of Joint Logistic Operations and Plans, (DJLOP), Financial Aspects, 99 28181

ADHQ Operation *Stabilise*—International Force in East Timor (INTERFET), 99 27708

ADHQ Operation *Warden*, 99 27064

ADHQ Operation *Warden*, 99 27320

ADHQ Operation *Warden*—Australian Defence Force (ADF) involvement in East Timor, 2002 41633

ADHQ Operation *Warden*—Integrated Logistic Support (ILS) Issues, AGB 99 03101

ADHQ Operation *Warden*, Australian Defence Force (ADF) Involvement in East Timor, 02 41633

ADHQ Operation *Warden*, Australian Defence Force (ADF), Involvement in East Timor, DGJOP Aspects, 99 26497

ADHQ Operation *Warden*, Australian Defence Force (ADF) Involvement in East Timor, DJLOP Aspects, 2000 6181

ADHQ Operation *Warden*, CDF Aspects, 99 26304

ADHQ Operation *Warden*, Daily Situation Reports (SITREPS), CDF Aspects, 99 28939

ADHQ Operation *Warden*, DLOGOPS (A) Aspects, 99 0272

ADHQ Operation *Warden*, DLOGOPS (A) Aspects AGB, 99 02721

ADHQ Operation *Warden*, East Timor, 99 29433

ADHQ Operation *Warden*, Support Command Australia, 2000 3231

ADHQ Operation *Warden*, Integrated Logistics Support (ILS) Issues, 99 0310

ADHQ Operation *Warden*, Support Command Australia, 2000 3231

ADHQ Operation *Warden*, SC Aspects, 2000 19128

ADHQ Operation *Warden/Stabilise*, Logistic Sustainability Issues, DJLOP Aspects, 99 33701

ADHQ Operation *Warden/Stabilise*, Mobilisation Issues, 99 33728

ADHQ Overseas Deployment Policy, Operation *Faber, Concord, Spitfire*, Australian Contribution, 99 15681

ADHQ Overseas Deployment Policy, Operation *Warden/Stabilise*, ADF Involvement in International Force in East Timor, 99 26459

ADHQ Support Planning, 99 27256

NAA, Sydney

LHQ ABCA Exercise 1998 (Ex *Rainbow Serpent*), K93 00765

LHQ ABCA Exercise 1998 (Ex *Rainbow Serpent*), K96 01254

LHQ Exercise *Rainbow Serpent* 98, Planning Aspects, K97 00489

Interviews

Staff Sergeant W.S. Anderson, 21 December 1999, Regimental Aid Post Sergeant, 2 RAR

Major M.C. Ashleigh, 20 January 2000, OC Battalion Support Group, 3 BASB

Brigadier Steve H. Ayling, Discussions with author in May 2000

Admiral Chris A. Barrie, AC (Retd), 6 September 2005

Commander Daryl W. Bates, 6 January 2000, Operations Officer, Navy Component, HQ INTERFET

Lieutenant A.R. Birch, 19 December 1999, OC 2 Platoon, 2 RAR

Lieutenant K.S. Black-Sinclair, 16 February 2000, Platoon Commander, 41 MP [Military Police] Platoon

Captain E.G. Boulton, 21 January 2000, 3 BASB, Operations Captain

Major Jim L. Bryant, 23 December 1999, OC C Company, 2 RAR

Group Captain Stewart R. Cameron, 20 February 2000, Air Component, CO Air Support Wing

Lieutenant Steve M. Casey, 23 December 1999, OC 9 Platoon, 2 RAR

Colonel G.D. Cavanagh, 17 January 2000, Commander FLSG

Corporal D.M. Cheung, 13 January 2000, Operator, 72 EW Squadron

Lieutenant Grant A. Chisnell, 28 December 1999, OC Reconnaissance Platoon, 2 RAR

Sergeant D.R. Commons, 7 February, HQ 3 Brigade, Intelligence Sergeant

Major General Peter J. Cosgrove, 2, 3, 4, 5, 6, 7, 18, 19, 20, 21 and 22 January 2000, Commander INTERFET

Lieutenant Colonel Don C. Cousins, 23 February 2000, SO1 Personnel and Logistic Operations HQ INTERFET

Captain D.J. Crowe, 16 January 2000, Civil Military Operations Centre Officer, 8/12 Medium Regiment, Royal Australian Artillery

Brigadier Mark Evans, 6 February 2000, HQ 3 Brigade, Commander WESTFOR

Major Marcus C. Fielding, 6 February 2000, Brigade Major, 3rd Brigade

Major Steve J. Grace, 13 January 2000, OC B Company, 3 RAR

Lieutenant Peter Halleday, 23 December 1999, OC 8 Platoon, 2 RAR

Captain J.G. Hawkins, 15 December 1999, Troop Commander, 3 Squadron, SASR

Major N.A. Herman, 10 January 2000, OC A Company, 3 RAR

Corporal A.M. Higgins, 11 January 2000, Section Commander 1 Platoon, 3 RAR

Lieutenant J.G. Hunter, 19 December 1999, OC 3 Platoon, 2 RAR

Lieutenant J.A. Jordans, 11 January 2000, OC 1 Platoon, 3 RAR

Lieutenant Colonel R.A. Joy, 22 January 2000, 1 JSU, CO JSU

Lieutenant Colonel D.W. Keating, 15 February 2000, 1 Field Hospital, CO Field Surgical Team

Lieutenant Colonel Mick C. Kehoe, 2 February 2000, CO 10 FSB

Lieutenant Colonel F.J. Kelloway, 18 December 1999, OC B Squadron, 3rd/4th Cavalry Regiment

Colonel M. Kelly, 1 January 2000, Chief of Staff, HQ INTERFET

WO2 S.J. Keogh, 11 January 2000, 3 BASB, IC Treatment Section

Lieutenant Colonel S.A. Kinloch, 20 January 2000, CO 3 BASB

Corporal N.K. Krishan, 23 December 1999, Section Comd 9 Platoon, 2 RAR

Lieutenant K.A. Lawton, 12 January 2000, 3 RAR, OC 5 Platoon

Major James F. McMahon, 15 December 1999, OC 3 Squadron, SASR

WO1 Peter F. Mele, 9 January 2000, RQMS, 2 RAR

Colonel David L. Morrison, 19 February 2000, Colonel (Operations), HQ INTERFET

Corporal C.M. Mosch, 28 December 1999, Section Commander, Reconnaissance Platoon, 2 RAR

Lance Corporal L. Moss, 11 January 2000, Section Commander 2 Platoon, 3 RAR

Major G. Murphy, 30 December 1999, Chaplain, 2 RAR

Corporal N.L. Murphy, 13 January 2000, Operator, 72 EW Squadron

Corporal P.R. Nichols, 23 December 1999, Medic C Company, 2 RAR

Major Robert V. Parker, 19 December 1999, OC A Company, 2 RAR

Captain R.J. Peterson, 29 December 1999, Intelligence Officer, 2 RAR

Captain A.R. Plunkett, 15 January 2000, Intelligence Officer, 3 RAR

Major M.D. Reilly, 27 December 1999, OC Administration Company, 2 RAR

Captain B.R. Rhodes, 15 January 2000, Air Operations Officer, 3 RAR

Commodore B.D. Robertson, 18 February 2000, Navy Component Commander, HQ INTERFET

Captain Lawrence T. Sargeant, 21 December 1999, Senior Nursing Officer, 3 BASB

Captain Kate L. Saunders, 7 February 2000, Movements Watchkeeper, HQ 3 Brigade

Private P.R.J. Shaw, 13 January 2000, Rifleman, 3 RAR

Major A.C. Shegog, 7 February 2000, 103 Signals Squadron, OC Signals Squadron

Lieutenant Colonel P.K. Singh, 16 January 2000, CO 3 RAR

Lieutenant Colonel Mick D. Slater, 9 January 2000, CO 2 RAR

Major Peter C. Steel, 15 December 1999, OC 5 Aviation Squadron Group, 5 Aviation Regiment

Colonel Paul B. Symon, 21 August 2000, Military Liaison Officer, UNAMET

Major R.M. Vivian, 7 February 2000, OC 72 EW Squadron

Major D. Weadon, 7 February 2000, HQ 3 Brigade, Linguist/S2 3 Brigade

Index

Abigail, Peter J. 55–8, 60–5, 71–5, 77–9, 81
administration vii, 2, 9n19, 21n18, 21n24, 45, 47, 62–3, 67, 87, 100–1, 104, 111, 118, 124n12, 124n13, 124n15, 124n24, 124n26, 172n5, 211
    administrative support 46, 72, 87, 119, 182, 203–4
    personnel administration 87, 160
Afghanistan ix, 166
Ahearn, Ian F. 47
aid 106n10, 145, 200
    humanitarian aid 145
        Office for the Coordination of Humanitarian Aid 145
    multilateral aid 50
    (*see also* AusAID)
aircraft 3, 5, 19, 22n52, 24, 35–40, 93, 105, 112–14, 136, 140–1, 156 (*see also under* Royal Australian Air Force)
Air Commander (*see under* Royal Australian Air Force)
air force (*see* Royal Australian Air Force)
alliances 3, 8n7, 16–17, 88, 183
Area of Operations vii, 2, 80, 105, 118, 150n38, 183
Arnison, Peter M. 35, 37, 55–62, 73–5, 77–8, 82n15, 115, 160
AusAID (*see also* aid) 118
Australia 79–81, 85, 88, 91n16, 93–5, 98, 100, 102, 104, 109–10, 115, 128–9, 135, 147, 158, 163, 165–6, 169
    Australian military forces 19, 86
    capabilities 159, 177
        lack of 47, 60, 97, 112, 126n58
        military vii, xvi, 2–3, 7n2, 12, 75, 136, 155, 181
    cities:
        Brisbane 86, 89, 99, 114, 122, 131, 146
        Canberra ix, 24, 33–5, 40, 45, 48, 54–5, 57–60, 62–3, 81, 85–7, 95–101, 117, 119–20, 130–33, 135, 137, 146, 155, 170–1
        Darwin 1, 16, 85–6, 89, 130–6, 138, 140–2, 145–7, 156
        Melbourne 12, 31, 61, 111, 113, 128, 156, 161
        Townsville 14, 24, 32, 35, 38, 40, 49, 56–7, 61–3, 65–7, 71, 77, 81, 99, 101, 105, 114–15, 130, 132, 139–40, 142: Townsville Air Base (*see under* Royal Australian Air Force: bases)
    Cocos Islands 28n10, 177
    Gulf of Carpentaria 55, 63
    Northern Territory 122, 133, 136, 138–9, 146
    reputation of 7, 127, 158, 160, 163, 168
    resupply from 112–13, 119, 122, 131, 138, 146
    strategic thinking of vii–iii, 1–127, 158–9, 163, 168, 187
        continental defence 13, 159
        'defence-in-depth', xv, 18, 23
        geographical frontline 85
        isolationism 1, 159
        sea and air gap 159
Australian Army 14–15, 18–19, 186, 193
    Army Joint Support Plan 47
    Army Office 35, 40, 47, 49
    Army Operations Support 78
    attaché 137, 149n18
    force projection 5, 13, 160, 162–3
    formations and units:
        3rd Brigade 24, 34:
            support to Operation *Bel Isi* (Bougainville 1997–98), 99, 122; Operation *Lagoon* (Bougainville 1994) 54–8, 62–3, 67, 78, 83n32; Operation *Morris Dance* (Fiji 1987) 32, 35, 37, 47, 49, 51n20; Operation *Spitfire/Warden/Stabilise* (East Timor 1999), 122, 132, 135–7, 139, 141–2, 145–6, 153n116
        9 Force Support Battalion (*see under* Logistic Support Force *under* logistics: headquarters, formations and units)
        10 Force Support Battalion (*see under* Logistic Support Force *under* logistics: headquarters, formations and units)

Advance Company Group (ACG): Operation *Morris Dance* (Fiji 1987) 32–3, 35, 37, 40, 42n34
Moorebank Logistic Group (*see under* logistics: headquarters, formations and units)
Royal Australian Regiment (RAR) 17, 140, 142: 1st Battalion (1 RAR) 17, 32, 35, 38, 41n17, 57, 63; 2nd Battalion (2 RAR) 140–1, 148, 169; 3rd Battalion (3 RAR) 142, 169; combat troops 79, 135, 139, 141: ammunition carriage 149n1; rapid response command 171
helicopters: *Black Hawk* 64, 71, 133
support to:
Butterworth Air Base, Malaysia, 22n52; Operation *Bel Isi* (Bougainville 1997–98) 93, 95, 103, 106, 115: cultural dimensions 123; ignorance of culture 119; welcoming ceremonies 102; Operation *Lagoon* (Bougainville 1994), 58, 66–7, 71–3, 76–7, 80–1, 83n32: culture, ceremony and status 66; Operation *Morris Dance* (Fiji 1987) 36–7, 49; Operation *Spitfire/Warden/Stabilise* (East Timor 1999) 133, 137
headquarters:
Deployable Joint Force Headquarters (DJFHQ) role 86–7, 89–90, 128, 155: support to Operation *Bel Isi* (Bougainville 1997–98) 96, 107n46; support to Operation *Spitfire/Warden/Stabilise* (East Timor 1999) 131: concept of operations 135, 137, 146
Land Headquarters: support to DJFHQ 122; support to Operation *Bel Isi* (Bougainville 1997–98) 96, 100–1, 103: command duplication 105, 106n14, 107n27, 109–12, 115; assessment of 120, 122–3, 124n22, 125n50, 126n58; support to Operation *Lagoon* (Bougainville 1994) 54, 56–9, 61–3: orders 64, 67; assessment 72, 75–7, 80–2, 82n15, 83n25, 83n32; support to Operation *Morris Dance* (Fiji 1987) 33, 36, 38, 40, 42n34: assessment of 47, 49; Operation *Spitfire/Warden/Stabilise* (East Timor 1999) 131, 150n37
Land Commander 36, 42n46, 55, 85, 95, 115, 119–20, 123, 131, 161
Australian and New Zealand Army Corps (ANZAC) 94, 98, 110
Australian Defence Force (ADF) xv, 19, 23, 55, 71, 74, 85, 94, 109, 165–6, 181, 186
ADF Warfare Centre 173n15
Australian CINC 89
joint environment 128
senior officers 155
commanders:
Commander—Australian Theatre 85–90, 91n3, 104, 128, 137, 160: bypass 152, 157; co-location 85, 157; commanders 98, 160; efficacy 128; environmental command 34; failure of theatre command 161; theatre command 111, 118, 121, 129
Commander—Air Command (*see* Royal Australian Air Force: Air Commander)
Commander—Land Command (*see* Australian Army: Land Commander)
Commander—Maritime Command (*see under* Royal Australian Navy as Maritime Commander)
Commander—Northern Command (COMNORCOM) 85–6, 89, support to Operation *Spitfire/Warden/Stabilise* (East Timor 1999) 131–2, 136, 138
Commander Support Command—Australia (*see under* logistics)
headquarters:
Australian Defence Force Headquarters (HQ ADF) 20, 24, 33, 45, 54, 87–9, 96, 132–3, 155, 185, 207: Australian Defence Force Command Centre (ADFCC) 77; Australian Defence Force Intelligence Centre (ADFIC) 60–1, 63; devolved decision-making 128,

133, 161; Joint Logistics Section 20
    Australian Defence Headquarters (ADHQ) 87–9, 96, 132–3, 155
    Headquarters Australian Theatre (HQAST) Australian Theatre Joint Intelligence Centre (ASTJIC) 85, 120: establishment of 85–90, 128–9, 149n11, 150n31, 206; failure of Theatre Command 161; transition from strategic to operational decision making 90, 105, 161
        support to Operation *Bel Isi* (Bougainville 1997–98) 96–7, 100–4, 108n58, 117: assessment 161; command and control duplication 105, 109, 126n58; joint logistic component commander 110; logistic instructions 111
        support to Operation *Spitfire/Warden/Stabilise* (East Timor 1999) 131–2, 147, 150n37: assessment 155; command and control, 133–4, 138, 152n89
    senior staff and committee:
        Assistant Chief of the Defence Force–Operations (ACOPS) 81, 93, 110
        Chief of the Defence Force (CDF) 20, 32, 46, 53, 76, 85, 128, 160, 166
        Chief of the Defence Force Staff (CDFS) 19
        Chief of the General Staff (CGS) 13, 36, 42n46
        Chief of Navy Staff (CNS) 36
        Chiefs of Staff Committee (COSC) 34, 45, 85, 128, 186, 206–7: examination of operational performance 156, 168
        Director Joint Operations (DJOPS) 33, 56, 61
        Vice Chief of the Defence Force (VCDF) 20, 54, 90, 117
Australian Government:
    Cabinet:
        consideration of Operation *Bel Isi* (*Bougainville* 1997–98) 95, 98
        consideration of Operation *Lagoon* (*Bougainville* 1994) 46, 57–8, 64, 78, 82
        consideration of Operation *Morris Dance* (Fiji 1987) 36–8, 38
        consideration of Operation *Spitfire/Warden/Stabilise* (East Timor 1999) 128, 135
    Department of Defence ix, 14, 163, 166–7, 168
        rapid response command 171–2, 175n37 179
        support to: Operation *Bel Isi* (Bougainville 1997–98) 95, 98, 100; Operation *Lagoon* (Bougainville 1994) 57–8, 60, 93; Operation *Morris Dance* (Fiji 1987) 48; Operation *Spitfire/Warden/Stabilise* (East Timor 1999) 130, 150n39, 152, 155
    Department of Foreign Affairs and Trade (DFAT)
        diplomats 54, 63, 81
        support to Operation *Bel Isi* (Bougainville 1997–98), 94: diplomats 95, 97–8, 104, 117–8, 122–3
        support to Operation *Lagoon* (Bougainville 1994) 57–8, 63: diplomats 54, 63, 81
        support to: Operation *Morris Dance* (Fiji 1987) 33–4, 46, 48: cables 49
    Department of Prime Minister and Cabinet 46
    Hawke Government 31–2, 37
    Howard Government 167
    National Security Committee of Cabinet (NSCC) 135–6
    Prime Minister of 25, 31, 71, 81, 93, 107n33, 129
    Whitlam Government 18
Australian Light Armoured Vehicle (*see under* vehicles)
Australian National Audit Organisation: Operation *Stabilise* audit 169
Australian Public Service:
    support to Operation *Bel Isi* (Bougainville 1997–98) 105, 117, 122

215

Australian Special Forces (*see* forces: Special Forces)
Australian Strategic Policy Institute (ASPI) 167, 173n6
Australian Theatre 128 (*see also* Australian Defence Force: Headquarters Australian Theatre)
Australian Theatre Joint Intelligence Centre (*see* Headquarters Australian Theatre *under* Australian Defence Force: headquarters)
Ayerbe, Tony 62
Ayling, Steve H. 74, 151n48

Baker, John S. 54, 58, 60–1, 76–7, 85, 87–9, 91n3, 96–7, 101, 105, 107n33, 107n46, 111, 116–19, 121, 123, 128, 160
Banister, Gary R. 125n50
Barnard, Lance 18
Barrie, Chris A. 90, 117, 128, 130–6, 138, 146, 152n89, 161
Bartlett, David J. 125n51
bases 37
    home vii, xv, 5–6, 11
    mounting and forward operating bases 61, 148, 159, 162: rapid response command 171
    mounting base operations 156, 160
    (*see also* Royal Australian Air Force: bases)
Bavadra, Timoci 24–5, 31, 36
Bean, C.E.W. 7, 14, 165, 168–9
Beaumont, Alan L. 53–6, 58–9, 61–2, 65–6, 75–8, 81, 121
Beazley, Kim C. 23, 31, 33–4, 37, 85
Bell, David 97
Bennett, Phillip 19–20, 24, 36, 45–6, 160
Bertram, John F. 47
Birks, Alan L. 93, 96–100, 104
Blake, Murray 105, 115, 160
Blaxland, John 135
Boer War (*see under* wars)
Bolger, Jim 93
Bonser, Mark F. 131–2, 136, 138
Bougainville (*see under* Papua New Guinea)

Bougainville Crisis Action Team (*see under* Papua New Guinea: Bougainville)
Bougainville Revolutionary Army (*see under* Papua New Guinea: Bougainville)
Boyd, Craig W. 115–6, 131
Bridges, W.T. 13
Britain:
    Australian military assistance to 11–16, 13, 16
    force projection 4, 174n36
    involvement in Fiji 25–6, 32
    involvement in Vanuatu 28n16
    strategic posture 172n5
    support to Operation *Stabilise* (East Timor 1999) 27, 139
    withdrawal East of Suez 17–18
Brown, Malcolm 32
Brownrigg, Ken A. 137, 139–40, 149n18
Bryant, Jim L. 142–4
Buchanan, David J. 80–1
Byrne, Michael J. 125n51

Cambodia xv
Cameron, Stewart R. 139, 153n101
Canada 139
    civil support capability 156
    land force capabilities 17, 159
    staff capability 155
Casey, Steve M. 143–4
Cassidy, Richard P. 95, 100, 106n16
Cavenagh, Grant D. 147
Chalmers, Don 58, 65
Chamberlain, Joseph 12
Chan, Julius 53–5, 59, 64–5, 67, 71, 74–5, 78–9, 93
Chidgey, Colin 63, 66, 82n2
China 11–12
Chisnell, Grant A. 143–4
coalition 135, 145, 167, 183
    contingents 147
    government 18, 25, 36, 93
    operations 6, 76, 131, 141, 145
Cockburn, Milton 38
Cold War 5, 11, 17, 19, 127, 165
    operations 22n52

Index

command and control viii, 2, 7n2
  arrangements for:
    Australian Naval and Military Expeditionary Force 5
    forward operating bases 180
    Operation *Bel Isi* (Bougainville 1997–98) 104–5, 111, 117–18, 120–1
    Operation *Lagoon* (Bougainville 1994) 58–9, 65
    Operation *Morris Dance* (Fiji 1987) 46–8
    Operation *Spitfire/Warden/Stabilise* (East Timor 1999) 155–7, 161, 200
    UK military 8n11
    US military 8n12
  chain of command 58–9, 90, 104, 117, 120, 122, 132, 159, 162, 169, 177–8
  joint command and control viii, 14, 17, 20, 85–7, 106, 123, 129, 159
    arrangements for 19–20, 76, 86
    centre 87
    consolidation viii
    joint logistic command and control 109, 122
    lack of rehearsal 159–60, 170
    Service opposition to 85, 121–2, 170, 172
    weakness in 109, 129, 155
  levels of command 3, 5–6, 48, 58, 131
    challenges to coordinate 48
    emphasis on operational and tactical 4
    integration for East Timor 1999 133
    operational 36, 76, 79, 88, 111, 118, 121, 130: assessment 47, 158–9, 161
    strategic 36, 48, 58, 79, 88, 90, 100, 130, 133, 155: assessment 158–9, 169
    tactical 55, 58, 76, 79: impact of Information Age on 4; pressure from higher levels viii, 40, 46–7, 54, 58, 78, 86, 103, 130, 149n10, 159, 162
    technical and administrative 65, 171–2, 175n36, 177, 183

  theatre 88, 98, 111, 118, 121: co-location 85, 157; commanders 98, 160; creation 160; failure of 161; negative assessment 129; positive assessment 128, 155
  unity of 86, 128
Commander—Air Command (*see under* Royal Australian Air Force as Air Commander)
Commander Australian Theatre (*see under* Australian Defence Force)
Commander—Joint Logistics (*see under* logistics: commanders)
Commander—Land Command (*see under* Australian Army as Land Commander)
Commander—Maritime Command (*see under* Royal Australian Navy as Maritime Commander)
Commander—Northern Command (see under Australian Defence Force: commanders)
Commander—Support Command–Australia (*see under* logistics: commanders)
communications vii, 2, 7n2, 17, 58, 77
  arrangements for:
    Operation *Bel Isi* (Bougainville 1997–98) 94, 96–8, 100, 102, 116–7, 121, 126n58, 145: Signals Squadron 116
    Operation *Lagoon* (Bougainville 1994) 58–61: problems 67, 72–6, 81, 82n15, 83n32, 103; Signals Squadron 83n32
    Operation *Morris Dance* (Fiji 1987) 36, 38, 40, 42n42, 45, 47–8
    Operation *Spitfire/Warden/Stabilise* (East Timor 1999) 131, 155
  Director General, Joint Communications and Electronics 72
  dysfunction 155, 178
  equipment 38, 116–17
    e-mail/email 154n127
    high-frequency receivers 72–3
    RAVEN tactical radios 73
    satellite (Inmarsat) 67, 72–4, 102, 131

217

telephone 37–8, 46, 58, 67, 72, 77, 101, 115
Joint Communications Planning Group 72, 75
low-level 79, 102, 117
personnel 36, 116
radio operators 73, 116
signals 67n4, 80, 102, 117, 124n22, 126n58
    signaller 144
Connolly, Jim M. 54, 58, 60–6, 81, 90–1, 96–9, 101–5, 107n33, 107n46, 110–11, 117–23, 128
contracting 14, 28n15, 93
opposition to 146, 154n125
control administrative 65
rapid response command 171, 175n36, 177
technical 65, 175n36, 183
cooperation 12, 15, 33
between Australian and New Zealand diplomats 94–5
between environmental commanders 86–7, 121, 129, 133, 163, 160–1
logistic 111, 160
with Indonesian security forces 134, 143
coordination 3, 28n16, 97, 107n27
air movements 35, 112, 124n13, 156, 139
collapse in Darwin 145
delegates 79
evacuation 33, 37, 40, 63
ineffective 103, 109–11, 120, 122, 134, 147, 161
intelligence 47, 60–1
joint operations 47
joint procedures 47
logistic 46
navy-army 72
ship loading 160
surveillance 85
withdrawal of PNGDF forces 66
Cosgrove, Peter J. 131–41, 145, 148, 161–2, 166–7, 170–1
Cronin, John O. 57, 63
Crouch, Harold 149n17

Cousins, Don C. 131, 139–41, 145, 147
Culleton, John J. 96–7, 100, 107n33, 107n35, 109–13, 115

D'Hage, Adrian S. 33
Dawson, Brian R. 42n34
Defence Intelligence Organisation (DIO) 57, 59–60, 76, 91n16, 130
dissatisfaction with 76, 81, 120, 155
Defence National Supply and Distribution Centre (DNSDC) 146, 157
dissatisfaction with 163, 164n14
Defence Papers:
Australian Approach to Warfare 167, 187
Australian Defence (1976) 19
    rapid response command 171, 175n37
Defence 2000: Our Future Defence Force 167, 187
Defending Australia 1994 187
Force 2020 166, 188
National Security: A Defence Update 167, 188
The Defence of Australia (1987) xv, 15, 23, 158–9, 177, 187
Defence Security Branch (DSB) 91n16
Defence Signals Directorate (DSD) 91n16, 152n81
radio intercepts 152n81
Dennis, Mike 47
Dennis, Peter 169
Deployed Forces Support Unit (*see under* logistics: headquarters, formations and units)
deployment (also known as force deployment) 178
arrangements for:
    Operation *Anode* (Solomon Islands 2003) 167–8: assessment 173n15
    Operation *Bel Isi* (Bougainville 1997–98) 104, 109, 117: dissatisfaction with 119, 121–2
    Operation *Lagoon* (Bougainville 1994) 71–2

Operation *Morris Dance* (Fiji 1987) 35–40
Operation *Solace* (Somalia 1993) 105
Operation *Spitfire/Warden/Stabilise* (East Timor 1999) 134–6, 138–9, 142, 146: assessment 155, 161; assignment of forces 162
    Vietnam 1966 133
    dependence on allies 155
    lack of rehearsal 159, 162–3
    rapid response command 171
    unsatisfactory 158, 160–1, 169
detention 64, 74
Dexter, David 7
Dibb, Paul 23–4, 158–9
Downer, Alexander 93–5, 97, 101, 104, 129, 132, 135
Draunidalo, Sevenaca 57, 64, 74, 78, 82n6
Ducie, Greg 57, 63

Earle, Rod 78, 80
East Timor vii, ix, xv, 134, 146
    auxiliaries (militia) 127, 129, 130, 134–7, 140, 142, 144–5, 149n19, 150n25
    Balibo 148
    Dili (1999) 127, 129, 134, 136–7, 139, 145, 147
        air bridge to 140–1, 153n101, 162
        establishing a secure environment 139–42, 145, 162, 168
        Dili Harbour 141, 145, 147
        Komoro Airfield 139, 147, 162
        UN compound 135, 137
    East Timorese 129–30, 134–5, 140
        punishment of 134, 137, 149n19, 152n81
    infrastructure 162
        destruction of 137, 152n81
    intelligence assessment 130
    Liquica 149n19
    Maliana 134, 148
    political status 130
    pro-independence forces 129–30, 134
    sacking of 135, 137
    stabilisation intervention in 3, 6–7, 127, 129, 131–3, 135–40, 145–8, 157, 160–3, 167, 169
    territorial battalion 127, 130, 138, 143–4, outriders 143
Egypt 15
    Suez 17–18
embassies, consulates and high commissions:
    Australian Consulate in East Timor 137
    Australian Embassy in Jakarta 139
    Australian High Commission in Fiji 35, 40, 49
    Australian High Commission in Port Moresby 55, 57
    New Zealand High Commission in Fiji 31
emergencies 7, 8n3, 11–12, 105, 116, 158, 166
    humanitarian 1
    contingency stocks for 141
    rapid response command 171–2
    regional emergencies 166, 172
    rehearsals for 50
    standby for 28n16, 28n24, 32, 34, 37, 161
Endeavour Accords 58 (*see also under* Papua New Guinea: Bougainville)
engineering 57, 97, 101–2, 104, 147–8
Espiritu Santo Rebellion (Vanuatu, 1980) 24, 28n16, 50
Europe 15
    Australian military projection to 13, 15
evacuation operations:
    East Timor 130, 136–7
    Fiji 34, 37, 47, 50
Evans, Gareth 31, 37, 53–4, 59, 67n4
Evans, Mark 132, 135, 137–8, 140–5, 152n73, 162
exercises:
    command-post exercises 66, 85
    Crocodile 85, 91, 129
    field exercises in the north 1, 138, 146, 159–60, 162
    Kangaroo 19, 85, 122, 129, 138, 153n91, 160
    Swift Eagle 56–7, 62–3

Faithfull, Kim 115
Fielding, Marcus C. 135, 153n116
Fiji 25, 27, society 25–7
    Bavadra Government 25–6, 27, 31–2, 37
    military coup 1987
        Air New Zealand hijacking at Nadi Airport, 35
        Constitution 25, 27, 31, 34–5
        Council of Advisors 36
        Council of Ministers 25, 31, 35–6
        Fijian Nationalist 'Taukei Movement' 26–7, 28n24
        Fijians' responses 25–6, 28n24, 31–2, 34, 37
        Governor General of 25, 31–2, 35–7
        Great Council of Chiefs of 35, 37
        Indians' responses 25–6, 28n32, 31–2, 34–5, 37–40
        police force 27, 33, response to rioting and looting 32, 37–8
        possible air or sea evacuation 42n47, 46
        Queen Elizabeth Barracks 24
        raids on media 27, 32
        Suva 24, 31–2, 34–5, 57
    Republic of Fiji Military Forces (RFMF):
        military coup 1987 24–7, 28n24, 32–6, 38
        support to Operation *Bel Isi* (Bougainville 1997–98) 119
        support to Operation *Lagoon* (Bougainville 1994) 53, 55–7, 61, 65, 81, 82n6
        threat from 47
force:
    command (*see* command and control)
    deployment (*see* deployment)
    employment (*see* functions of force projection: employment)
    preparation (*see* functions of force projection: generic force preparation; *see* functions of force projection: specific force preparation)
    projection:
        Australian xv–xvi, 3, 7, 11, 89, 128, 157, 163, 167
        cycle of xv, 3
        enabling functions of (*see under* functions of force projection)
        history of 11–17, 19
        planning 61, 78
        political and cultural dimensions of 3, 123
        synchronisation of 89
        protection (*see* functions of force projection: protection)
        reconstitution (*see* functions of force projection: reconstitution)
        redeployment (*see* functions of force projection: redeployment)
        rotation (*see* functions of force projection: rotation)
        sustainment (*see* logistics)
Force Structure Review 146
forces:
    1st Australian Imperial Force (AIF) 13–15, 49
    1st Australian Task Force (1 ATF) 21n36
    Australian Force-Somalia 83n28, 83n40
    Australian Naval and Military Expeditionary Force (AN and MEF) 7, 9n19, 13–14, 17
    Combined Force Operation Anode (Solomon Islands 2003), 167
        Operation Lagoon (Bougainville 1994) 55–6, 60, 62, 64–6, 69n57, 71–2, 78–9, 81, 83n25, 83n32, 118: maritime component 66
    Commonwealth Military Forces 13
    deployed forces responsiveness to 86
        sustainment of 123, 156–7
    Special Forces 2, 8n5, 47, 57, 87–8, 133, 139, 141, 179, New Zealand 116
Ford, Tim 99, 107n46
Forrest, Athol 101–2
France (Espiritu Santo Rebellion, 1980) 28n16
functions of force projection vii, 2–3
    command (*see* command and control)

deployment (*see* deployment)
employment vii, xv, 2–4, 6, 11, 158, 181
    independent Service 160, 163
    Operation *Bel Isi* (Bougainville 1997–98) 105
    Operation *Lagoon* (Bougainville 1994): 73, 83n25
generic force preparation vii, xv, 2, 7n1, 13, 15
protection vii, xv, 2, 5–6, 8n5, 15, 26, 33, 48, 159
    arrangements for Operation *Bel Isi* (Bougainville 1997–98) 100, 105, 121
    arrangements for Operation *Lagoon* (Bougainville 1994) 59, 79, 82n6, 83n25, 83n27
    arrangements for Operation *Spitfire/Warden/Stabilise* (East Timor 1999) 136, 141, 158
    rapid response command 171, 173n9, 179:
reconstitution vii, xv, 2–3, 5, 7, 7n1, 13
redeployment vii, xv, 2, 6, 13, 32, 83n25, 179, 182
rotation vii, 2, 4–6, 75
    arrangements for Operation Bel Isi (Bougainville 1997–98) 119–20, 125n50
    arrangements for battalion groups 16, 18
specific force preparation vii, xv, 2–3, 6, 11–15, 17, 20n3, 89, 158–60, 167, 169
    arrangements for Operation *Bel Isi* (Bougainville 1997–98), 90, 97–104, 109, 119–20, 122, 125n50
    arrangements for Operation *Lagoon* (Bougainville 1994) 6, 61, 63, 65, 67, 79, 83n25, 83n32
    arrangements for Operation *Morris Dance* (Fiji 1987) 33–4, 37, 86
    arrangements for Operation *Spitfire/Warden/Stabilise* (East Timor 1999) 133, 155

    number capping 109, 122, 126n58, 167; rapid response command 171
sustainment (*see logistics*)

Ganilau, Ratu Sir Penaia 25
Gillespie, Ken J. 174n34
Glossop, J.C.T. 14
Gordon, Charles 12
Gorton, John 22n40
Gould, John 151n59
Grace, Steve J. 57, 63
Gration, Peter C. 24, 32–3, 35–7, 39–40, 46, 48–9, 76, 85, 121, 160
Grey, Jeffrey 13, 15, 169
Gubb, Matthew 34, 39, 50
Gulf War (1991) (*see under* wars)
Gunder, Ashley L. 96, 107n27

Habibie, Jusuf 129–30, 135, 138, 146
Haddad, Peter F. 156
Halleday, Peter 144
Harris, Mick J. 33, 35–7, 42n34
Hart, Basil H. Liddell 170
Hartley, John C. 119–20, 122–3, 131, 134, 147–8, 161
Hawke, Robert J. 25, 27, 31–4, 48
Hayes, John 93, 106n18
headquarters (*see under* Australian Army; *see under* Australian Defence Force, *see under* logistics)
Hickling, Frank J. 95–101, 104–5, 106n14, 107n35, 107n37, 107n46, 110–11, 115–18, 121–2, 123n5, 123n6, 161
Hill, Robert 31, 167, 170
Hill, Roger A. 59–60, 63, 81
Hingston, Colin M. 156
Holmes, Roger 97
Holmes, W. 14
Homer 168
Horne, Donald 165
Horner, David M. 5, 18–19, 136, 152n89
Houston, Angus G. 96, 171
Howard, John W. 25, 93, 95, 97, 107n33, 129–31, 161
Hudson, Mike 36
Hughes, Ian K. 56, 62–3, 67

221

Hurford, Gordon 56, 61
Hurley, David J. 68n17, 74, 95–6, 107n27

Indonesia xv, 18, 34
    involvement in East Timor (1999) 127–49
    relations with Australia 127, 130, 135, 137–8, 143, 152n88
intelligence 3, 93
    agencies/organizations:
        ADF Intelligence Centre support to Operation *Lagoon* 60, 63
        Australian Theatre Joint Intelligence Centre (ASTJIC) 85, 87, 91: criticism of support 120
        Defence Intelligence Organisation 57, 76: criticism of support 120; 155 leaks 130
        Joint Intelligence Organisation (JIO) 33, 47: denial of access to Army Office 47
        Office of National Assessments (ONA) criticism of support 120
    challenges at HQAST 87
    concept of operations 178
    failure to deliver at the tactical level 170
    human intelligence 60, 79
    need for more capability 166, 171
    rapid response command 171
    reforms 76, 85–6, 91n3
    relationship to force protection vii, 2, 8n5, 179
    Suharto regime 152n81
    support to:
        Operation *Bel Isi* (Bougainville 1997–98) 96, 106n14, 117: criticism of support 120
        Operation *Lagoon* (Bougainville 1994) 55, 58–61, 63, 68n17, 74–5, 77, 79, 84n49: assessment 80, 83n32; Bougainville Crisis Action Team 60, 80–1; lack of independent communications 81, 82n15; lack of liaison officers, 57
        Operation *Morris Dance* (Fiji 1987): assessment 47, 49
        Operation *Solace* (Somalia 1993): human intelligence 60, 201
        Operation *Tamar* (Rwanda 1994–95): human intelligence 60
        Operation *Warden/Stabilise* (East Timor 1999) 130–2, 135–6, 143: criticisms of support, 155
International Force—East Timor (INTERFET) involvement in East Timor 127–49
Iran 166, 173n6
Iraq xv, 166, 173n6
Irian Jaya xv
Irvine, David 106n18, 119

Jamieson, Ian 138
Joint Administrative Branch 91
    Administrative Cell 87
    Communications and Electronics 72
    Communications Planning Group 72
    distribution centre 157
    Exercise Planning Staff 45
    Joint Intelligence Organisation (*see under* intelligence: agencies/organisations)
    Joint Logistic Unit (*see under* logistics: headquarters, formations and units)
    Joint Movements Group (*see under* logistics: headquarters formations and units)
    Joint Operations Command (JOC) 170
    Parliamentary Committee on Foreign Affairs, Defence and Trade 20
    staff groups 121, 128
    task force 118, 128, 155
Joske, Steve K. 97, 100–3, 105, 107n46, 114, 121

Kauona, Sam 55, 64, 80
Keating, Mick 133–4, 138
Keating, Paul 71
Kehoe, Mick C. 131–2, 134, 147
Kelly, Paul 32
Kenny, Laura 125n51
Killen, D.J. 22n50, 175n37
Korean War (*see under* wars)

Land Commander (*see under* Australian Army)
land force commander 14, 162
land force projection 5, 16, 136, 160
    land power 9n16, 9n18, 180
    land warfare 19
    operations 122, 160, 163
Lange, David 25, 27, 31
Legge, J.G. 13–14
liaison 45, 78, 57
    high-level liaison and reconnaissance 78–9, 100
    inter-departmental 46, 48, 78
    officers 38, 46–7, 51n19, 60, 100, 109, 112, 124n13, 137, 154n127, 155
        hasty deployment of 57, 96
        Military Liaison Officers (UNAMET) 130, 134
    secessionist liaison team ambush 75, 80
Lilley, Clive W. 101–2
Lincoln Agreement 116–18
Lini, Father Walter Hadye 28n16
Logistic National Interim Demand System (*see under* logistics: headquarters, formations and units)
logistics viii
    commanders:
        Commander—Joint Logistics (CJLOG) 110, 114, 156–7, 170
        Commander—Logistic Support Force 104, 110, 115, 131: Logistic Component Commander 134, 138, 161
        Commander—Support Command-Australia (COMSPTAS) 89: support to Operation *Bel Isi* (Bougainville 1997–98) 111, 113: assessment 113, 121–3, 128; support to Operation *Spitfire/Warden/Stabilise* (East Timor 1999) 131–3, 147: assessment 147–8, 154n125, 156, 161
    Commercial Support Program 146
    Force Structure Review 146
    headquarters, formations and units:
        Defence National Supply Distribution Centre (DNSDC) 62: assessment 115, 121, 123, 124n22, 157, 163, 164n14; Operation *Bel Isi* Coordination Cell 110–11, 115, 123; support to Operation *Bel Isi* 110–11; support to Operation *Warden/Stabilise* (East Timor 1999) 147
        Deployed Forces Support Unit 104, 119
        Headquarters Logistic Command: support to Operation *Lagoon* (Bougainville 1994) 62, 67, 80; support to Operation *Solace* (Somalia 1993) 164n14
        Headquarters Movement Control support to Operation *Lagoon* (Bougainville 1994) 80: 1 Joint Movements Group (1 JMOVGP) 85, 110: assessment 115, 124n13, 124n22, 156; challenges 87; expectations 91; support to Operation *Bel Isi* (Bougainville 1997–98) 111; support to Operation *Warden/Stabilise* (East Timor 1999) 138, 146
        Logistic Support Force (LSF): support to Operation *Bel Isi* (Bougainville 1997–98) 96, 103–4: assessment of 120, 123, 147–8, 155–6; Logistic Management Centre 115; Logistic National Interim Demand System 116; logistic planning 131, 138, 145–7, 150–7; mounting headquarters 104, 109–10, 116–17; Operation *Warden/Stabilise* (East Timor 1999) 146; *Operation Anode* (Solomon Islands 2003) 168; Force Logistic Support Group support to *Operation Warden/Stabilise* (East Timor 1999) 134, 147
        9 Force Support Battalion (FSB): support to Operation *Bel Isi* (Bougainville 1997–98) 98–9; support to Operation *Warden/Stabilise* (East Timor 1999) 131, 134
        10 Force Support Battalion support to Operation *Warden/Stabilise* (East Timor 1999) 131
        Joint Logistic Unit—North (JLU-N) 132, 146, 154n127
        Moorebank Logistic Group 121, 164n14

lack of rehearsal 162
logistic redevelopment projects 146
rapid response command 171
reforms 48, 85, 89, 91n3
supply:
    basic commodities/items 59, 139, 146, 159, 164n19: backlog 148; bottled water 141–2; camp stores 103, 148; canteen service 116, 148; construction stores 147; contingency stocks 141; fuel 114, 140, 145, 147; generators 113, 124n17; maps 38, 106n14, 136; refrigeration 113; spare parts 46, 59, 112–13, 115–17, 121, 124n17, 147–8, 162; tents 15, 103, 147–8
    chains: *ad hoc* supply chain (Operation Stabilise East Timor 1999) 145; air force resupply chain 86, 113; failure of joint logistics 162, supply chain management 120, 122, 156, 158, 160, 162; under-rehearsed supply operations 163
support to:
    Operation *Anode* (Solomon Islands 2003) 168
    Operation *Bel Isi* (Bougainville 1997–98) 103, 108n58: supply chain management 109–10, 115; assessment 120, 122, 160
    Operation *Hardihood* (Vietnam 1966) 21n36
    Operation *Lagoon* (Bougainville 1994) 54–5, 57–9, 62, 72: planning 61–2; assessment 80, 83n32, 160
    Operation *Morris Dance* (Fiji 1987) 46: assessment 48
    Operation *Spitfire/Warden/Stabilise* (East Timor 1999) 131, 135, 140, 145–8: ANAO audit 169; assessment 156
    Vanuatu 1980 28n16
theatre level arrangements 128
weaknesses 109, 157, 161–3, 170
Loosely, Stephen 53

MacKenzie, S.S. 7
mail:
    absence of mail during Operation *Lagoon* (Bougainville 1994) 80, 82n32
    arrangements for mail during:
        Operation *Bel Isi* (Bougainville 1997–98) 109, 114–15
        Operation *Morris Dance* (Fiji 1987) 46, 59
        Operation *Warden/Stabilise* (East Timor 1999) 148
Mara, Ratu Sir Kamisese 25
Martin, Ian 135, 137
Martin, Ray 57
Martinkus, John 152n81
Mataparae, Jerry 116
McCarthy, Dudley 7, 169
McDonald, Hamish 152n81
McDowall, Greg 86
McKinnon, Don 93–4
McLachlan, Ian 95, 97, 101, 104
McMahon, James F. 151n49
McMahon, William 22n40
McManus, Barry 131, 134, 147
McNamara, Phil J. 56, 58
McNeil, Ian 17, 169
media 90, 141
    classified news 155
    coverage of:
        Operation *Bel Isi* (Bougainville 1997–98) 93–4
        Operation *Lagoon* (Bougainville 1994) 54, 67n4, 76, 96: early warning 122
        Operation *Morris Dance* (Fiji 1987) 27, 31, 33–4, 36–7, 48–9
        Operation *Spitfire/Warden/Stabilise* (East Timor 1999) 130, 132, 134
    magnification of tipping points 6, 160–1, 168
    newspapers:
        Age 94, 106, 201
        Australian 106, 149–50, 173: *Weekend Australian* 150, 152
        Fiji Sun 27

Fiji Times 27
Sun-Herald 31
Sydney Morning Herald 12, 27–9, 32, 38, 41–2, 106, 130, 132, 149–52, 197, 201
radio stations 49
    Radio Australia 67n4
    scrutiny by 4–5
television 90
    Cable News Network 122
Medical Support Force (*see under* operations: Tamar)
military:
    capability 181
        modernisation 3, 181
    competence 3, 127
        framework of force projection 7
    efficiency colonial 11, 129
    force projection (*see* force: projection)
    force protection (*see under* force: projection)
    intelligence agencies/organisations (*see under* intelligence)
    logistic support (*see* logistics)
    matériel 77, 99, 102–3, 120, 138, 150n38, 162, 175n36
        Australian Materiel Issue and Movement Priority System (AUSMIPS) 111
    medical support 14, 58–9, 65–6, 94, 97, 116, 141
    mobilisation vii, 1–2, 8n3, 14
    operations (*see* various military operations *under* operations)
    readiness vii, viii, 2–3, 8n3, 24, 34, 37, 151n39, 174n35, 181
        operationally ready 182
        rapid response command 171
    self-reliance 75, 127, 163, 168, 191
    strategic culture 3, 199
    strategy 17
        defence-in-depth xv, 4, 18, 23
        operational art 181
        operational level of war 181
    sustainability vii, 2–3, 7n2, 181
militia 14 (*see also* East Timor: auxiliaries (militia))

Miriung, Theodore 75
Molan, Jim 134, 136–7
monitoring groups:
    Peace Monitoring Group 116–20
    Truce Monitoring Group (TMG) 95–105, 110–11, 115–17
        Resource Group 95–7, 107n27, 108n58: transition to PMG 119
Moore, John 132–3, 135
Moriarty, Greg L. 106n18, 118
Morrison, David L. 55–8
Mortlock, Roger C. 93, 95, 97, 100, 105, 106n16, 106n18, 116
Mueller, Des 89, 111, 113, 121–3, 128, 131–2, 147–8, 156, 161
Murdoch, Lindsay 94
Murray, Alan A. 154n127

Nailatikau, Ratu Epeli 25, 32
National Security Committee of Cabinet (*see under* Australian Government)
New Guinea, German 14–15
New Hebrides 28n16 (*see also* Vanuatu)
New Zealand:
    Auckland gathering of world leaders (APEC) 138
        TMG planning 98, 101, 110, 112
    Australian relations with 93–4
    Burnham (Army Camp) 93–4, 120
        Burnham Declaration 94, 106n5
        Burnham talks 94–5
        Burnham Truce Agreement 95, 106n14, 120
    Linton, HQ TMG 100, TMG reconnaissance 101
    Ministry of Foreign Affairs and Trade (MFAT) New Zealand diplomats 93–5
    New Zealand Centre for Strategic Studies 136, 198
    New Zealand Defence Force (NZDF):
        support to Operation Bel Isi (Bougainville 1997–98): drivers 116–17
    serviceability of vehicles 116–17
    New Zealand Land Force Headquarters 112

Logistic Support Agency 110
Royal New Zealand Air Force (RNZAF) 111, 116
Royal New Zealand Navy (RNZN) 113: vessels HMNZS *Canterbury* 105; HMNZS *Endeavour* 105, 113
Special Forces 116
Tasman Sea 100, 111–12
Wellington TMG planning 95, 98, 100–1
Newham, Jim 36
Nixon Doctrine 18
Northern Command (NORCOM) (see Commander Northern Command *under* Australian Defence Force: commanders)

O'Connor, Justin 55–6, 58
O'Donnell, Laurie 36, 40
O'Hara, Jim S. 58, 65, 67, 71, 74, 80
O'Neill, Robert J. 169, 173n6
Office of National Assessments (see *under* intelligence: agencies/organisations)
Ona, Francis 118
operations:
    Anode (Solomon Islands 2003):
        assessment 167
        logistic support 174n31
        operational history 167
        Post Operation Report 173n15
    Bel Isi (Bougainville 1997–98):
        assessment 121–3
        logistic support 111–16, 124n7, 124n12
        operational history 111–20
        Post Operation Report 125n47, 126n58
        withdrawal of NZDF logistic support 116–17
    Faber (East Timor 1999):
        operational history 130–1, 150n26
        Post Operation Report 150n26
    Gateway (Cold War) 22n52
    Hardihood (Vietnam 1966) 147: logistic aspects 21n36
    Lagoon (Bougainville 1994) 6, 9n19, 53–75
        observations 75–82 157, 160
        operational history 53–84
        Post Operation Report 68n22, 83n45
        Status of Forces Agreement (SOFA) 57, 64
    Morris Dance (waters off Fiji 1987):
        operational history 6, 23–7, 31–41
        Post Operation Report 41n14, 41n19, 51n15
    Polygon (renamed *Bel Isi*) 98, 107n39
    Rausim Quik (PNG 1997) 93
    Sierra (PNG Highlands 1997) 97
    Solace (Somalia 1994) 110, 115, 122, 128, 136, 164n14
        operational history 191
    Spitfire (East Timor 1999) 6, 130, 132–3, 135–7, 146
        operational history 191
    Stabilise (East Timor 1999) 127–48
        ADF operational history 191
        reflections and observations 157–63
    Tamar (Rwanda 1994–95): 78, 122
        Medical Support Force in 56, 60, 63
    Terrier (renamed *Bel Isi*) 107n41
    Warden (East Timor 1999) 127–48
        operational history 191
Oram, James 34, 38
Osborn, Bruce V. 117–22, 126n58
Oxenbould, Chris J. 85–90, 128

Pacific Command (US) (PACOM) 88, 91n16
Pacific Patrol Boat program 33
Papua New Guinea (PNG) xv, 27, 28n10, 60, 97
    Bougainville:
        Arawa site: for monitoring operations (Operation *Bel Isi* 1997–98) 93, 99, 102, 105, 111, 114; as peace conference site (Operation *Lagoon* 1994) 55, 58, 64–6, 71–4, 78–81, 82n6
        Bougainville Crisis 53, 58: hopes for ending 93–4, 116, 118

Bougainville Crisis Action Team (BCAT) 60, 81
    Bougainville Reconciliation Government 120
    Bougainville Revolutionary Army (BRA) 54, 76, 80, 94, 102
    Bougainville Watch Group 106n14, 107n27
    Bougainvilleans 66, 73–5, 119: welcome for TMG 101
    Buin 105, 108n55
    Buka 71, 80, 97, 101–2
    Commitment for Peace on Bougainville 55
    Endeavour Accords 54
    Kieta airfield 102, 105
    Loloho 72–3, 78, 99, 102–3, 105, 109, 111, 113, 118
    neutral zones 55, 64–6, 72, 74, 79
    Panguna copper mine 93
    secessionists 53–4, 64, 74–5, 94, 121
    Tonu 105
Chan Government 93
government involvement with:
    Operation *Bel Isi* (Bougainville 1997–98) 93–5, 99, 101, 104
    Operation *Lagoon* (Bougainville 1994) 32, 54, 64–5, 67, 71, 75, 78–9, 81, 83n24
Papua New Guinea Defence Force (PNGDF) 19
    involvement with: Espiritu Santo Rebellion (Vanuatu 1980) 28n16; Operation *Bel Isi* (Bougainville 1997–98) 93–5; Operation *Lagoon* (Bougainville 1994) 53, 66, 73–6, 79–80, 84n49
    differences with PNG government 81
Port Moresby 16, 55, 57, 64, 78, 94, 101, 119
Rabaul 14, 49
Skate Government 94
Patey, George E. 14
Peniai, Nick 73–4

People's Republic of China (*see* China)
planning:
    combined planning Operation *Bel Isi* (Bougainville 1997–98) 95, 99, 103
    compartments:
        Operation *Lagoon* (Bougainville 1994), 60, 76
        Operation *Warden* (East Timor 1999) 130, 133, 135
        rapid response command 171
    contingency planning 86, 89–90
        Operation *Bel Isi* (Bougainville 1997–98), 95–6, 106n14, 107n27, 122
        Operation *Lagoon* (Bougainville 1994), 54, 59, 76, 81
        Operation *Spitfire* 130–3
    cryptographic plans
    devolution of planning and decision-making 133, 161
    Immediate Planning Group ADFCC 77–8
    Plan *Benefactor* 47
    planning and conduct of campaigns and operations 90, 157
    planning cycle 61, 78
    planning directive 85
        Operation *Bel Isi* (Bougainville 1997–98) 98
        Operation *Lagoon* (Bougainville 1994) 55–6, 61–2, 77
        Operation *Morris Dance* (Fiji 1987) 46
    transition from strategic to operational planning 89
Portugal 129–30
Powell, Roger 120–1
power:
    air 5, 9n17, 159, 164n21
    land 180
    littoral 180
    maritime 180
preparedness vxi, 2, 132, 177
    generic preparedness 3, 7n1
PricewaterhouseCoopers report on HQ AST 129
Puddicombe, Reece 117
Pursey, Peter 32–3, 35, 42n34

Rabuka, Sitiveni 24–7, 31, 35–6
Radford, Ted 36
Rapid Deployment Force (US) 4, 8n10
rapid response command, case for 171–2
Ray, Robert 53–4, 58, 65–6, 71
reconnaissance vii, 2–3, 5, 8n4
   arrangements for:
      Operation *Anode* (Solomon Islands 2003) 167
      Operation *Bel Isi* (Bougainville 1997–98) 95, 97–104, 109
      Operation *Lagoon* (Bougainville 1994) 57, 63–5, 74–5, 77–9
      Operation *Spitfire/Warden/Stabilise* (East Timor 1999) 131, 159
   challenge for HQ AST, 86, 182
   rapid response command 171
Republic of Fiji Military Forces (*see under* Fiji)
Richardson, G.F.T. 21n36
Rimington, Hugh 27
Ritchie, David 117–19
Robertson, B.D. 153n102
Robertson, John 15
Rogers, Paul M. 98–9, 101, 103, 109–10, 112–15, 119, 121
Royal Australian Air Force 11, 38, 80, 111
   Air Commander 24, 36, 42n46,46, 118, 128
   aircraft 42n47, 46, 80, 95, 111–12, 114–15, 127, 145, 157, 160, 162
      A-4 Sky Hawk 136
      C-130 *Hercules* 38, 51n19, 71, 80, 112, 133, 137, 139–40, 153n101
      Caribou 71
      F-16 *Fighting Falcon* 136
      F-111 strike aircraft 136
      forward air control 136
      P-3C *Orion* aircraft 22n52
      rapid response command 171
      sorties 141, 153n101
      transiting 114–15
      transport 38, 71, 51n19, 127, 133, 139
   bases 112
      Amberley Air Base 114
      Butterworth Air Base (Malaysia) 22n52
      Richmond Air Base 80, 104, 111–12, 114, 124n22
      Tindal Air Base 133, 136
      Townsville Air Base 38, 114
   helicopters:
      Sea King 74, 80, 105
      Wessex 39
   higher command 5, 34
   personnel 38, 85, 114, 124n22 ,128, 137, 141,
   support to:
      DJFHQ 128, 137, 155
      land forces 5, 24, 80, 86, 103, 105–6, 109–15, 112, 118, 121, 160, 162–3
      Operation *Bel Isi* (Bougainville 1997–98) 103, 105, 109–15, 118, 121, 124n22: Air Lift Group (ALG); Richmond 111; automated cargo visibility system 115, 121, 124n22
      Operation *Lagoon* (Bougainville 1994) 55, 59, 73, 80: supply chain 86, 95 156
      Operation *Morris Dance* (Fiji), 38, 42n47, 51n19
      Operation *Solace* (Somalia 1993) 105, 160
      Operation *Spitfire/Warden/Stabilise* (East Timor 1999) 136, 139–41, 145–7, 150n38, 156, 162: air bridge 147; Combined Air Wing Group 139–40
Royal Australian Navy (RAN):
   Cold War operations 11
   force projection role 5, 13–15, 19, 24, 58, 159, 162
      maritime power 180
   Maritime Headquarters vii, 39, 47
      Maritime Commander 36–7, 42, 46, 58 environmental title 20, 24; role in raising HQ AST 85, 88
      maritime power 9n17
      support to Operation *Bel Isi* (Bougainville 1997–98) 96, 103: assessment of 105, 118, 121–2, 128, 156, 161
      support to Operation *Lagoon* (Bougainville 1994) 58, 66–7

support to Operation *Morris Dance* (Fiji 1987) 36–7, 42n47, 46
Navy Office Contingency Co-ordination Centre (NOCCC), Australian Navy Supply 83n32
support to:
    DJFHQ 128, 137, 155
    land forces 17, 136, 138, 156, 159, 162–3
    Operation *Bel Isi* (Bougainville 1997–98) 103, 106, 110, 118
    Operation *Lagoon* (Bougainville 1994) 55, 58, 65–6, 72–4, 74, 80, 83n32
    Operation *Morris Dance* (Fiji 1987) 31, 33–4, 36–8, 42n40, 43n69, 51n19: tensions with Fiji 35, 40, 49
    Operation *Solace* (Somalia 1993) 160
    Operation *Spitfire/Warden/Stabilise* (East Timor 1999) 136, 140–1, 145, 156–7
vessels:
    HMAS *Adelaide* 39, 43n69
    HMAS *Jervis Bay* 133, 141–2, 142, 150n39: assessment 162
    HMAS *Parramatta* 39, 43n69
    HMAS *Stalwart* 43n69, 45
    HMAS *Success* 37, 39, 42n40, 43n69, 56, 58, 65, 71, 80, 105, 109, 141, 145
    HMAS *Sydney* 35, 43n69
    HMAS *Tobruk*: support Operation *Bel Isi* (Bougainville 1997–98) 97, 99, 102–5, 109, 118; support to Operation *Lagoon* (Bougainville 1994) 56–8, 62, 66–7, 71–3, 76, 81; support to Operation *Morris Dance* (Fiji 1987) 36–7, 39, 42n47, 43n69; support to Operation *Warden/Stabilise* (East Timor 1999) 141–2, 145
Royal New Zealand Air Force (*see under* New Zealand)
Royal New Zealand Navy (*see under* New Zealand)
Rules of Engagement (ROE) 8n9, 182
    Operation *Lagoon* (Bougainville 1994) 74, 78

Operation *Warden/Stabilise* (East Timor 1999) 142
Russia 12
Rwanda xv (*see also under* operations: Tamar)
Ryan, Alan 170

Salter, John P. 39–40, 41n17, 47, 49
Sanderson, John M. 95, 107n46
Sargeant, Lawrence T. 153n105
Saunders, Kate L. 153n106
Scully, Peter J. 33–4, 45–6
secrecy, impact of, on:
    operational planning 86, 89–90, 149n10, 159: rapid response command 171
    Operation *Anode* (Solomon Islands 2003) 167
    Operation *Lagoon* (Bougainville 1994) 59, 61
    Operation *Morris Dance* (Fiji 1987) 46
    Operation *Spitfire/Warden/Stabilise* (East Timor 1999) 130, 132
Sharp, Russ W. 61–2
Shoebridge, Robert W. 55, 58
Sinclair, Peter 36–7
Singarok, Jerry 93
Skate, Bill 93–4
Slater, Mick D. 142–4, 153n112
Slip, Murray 109–10
Smith, Neil 112, 124n13
Solomon Islands 53–4, 71, 78, 95, 167
    Honiara 53, 55, 64, 71–2, 78, 95
Somalia 78
    Operation *Solace* (1993):
        command and control 105, 115, 121
        human intelligence 60
        lessons from 110, 122
        logistic support to 80, 109, 156, 160
        ship loading 62, 67, 75
South Africa 11–13
South Pacific:
    political volatility in 50
    South Pacific Defence Cooperation Program 32

South Pacific Forum 28n16, 32, 61
South Pacific Peace Keeping Force (SPPKF) 53–6, 58–9, 63–6, 71–6, 78–81
South Pacific support to Operation Lagoon (Bougainville 1994) 62–4, 66–7, 73
    assessment of 82n2
specific force preparation (*see* functions of force projection: specific force preparation)
Steel, Peter C. 151n50
Steketee, Mike 32, 34
Stevens, David 135
Stevenson, J.B. 14
Stokes, Captain 126n58
Stone, Gary J. 32–3, 38–40, 47, 49
Strategic Watch Group 96
strategy (*see* Australia: strategic thinking of)
Strickland, Edward 12
Suakin (in the Red Sea) 11
submarines (*see under* vessels)
Sudan (*see under* wars: British Sudan War)

supply (*see under* logistics)
Support Command—Australia (*see under* logistics: headquarters, formations and units)
surveillance vii, 2, 131
    air 11, 22n52
    maritime 11, 22n52, 83n20
    operations 19, 85
    technical 79
Syahnakri, Kiki 138–9, 143, 145
Sydney Morning Herald (*see under* media: newspapers)
Symon, Paul B. 130–1

Takal, Sevle 57, 64, 78–9
Tambea Accords 54
Tange, Arthur 18, 20, 22n43
    Tange Reforms 22n43
    Tange Report 18–19
Teece, William G. 72
tipping points 127
    definition vii, 4
    Kokoda Track 1942 vii, 11, 127, 157, 165
    Long Tan, Vietnam 1966 vii, 4, 6, 11, 127, 157, 165
    media creation of 4, 6
Tonga:
    support to Operation *Lagoon* (Bougainville 1994) 55, 57, 64, 69n56
Treloar, Bob 128–9, 131–8, 147–8, 155, 161
Truce Monitoring Group (*see under* monitoring groups)
Tupou, Feto 57, 64, 73–4, 78
Tyrell, Phillip R. 173n15

United Kingdom (*see* Britain)
United Nations 1, 16, 19
    Fijian service with 26
    involvement in East Timor 129–31, 134–9, 141, 145, 148
    United Nations Assistance Mission–East Timor (*see* United Nations: involvement in East Timor)
    United Nations Security Council Resolution 1264 138
United States 18
    CINC arrangements 88–9
    condemnation of Fiji coup 1987 27
    expectations of Australia 34
    force projection 4, 166
    support to Operation *Stabilise* (East Timor 1999) 135, 137, 139, 141
    support to South West Pacific Campaign 1942 16

Vanuatu (*also* Ni Vanuatu) 24
    support to Operation *Bel Isi* (Bougainville 1997–98) 97, 104, 109, 119
    support to Operation *Lagoon* (Bougainville 1994) 55, 57, 64, 69n56, 82n6
    support to Operation *Morris Dance* (Fiji 1987) 27, 50
vehicles:
    Australian Light Armoured Vehicle (ASLAV) 142–4
    support to Operation *Warden* (East Timor 1999) 127, 139, 142, 144, 149n1

vessels:
    Coalition vessels 141
    landing craft 36–7, 124n17
    submarines 21n23, 22n52, 24
        Indonesian submarine 136
        Soviet submarine 22n52
    Vietnam War (*see under* wars)
    (*see also* Royal Australian Navy: vessels)

Walker, Frank 31
Walsh, Vince 38, 46–7, 51n19
Walters, Patrick 24
Wardlaw, Mark J. 110–11
warning orders:
    Operation *Bel Isi* (Bougainville 1997–98) 96, 99–101
    Operation *Lagoon* (Bougainville 1994) 54, 58–9
    Operation *Morris Dance* (Fiji 1987) 34, 46
    Operation *Spitfire/Warden/Stabilise* (East Timor 1999) 128, 135
warning time 1, 76, 94, 158
    dissatisfaction with 161
    lack of rehearsal and 159
    media and 122
    rapid response command and 171
    secrecy and 159
wars:
    Boer War 12–13
    British Sudan War (1885) 11
    First World War 13–15
    Gulf War (1991) 18
    Kokoda Campaign 146, 157, 169, 174n22
    Korean War 16–17, 19, 169, 174n23
    Second World War 1, 7, 9n19, 11, 15–16, 138
    Vietnam War 4, 11, 17–18, 172n26
Watman, Gary 97, 100–1
weapons 142
    carriage of 140, 144
    confiscation of 74
    infantry preference 49
    safety of 66
    ship storage of 39

Wells, John 66–7, 71
Weston, Brian G. 87–90
Whitlam, Gough 18
Wilkinson, Jeff B. 104, 110–11, 114, 116–17, 121–3, 123n5, 123n6, 131–2, 134, 138, 145–8, 155–6, 161
Wilton, John 22n44
Wiranto, General 132, 135, 137–8
Woodley, Brian 34
Woods, Alan 33, 37

Young, Gary 57, 68n17

www.ingramcontent.com/pod-product-compliance
Lightning Source LLC
Chambersburg PA
CBHW060930180426
43192CB00045B/2874